ADAM M. LOWENSTEIN spent eigh
government and politics, most recently a:
communications advisor in the United Stat

Today, Adam lives in London with his partner, Erin, and writes
frequently about politics, work, and life. Visit his website, see his latest
work, and subscribe to his newsletter at www.adaml.blog.

Reframe the Day

Embracing the Craft of Life,
One Day at a Time

Adam M. Lowenstein

SilverWood

Published in 2020 by SilverWood Books

SilverWood Books Ltd
14 Small Street, Bristol, BS1 1DE, United Kingdom
www.silverwoodbooks.co.uk

ISBN 978-1-78132-942-9 (paperback)
ISBN 978-1-78132-943-6 (ebook)

British Library Cataloguing in Publication Data
A CIP catalogue record for this book is available from the British Library

Page design and typesetting by SilverWood Books

"*When the day is done, and the lights are out, and there is only this other heart, this other mind, this other face, to assist in repelling one's demons or in greeting one's angels, it does not matter who the president is.*"

David Brooks, *The Road to Character*[1]

For Erin

Contents

What (and why) is this?

"Write a bit, just for yourself. Give that maelstrom in your head a place to land. Look at everything swirling around in there!"

Lin-Manuel Miranda[2]

Trial and Error

Some people have always known what they want to do with their lives. Or at least it feels that way. In the world of politics, it seems as if the most successful people began plotting their career paths when they were twelve years old. My parents would be the first to tell you that's not me. They've watched me evolve from studying mathematics and computer science, to working in the skiing and music industries, to stumbling into nearly a decade in politics on Capitol Hill, to living in the United Kingdom and writing reflections on life.

Like most chapters of this journey, until I found myself in politics in my early 20s, I hadn't planned on making it a career. I studied computer science long enough to realize I didn't want to be a programmer. I spent years DJing and working in college radio, only to discover I wanted nothing to do with the music industry. It took two internships and a lack of other realistic job prospects in Colorado for me to wind up working in politics in Washington, DC. It took leaving Capitol Hill and moving home to Colorado to work in state politics to realize I actually wanted to be back in Washington working on Capitol Hill. After eight-ish years working in the U.S. Senate and U.S. House of Representatives, it took moving away from the nonstop world of politics to make some sense of what fulfills me. It took moving away from a group of people I was close to, and one in particular, to learn that home isn't where I grew up or where I work but where I'm with the people I care about.

For better or worse, this trial-and-error approach has been the *modus operandi* of my adult life. There's a lot of privilege inherent in such an approach. Not everyone is lucky enough to have so many chances to try, stumble, and try again (and to do so over and over again). I've been fortunate to have been able to do a lot of stumbling and continue to land on my feet. But there's also something universal in my trying and stumbling and trying again, something not limited to those of privileged circumstances or connections or means.

To some degree, we *all* live our lives through trial and error. No one really knows what they're doing or where they're going. No one is really in control of their trajectory, let alone the trajectories of the people they love or the things they care about or the world as a whole. No one can predict the future. No one gets it right every time, even though life can sometimes make us feel as though we're the only ones always getting it wrong. No one has unlocked *the* secret to being happy or finding inner peace or leading a meaningful life. We're all learning as we go, trying to nudge our lives in a slightly more fulfilling direction. That's what this book is about: finding ways to reframe our regular, routine, everyday lives to squeeze a little more fulfillment out of each day.

This book is not about me, although my story runs through it (that's my author's prerogative, I guess). It's not entirely about politics, either, though my perspective is inseparable from the world of politics that I inhabited for eight years and that has shaped the person I am today. Nor is the book solely for or about millennials, even though every idea underpinning the next ten chapters is a product of a world dominated by the constant striving and constant uncertainty that define the millennial experience.

While it's not *about* politics or millennials, those two perspectives have, perhaps more than anything else, shaped my worldview and guided me toward the ideas in this book. Take the first one. American politics is defined by constant uncertainty. It's obsessed with striving—for the next election, the next achievement, the next promotion, the next connection, the next opportunity to inch a bit closer to power. On a Venn diagram of all things millennial and all things political, there's probably not a great deal of overlap. But in one key area, at least, they intersect entirely: constant striving in a constantly uncertain world. That's life as a millennial. That's life in politics. That's...life. Life for all of us, it seems, is about constant striving in a constantly uncertain world. That doesn't only apply to those born between 1981 and 1996 or those working in the business of government.

A world characterized by striving and uncertainty is exhausting. It's overwhelming. It's stressful. It leaves you restless and unsatisfied. It keeps you perpetually distracted. It hijacks your focus and trains you to obsessively wonder, "What's next?" None of us can change that reality, at least not overnight. But what if you were to reframe how you perceive it? What if your days were a little less frantic and a little more fulfilled? What if your days contained a little less striving and a little more stillness? What if they included a little less busyness and a little more time for the people and activities that matter to you?

Millennials

Before we go further, a little scene-setting about the two perspectives I mentioned is in order. Let's start with millennials. Oh, the millennials. Those constantly scrutinized, oft-analyzed, ever-mysterious millennials. That contingent, that generation...those are my people. And we have some thoughts.

For reasons we'll discuss in the chapters ahead, millennials have grown up in an era starved of stillness and self-awareness. From classrooms and offices to extracurricular activities and entire economies, we've only ever known environments characterized by busyness, striving, and never-ending distractions. We came of age with the smartphone and social media. Many of us entered the world of work during the worst economic downturn since the Great Depression, leaving us with few expectations of professional certainty or personal stability. As Anne Helen Petersen writes, since birth, many millennials have been "trained, tailored, primed, and optimized for the workplace."[3] The only world we know is one in which we're expected to always be "on"—working, striving, networking, climbing, aspiring, achieving—and always online. As we've aged, we've become an increasingly large population and workforce demographic, and we've brought our habits with us—constant connectivity, relentless life plotting, an obsession with the hustle, and doubt that the premise of "work-life balance" is anything but a myth of corporate recruiting.

These attributes may be characteristic of our generation, but—here's why this book isn't only for my fellow millennials-in-arms—they aren't unique to us. As the (millennial) writer Michael Hobbes put it in a deeply reported piece entitled simply, *Millennials Are Screwed*, "What is different about us as individuals compared to previous generations is minor. What is different about the world around us is profound."[4] The world has changed. And this chapter in our collective history, for all its advances and advantages, has raised some troubling questions that impact all of us, not just millennials.

Why are so many of us so frazzled and overwhelmed so often? Why are we so obsessed with productivity and so addicted to busyness? Why do we idolize the "grind" and sacrifice what we care about for the "hustle," all while yearning for some abstract point in the future when we can grind and hustle less and spend more time doing what we care about? Why do we wear multitasking and sleepless nights and early-morning emails like badges of honor when we know, intellectually at least, that there's more to life than working seven days a week to never reach the finish line? Why are we so accustomed to feeling stressed and swamped with endless to-do lists that we forget there's any other way to feel? Why does it feel like everyone else has time to do it all? Why can't *we* find the secret pause button?

Anne Helen Petersen offers one theory. "Why am I burned out?" she asks. "Because I've internalized the idea that I should be working all the time. Why have I internalized that idea? Because everything and everyone in my life has reinforced it—explicitly and implicitly—since I was young."[5] Petersen's description captures much of the human experience today, and not just that of millennials. "Things that should've felt good (leisure, not working) felt bad because I felt guilty for not working," she writes. "[And] things that should've felt 'bad' (working all the time) felt good because I was doing what I thought I should and needed to be doing in order to succeed."[6] Where do these compulsions come from? What are we seeking? Why are we striving? Isn't there something more fundamental, something that exists beyond the searching and striving and suffering, beyond the momentary triumphs of another completed task with yet another already looming on the horizon?

Politics

For answers to some of life's most fundamental questions, we turn, of course, to politics…said no one ever. The political universe is decidedly *not* the lens through which many of us expect to find guidance about how to build more meaningful lives, or about how to do much of anything, for that matter. The popular impression of politics today is of angry screaming on cable news, relentless barrages of patronizing TV commercials, endless streams of questionable and fringe-y content on social media, clickbait headlines designed to mislead and stir up outrage, and shameless pandering and condescension from politicians. I'm agitated just writing this. We long for a politics like *The West Wing* but instead get a depressing blend of *Veep* and *House of Cards*, seasoned with a hint of *The Office*. Or we did, at least, before politics became a never-ending season of *The Apprentice*. (Ugh.) It's no surprise that everyone is at least a little exhausted and cynical about it all. So why start a book about building more fulfilling lives by talking about politics?

The universe of American politics is a strange one to work in. It's hopeful, hopeless, fun, exhausting, inspiring, depressing, addictive, insular, unique, toxic, and invigorating. It's often all of those things at the same time, in doses far more intense than one realizes in the middle of it. As a political staffer (as people working for politicians are often known), politics can offer proximity to power and influence at an uncomfortably young age. It attracts some of the country's most hardworking, dedicated, idealistic, and service-oriented people (together with a few of the most cynical and disingenuous ones, too, though they are, thankfully, outnumbered). Politics casts aside the idea of work-life balance for a pseudo-reality in which work, life, the news cycle, and current events are all the same thing. Unlike most industries that seek and depend on stability and long-term planning, politics assumes the likelihood of neither. The political world can be, and often is, completely transformed overnight by an election, a scandal, or a national disaster.

For many staffers, compensation for the low pay and lack of work-life balance comes from the conviction that they are working at the heart of the fight for something they care deeply about. But that doesn't make it any less challenging or any less exhausting. Politics is an environment characterized by burning ambition, relentless striving, and perpetual calibration and recalibration of one's status within concentric circles of connections and networks. Underlying a staffer's day-to-day worries is an ongoing assessment of career trajectory. *Where am I now? Who do I already know? Where do I want to go next? Who do I need to know to get there? Oh, and what happens to me if we're not reelected?* This uncertain state of affairs is an inevitable byproduct of having too much to do and working in an unpredictable environment where careers are guaranteed until they're not, where elections and scandals can change the course of history, and where even the best-laid career plans can be annihilated in an instant.[*]

---

[*] Consider the fallout from Hillary Clinton's 2016 election loss, when the career paths of thousands of hardworking political operatives were permanently redirected on November 9th. Consider also the legions of staffers working for Senator Barack Obama in the mid-2000s who, following the 2008 election, suddenly found themselves in the White House. Both cohorts contained a lot of skill, hard work, and dedication. But it's impossible to overlook the element of fortune that sends one group of staffers to 1600 Pennsylvania Avenue and the other home to update their resumes after the polls have finally closed.

◆

I may have stumbled into (and later out of) a career in politics, but I'm no political outsider. For nearly eight years, I worked in state and national politics, in four different congressional offices, and on political campaigns. My friend Shad and I once set up a networking organization to help aspiring staffers gain access to job opportunities that we came across on the inside. I've given (and asked for) countless informational interviews about working in politics. Most of those discussions about political job-hunting can be summarized in one question: Who do you know? That can feel like pretty swampy stuff.

Yet falling into this world through a series of internships, and moving to Washington, DC without understanding how politics works, forced me to learn the game through trial and error. Being surrounded by so many people who seemed to have known what they wanted to be all their lives gave me sense of separation from the world I inhabited. Over the course of multiple leaves of absence from politics, most recently decamping to my current home in the United Kingdom, I've begun to separate my own identity from my political career path. Feeling like an outsider can lead to chips on shoulders, among other downsides, but a sense of separation can also yield a bit of perspective. Somehow, my circuitous path has deposited me in London with a small air bubble amidst an avalanche of life transitions, giving me just enough space to catch my breath and reflect. I've come to realize that, as both a work environment and a reflection of culture and society as a whole, politics is a microcosm of many of the twenty-first century's toxic forces that leave us exhausted and overwhelmed.

Like many workplaces, most of the day-to-day challenges of Capitol Hill are thoroughly ordinary. From being tethered to email and bombarded with incoming information, to equating busyness with importance and stress with status, to burying lingering questions concerning the point of all this work and overwhelm, the trials of working in politics aren't specific to that particular profession. According to a 2018 Gallup survey, two-thirds of full-time employees report feeling burned out at work at least some of the time.[7] (Those ever-intriguing millennials report even higher levels of burnout.[8]) A 2016 study by Groupon found that "60% of Americans have an unhealthy work-life balance," while almost as many report that "there simply are not enough hours in the day to do what the[y] must do."[9] In the UK, respondents to one survey said they don't have enough time for, among other things, sleep, exercise, or "me-time."[10] (The same respondents also reported wanting more wine, cups of tea, and Instagram likes, for what that's worth.)

As with any workplace, politics is simply a collection of human beings trying to balance a challenging professional life with a fulfilling personal one. Like any workplace, it's a world in which everyone is expected to constantly reach for the next job or promotion. It's a world that thrives on the illusion of planning, plotting, and controlling things beyond anyone's control. It's a world that rarely encourages people to make time for the things that matter to them outside the office. (This challenge is exacerbated by an environment where news is the job, and news doesn't take evenings or weekends off.) It's a world characterized by an always-on, always-multitasking, status-obsessed mindset, and dominated by short-term, often superficial, thinking. It was a world, for me, where dinner with my grandparents or a weekend away to celebrate my in-laws' twenty-fifth wedding anniversary was supplanted, or at least supplemented, by frantically drafting a statement condemning the president's latest tweet or rewriting a memo for a subcommittee hearing that even the most dedicated online viewers of congressional hearings probably wouldn't watch.

A career in politics does not lend itself easily to personal fulfillment. It doesn't encourage stepping back and making sense of who you are beyond party affiliation and professional accomplishments. In politics, separating your identity from your work can be close to impossible. (If you're thinking, "Wait, that sounds like *my* life," that's precisely where we're going.) Politics is an all-consuming world in which busyness and burnout too easily obscure a fundamental fact of life: It's up to each one of us to discover and carve out time for the activities that most fulfill us and the people we care most about. No one else is going to do it for us. And if we wait for the perfect time to do it, we'll be waiting forever.

You might be wondering, "Why the lengthy political backstory?" Because working in politics has left me more confident than ever that every one of us, regardless of age, occupation, or circumstance, can take small steps to make our lives more manageable and meaningful. Stepping away from a world where personal success is too often defined by job title, status, and proximity to power has deepened my understanding of what it means to live a fulfilling life. It's instilled in me the conviction that, no matter who you are, where you live, or what you do, you have within you the power to make your day-to-day experience more fulfilling.**

In life, as in politics, so much is out of your control. In life, as in politics, you can't plan for many of the opportunities you encounter or the setbacks you face. In life, as in politics, you can and must find meaning in the struggle itself, not just in the outcome. In life, as in politics, no matter how angry or victorious or depressed or motivated or frustrated you feel, you only determine a tiny sliver of your own experience, let alone that of the world around you. That means that you have to find your own ways to recharge. You have to seek out your own moments of stillness. You have to learn to cultivate and maintain a sense of self-awareness and carve out time and attention for what you truly care about.

In life, as in politics, simply reacting to whatever the world throws your way, or having your days dictated by others' emails, tasks, tweets, and to-dos, will wear you down and burn you out. And in life, as in politics, we need enthusiastic, energetic, and fired-up people more than ever.

** Working in politics has left me optimistic in another way, too. As dysfunctional and depressing and infuriating as it can be, I remain convinced that most people working in politics are there for the right reasons. I worked with too many dedicated, talented, and selfless fellow staffers over the years to be entirely hopeless about our future. Things may be bleak right now, and rebooting our politics and our democracy will require a lot of struggle in the years ahead, but there's too much at stake, and too many good people ready to get in the trenches and do that work, for anyone to give up hope.

Everyone

"**B**ut I'm not a millennial," I hear you say. "No amount of money could convince me to work in politics," you may be thinking. (If money is the goal, it's probably the wrong line of work, anyway.) "What does all this stuff have to do with me?" From my relatively brief experience, everything. Constant striving in a constantly uncertain world doesn't only describe the life of this one millennial former political staffer. These days, it defines an entire era in which nearly everyone, nearly all of the time, feels overworked, over-busy, overstimulated, over-distracted, and overwhelmed.

No matter who we are or where we live or what we do, it seems that, from before we wake up until after we fall asleep, requests and to-dos and burdens bombard our phones and inboxes, sparing no time for reflection or deliberation. Information, distractions, and stimuli assault our minds, creating an impenetrable wall between us and stillness. Social media leaves us lonely and depressed, while political news leaves us lonely, depressed, and outraged. Our brains, which evolved to help hunter-gatherers navigate the immediate demands of survival, are completely overwhelmed and incapable of processing so much all at once, so we spend our days in an unfocused frenzy, scrambling from one thing to the next as we try to fit everything in.

Meanwhile, the broader trajectory of our lives is characterized by a relentless agitation, a constant sense of seeking and striving. There is always too much to do. We constantly compare ourselves to others, worried about what we've done in the past and what we have to do in the future. We try to be productive, whatever that means, but we never feel productive enough. We're always busy, but everyone else's busyness seems more productive and useful than our own, so we feel compelled to work even harder and take on even more. Our lives feel like an endless series of "what's nexts"—what's our next task, our next obligation, our next career progression, our next accomplishment?

Beneath it all, we're grappling with the cultural expectation that we *should* be able to do everything while staying fit, healthy, and happy.

We *should* be able to find careers that inspire us and change the world. If we tap into the secret stash of time and productivity that other high-performers and life-hackers have unlocked (just subscribe to their email newsletters to learn how!), we *should* be able to read and retain as many books as we want, maintain a robust social life, build a beautiful family, achieve career success as a disruptive entrepreneur-turned-thought leader, attend regular high-intensity interval training classes to stay fit, and perhaps take up a new habit such as journaling or baking or growing a rooftop garden. Even though our lives feel fuller than ever, they can somehow manage to feel incredibly empty. No wonder many of us are exhausted. No wonder we're starting to question the point of all this striving and busyness.

And yet, by many measures, human progress has moved inexorably in a positive direction. As scholars like Steven Pinker and Hans Rosling argue compellingly, as a species we have never been safer, healthier, better educated, or more prosperous.[11] Huge swathes of the global population have never had greater access to knowledge, entertainment, and information, nor have we had so much free time to consume it all. During and after his presidency, Barack Obama repeatedly noted that, despite all the very real challenges in the world, if you had to choose any time in human history to be born, you'd choose this one.[12] It's hard to argue with him there (though his political opponents would surely find a way).

So why does it feel like something's missing?

What It's Not

This book is a product of my journey to find stillness and fulfillment in a world that can make stillness seem nonexistent and fulfillment unobtainable. I've come across a lot of the ideas in this book through trial and error, through making constant course corrections, through thinking I knew myself and then finding out that I didn't. I've often found what works for me by slowly eliminating what doesn't (usually while worrying there was something else I was supposed to be doing or achieving), and I've generally discovered who I am by figuring out who I am not.

In that spirit, let me make it clear what this book is not. It's not about making radical changes to your life. It's not about finding everlasting happiness. It's not about pursuing a true calling or discovering a hidden passion that will allow you to change the world. It's not about unlocking secret reserves of time and productivity so you can work more efficiently and squeeze more stuff into each day. If that's what you're looking for, there are lots of great books out there that cover many of these topics. This book is not one of them.

Here's why. As far back as I can remember, whenever I considered that existential question—"What's the purpose of life?"—I assumed the answer was happiness. From a young age I had the good fortune to realize that fame and status were fleeting (though, like most people, I still think they sound pretty nice). Material possessions and power didn't seem to be the answer, either. Religion never held particular sway for me. Evolution aside, "to be happy" seemed to be the only answer to the purpose of our existence.

But can happiness really be the answer? No one can be happy all the time. Not only is eternal happiness impossible, but striving for it comes with all sorts of painful side effects. We bury resentments and vulnerabilities. We shun uncomfortable emotions. We wear an outer shell to project confidence and contentment, and an inner shell to protect ourselves from disappointment and discomfort. In our obsession with the next plan, goal, or success that we hope will bring us more happiness, we neglect the present moment right in front of us. We spend our days striving relentlessly to accomplish accomplishments and achieve achievements, anticipating permanent, peaceful bliss when all of this striving eventually pays off.

It never quite turns out that way, of course. Considering the famous words of America's Declaration of Independence, Aldous Huxley wrote, "The right to the pursuit of happiness is nothing else than the right to disillusionment phrased in another way."[13] To seek perpetual happiness is to achieve only perpetual exhaustion and perpetual dissatisfaction. Certainly, we should seek out people and activities that make us happy. But anyone who tries to be happy all the time inevitably avoids potentially rewarding opportunities because the price of vulnerability is sometimes rejection, which can be a deep source of pain and unhappiness. Anyone who tries to be happy all the time forgoes some of the most powerful and meaningful parts of the human experience, those parts that challenge and sometimes even hurt us, but from which we often grow the most. "Happiness is not the surplus of pleasant over unpleasant moments," Yuval Noah Harari writes. "Rather, happiness consists in seeing one's life in its entirety as meaningful and worthwhile."[14] Anyone who tries to be happy *all* the time risks overlooking the moments of happiness that come to us *some* of the time, often when we least expect it.

A couple years ago, I wrote a note to myself in the back of a small Moleskine notebook: "Have long thought the pursuit of life is happiness. But perhaps it's actually fulfillment, meaning." I have no idea what triggered that particular thought at that particular time, but it echoed what the philosopher Henry Sidgwick called the "Paradox of Hedonism." In the words of Dov Seidman, Sidgwick's insight suggests that "if you pursue happiness directly it tends to elude you, but if you pursue some higher, more meaningful purpose, you can achieve it."[15] A happy life, the paradox suggests, arises from a meaningful and fulfilling one. But what constitutes such a life? How do you define "fulfillment?" If happiness is so unattainable, why would meaning and fulfillment be any more likely? And even if this is indeed what you're after, how do you build a life of it?

To sum that up: This book isn't about finding perpetual happiness. Nor is it about uncovering a personal mission that will empower you to change the world. It's not about unlocking your undiscovered passion. It's not about finding a "true calling" hidden deep within you. I hope readers can find such a mission or such a calling, if such things exist for you. If that's what you seek, I'm confident the ideas in the chapters ahead will help you to find and make more time for that pursuit. But the very expectation that within each person is an invigorating, world-changing passion, and the assumption that what makes a person successful is stopping at nothing to pursue that passion, is precisely what has driven so many of us into lives defined by busyness and striving. That's especially true for millennials. Many of us have grown up with the expectation that we should be spending our lives in pursuit of the vague notion of "changing the world." (Why we've been told that the best way to change the world is through working 80-hour weeks in finance or consulting is a conversation for another day.)

Don't get me wrong: changing the world isn't a bad thing. The world needs a *lot* of changing. But the assumption that we will all inevitably spend our lives changing the world is a dangerously addictive notion. If we take this world-changing generational call-to-arms too far, we can easily find ourselves disheartened, burned out, and cynical. That doesn't help *anyone*. The Tibetan Buddhist teacher Yongey Mingyur Rinpoche observes, "People everywhere try so hard to make the world better. Their intentions are admirable, yet they seek to change everything but themselves. To make yourself a better person is to make the world a better place."[16]

No single person can solve all of the world's challenges, and most of us will never change the world the way society tells us we're supposed to. *And that's ok.* Like the quest for perpetual happiness, assuming that you must single-handedly fix the world is to fail if you don't. That's an impossible standard. It impedes the slow-but-steady progress and collective, often anonymous, effort that lasting, systemic change demands. And it causes us to overlook the many opportunities to do a little good that are right in front of us right now. "Nothing is more essential for the twenty-first century and beyond than personal transformation," Mingyur Rinpoche writes. "Transforming ourselves is transforming the world." For a less metaphysical take, consider the simple suggestion of Stanford professor Robert Sapolsky, who has spent decades studying how stress impacts our bodies and minds. "In a world of stressful lack of control," he writes, "an amazing source of control we all have is the ability to make the world a better place, one act at a time."[17]

As we'll soon discuss, cultivating slightly more fulfilling days empowers us to be more supportive of those around us. It helps us see more clearly the opportunities we have right now. And it gives us more strength for the daunting, lifelong struggle of—you guessed it—changing the world.

So, this book is not about finding permanent happiness, nor about changing the world, nor about discovering a true calling. While it is a tool for self-reflection and self-discovery, it is not a silver bullet. You won't find quick fixes in the pages ahead. The book doesn't offer an overnight solution to hack your life. I can't promise that if you read and implement the ideas in the next ten chapters, you'll unlock hidden reserves of time and energy that will enable you to work more, produce more, or survive on less sleep. In fact, my hope is that we can all learn to scrap these types of productivity obsessions entirely.

That's often what the modern-day notions of self-improvement and life-hacking mean, though. They mean doing *more*. Being more busy. Producing more. Checking more things off the to-do list. Handling more tasks. Taking on more responsibilities. Consuming more content. Sending more emails. Packing calendars more tightly. Saying "yes" to more requests. Feeling more rushed and more overwhelmed. If you take the all those productivity blogs and books at their word, as I did for years, you can do more—in fact, you can do it *all*—if you just work more efficiently for more hours. If you just do *more*.

As I worked my way in and out of politics for the better part of a decade, I was convinced that all my life was missing was the time and space to do *more*. If only I hacked my life better, I could develop deep expertise in every policy area while becoming a well-connected campaign strategist while maintaining a dedicated fitness regimen while reading all the best books of the year every year while seeing friends and family most nights of the week while volunteering regularly while doing everything that others asked me to do. This search for self-improvement shortcuts and miracle-cure life-hacks led me through dietary supplements phases, to-do list phases, hustle-at-all-costs phases, socialize relentlessly phases, disappear-from-the-face-of-the-earth phases, minimalist phases, fitness phases, read-and-implement-self-help-books phases, politics phases, relentless-social-media phases, and delete-social-media phases. I was constantly experimenting and searching, trying to find the hidden stash of *more*. I was convinced that permanent happiness and inner peace awaited me around the next professional corner. I was sure some future accomplishment or achievement would finally deliver the everlasting contentment and renown I craved, and that all I had to do to unlock that contentment and renown was find more time to work toward it. But—spoiler alert—it didn't.

What I was seeking with all that life-hacking was something that life-hacking could never unlock. The working and striving to which I became accustomed, even addicted, made it impossible to see what was right in front of me. I was searching for a sense of presence, clarity, and contentment. Of stillness, calmness, and confidence. A state of being in which I could be freed from worrying about missing something, needing to be somewhere else, falling into mind-racing loops of to-do lists and tasks and drafting and redrafting emails in my head, and feeling inadequate or guilty for not working enough.

These days, I'm learning to *not* define self-improvement as the search for the time and space to do more. Instead, my journey toward self-improvement is about taking small steps to shape more fulfilling days, with each new day an opportunity to nudge my life in the general direction I want it to go. That means learning to experience the present and to live with my emotions, no matter how unpleasant they are. It means distinguishing what actually makes me happy from what I project, or what the world projects for me. It means training myself to quiet the inner noise and let go of the grass-is-always-greener restlessness within. It means investing energy in learning a craft and spending time with people I care about in ways that leave me with a sense of peace and contentment. It means not just accepting but *embracing* the fact that I can't do it all. "More," it turns out, is not always the answer.

What's Next

As individual human beings, we have very little influence on the world around us. What does and does not happen to us is rarely in our control. "All kinds of things might happen to you in life," Michael Lewis writes. "By sheer accident only a few of them do. That tiny subset shapes your view of the world, to an alarming degree."[18] Plus, whether it's how we vote, how we spend our time, how we make decisions, how we respond to emotions, or how we interact with other people, our behavior operates on autopilot a lot more than we think. As journalist Robert Wright puts it, "If you ask the question 'What kinds of perceptions and thoughts and feelings guide us through life each day?' the answer, at the most basic level, isn't 'The kinds of thoughts and feelings and perceptions that give us an accurate picture of reality.' No, at the *most* basic level the answer is 'The kinds of thoughts and feelings and perceptions that helped our ancestors get genes into the next generation.'"[19] We're not wired for things like happiness, fulfillment, and meaning to come easily.

But we need them all the same. Despite the biological instincts and compulsions that natural selection has gifted-slash-burdened us with, we're social animals. We need companionship. We thrive on connection. We crave camaraderie. We seek contentment. We laugh. We smile. We have fun. And we *do* have some control over at least one aspect of our lives: how we perceive and shape our days. That means we can work to build days with more of the things that fulfill us, and less of the things that don't.

This book argues that if you can hone in on this one slice of existence that you surely do control—if you can reframe how you perceive and spend your time each day—you can, over time, nudge your life in a more fulfilling direction. In the pages to come, you'll find ten ideas, ranging from specific activities to broader philosophies on work and life, that have emerged from my journey and helped me build more fulfilling days. These ideas aren't hard-and-fast rules, overnight solutions, or radical lifestyle changes. They don't require you to uproot your life or transform into someone else. You don't have to quit your job, move halfway around the world, live off the land, or give all your income to charity. You can simply adjust, ever so slightly, how you see the life you're already living and make little tweaks to how you spend your days. These adjustments and tweaks, whether daily practices or broader ways of interpreting the world, might not feel like much in the short term. But with steady commitment over time, they can fundamentally alter the trajectory of your life.

I started this book by talking about politics and millennials, but the ideas in the chapters ahead are applicable to anyone. They aren't replacements for whatever journey you're already on. They're tools to help you reflect on that journey. Tools to strengthen you for that journey. Tools to help you unlock awareness and appreciation for the life that's happening right now, right in front of you. Tools to make the good times better and the tough times more endurable. Tools to allow moments of joy and contentment to emerge. Tools to help you enjoy the ride of life a little more and be a little more present in it, even in maelstroms of activity and anxiety, such as Capitol Hill.

By building a practice for cultivating awareness, you can seize a bit of control over how you respond to the crazy world around you. By breaking your addiction to busyness and defeating your obsession with productivity, you can reclaim a bit more time to focus on what you really care about and feel a little less guilty when you do. By choosing to view work as a craft to be honed instead of a series of tasks to be checked off, you can find more meaning and enjoyment in daily obligations, no matter how mundane they may feel. By thinking more about mortality, you can unlock a deeper appreciation of the fleeting nature of life. By taking a few steps to live your life with more stillness and more intentionality, you can reclaim a modicum of control in what feels like an increasingly out-of-control world.

If you tip your days in a slightly *more* fulfilling direction, you can be *more* supportive of the human beings around you and have a little *more* strength for the daunting undertaking of improving the world. You can live your life *more* intentionally and with less stress. You can spend *more* time doing what you care about with the people you care about, and be *more* present and aware while you're with them. You can find *more* fulfillment in what you already do. That sort of "more"—the marginal, incremental, routine, bit-by-bit kind—is the one worth pursuing. That's what this book is about.

Perpetual happiness is unattainable. But if you string enough fulfilling moments together, you can build a pretty happy life. Changing the world is an exhausting metric for success. But if you cultivate fulfillment in your own day-to-day experience, you can be more in touch with the world and better equipped to make an impact. Transforming your life overnight is an unrealistic and self-defeating expectation. But if you reframe each day, you can, over time, fundamentally reshape your life.

That was a lengthy introduction. Let's get started.

1

Create stillness

"Stress is a perverted relationship to time, so that rather than being a subject of your own time, you have become its target and victim, and time has become routine."

John O'Donohue[20]

Thinking

Think about how little time you spend thinking

It's a Tuesday in April 2016. I plan to get up early to do some work, or maybe read for a bit, but I sleep in instead. Not the good kind of sleep, but the non-restful, half-awake form of horizontal semi-consciousness interrupted every nine minutes by the cell phone alarm being snoozed and snoozed again. I finally get up and sit for a distracted ten-minute meditation. By now I'm behind. I hop in the shower, already thinking about being late for work, and hop out of the shower, my mind feverishly switching back-and-forth between thinking about being late and rehearsing all the work I have to do today. I start to clean up the kitchen and pick up clothes to do some much-needed laundry, only to realize— yep, I really needed to leave the house eight minutes ago. I stop tidying and gathering the laundry. I leave the house, jump in the car, hoping I have everything I'll need for the day. I drive to the Senate, calculating and recalculating the time it'll take to get there. Maybe *this* will be the lucky morning when every other human being in the nation's capital has decided to stay off the roads? As I make my way to the office, I honk and gesture self-righteously at other drivers, while listening to a podcast, while also refreshing my email at each red light. Requests are already coming in; the to-do list is already getting longer. I haven't yet had time to read the morning news alerts. Maybe it's time to unsubscribe from some of them, but they seem too interesting and necessary. I don't want to miss out on anything.

I finally reach the Senate staff parking lot. I walk briskly toward security, but not too briskly. I'm wearing a suit, and even in April, once you start sweating in hot and humid DC, it never stops. My backpack is pretty heavy because, in a moment of naïve optimism, I decided I would try to squeeze in a workout this afternoon, even though each new message landing in my inbox makes that increasingly unlikely. I finally get through security and to my desk, a standard and embarrassing fifteen minutes late. Everyone is walking around frantically, looking at their phones. Cable news is playing on the TV in the background. Emails pouring in now, with lots of the *Just wanted to follow up this...* variety. I should probably follow up on those.

The day was already going to be busy, and that was *before* the latest Trump tweet. Now a forceful statement in response becomes my new first priority, and everything else is pushed down the priority list, even though all the other priorities still have to get done this morning. My mind sifts through a few of them: *Confirm Brookings Institution speech on Russian interference in U.S. elections... Need to find time to brainstorm ideas... Few sets of talking points to write. Maybe I could repurpose health care points from last month... Need to finish that memo—when's it due again? Why have I been putting this off? Oh right, I need to reach out to that guy—what's his name again... Why did CNN reject that op-ed? Try pitching it to the* Post... *What was that thing I remembered when I was meditating that I need to pick up on the way home? It's...it's...oh well, better start that Trump statement.* "The President's tweets this morning were deeply disappointing..." *Hmm, what's a deeper expression of disappointment than "deeply disappointing?" I wonder what Twitter has to say? When am I gonna start working on that Brookings speech? Man, I am HUNGRY. If I have another cup of coffee will I get jittery? Oh, that's what I needed to do—buy more coffee on the way home.*

Another day in the Senate has begun.

For most of us, tucked in between each step in our frantic morning routines are some of the moments that make life worth living—a tender or funny moment with your partner, for instance, or laughing with coworkers when you get to the office. But those brief highlights aside, amidst the chaos and craziness of our days there's often something decidedly *not* present. It's something we need—or, at least, *I* need—but rarely make time for. It's something that modern life has stolen from us in tiny, subtle increments, to the point where it's almost entirely nonexistent in our lives. We haven't really noticed that it's gone. We've simply grown used to living without it.

What is it? As I got ready that morning, like so many others, there was no stillness. No space. No time to pause. No opportunity to think. No moment when I wasn't planning, counting down, or counting up to something. No moment when I wasn't worrying about what was next, and what was after that, and would I ever have time to do all of it? This reality isn't unique to me. It's not limited to jobs in politics. It's not simply a problem of mornings, or of particular days of the week. Everyone's life is different. But even if the details of our days are unique to us, we all exist in the same over-busy, overstimulated, overwhelmed world. More than ever, we need to find time and space to make sense of it all.

Yet most of us do the opposite. Think about how little time you *actually* spend thinking. I'm talking about a very specific kind of thinking. Not running through a to-do list. Not mentally composing a text message. Not prepping a retort to someone who has upset you. Not counting down the minutes until the end of a workout. Not organizing your calendar while a YouTube video plays in a different tab. Not worrying about how you're going to finish everything you want to finish before a friend comes to visit. I'm talking, instead, about conscious, intentional thinking.

How much time in any given day do you spend thinking constructively? How much time do you set aside for mentally chewing on a single challenge or problem? How much time do you carve out to connect different ideas or concepts in your brain? How much time do you give yourself to simply daydream or reflect? How long do you allow yourself to do nothing before grasping instinctively for your phone, whether out of self-consciousness, habit, or just sheer boredom?

Like many people, I've spent years existing in mental clouds of varied density and fogginess. I've operated essentially on autopilot, far less conscious of the thoughts and emotions and impulses flitting in and out of my brain, and far less in control of my consequent decisions and behavior, than I assumed. This brain fog is due to more than just lack of awareness. I've come to realize that it's also the result of spending all my waking hours focused intently on what's next and what still has to be done, rather than what I'm doing right now or what I've already done. This fogginess is the result of over-scheduling my days, over-programming my brain, and undervaluing the importance of stopping to make sense of it all. It's the result of slowly drifting into a routine in which intentional thinking, whether conscious mind-wandering or the simple decision to flip the switch to "off" for a while, has been sacrificed at the altar of productivity and getting things done.

I don't live in DC or work in politics anymore. These days, I work for an organization that prioritizes flexible working in a country that takes work-life balance a lot more seriously than I had known was possible. I don't have children. I don't make many extracurricular commitments. I spend a lot of time reading and thinking and writing. If the goal is having quiet time to think, my current lifestyle has a lot working in its favor. But even so, my life isn't automatically infused by moments of stillness.

Consider a Thursday in April 2018, two years after the frantic morning in the Senate I described earlier. This one took place about six months after I'd moved to the UK, right around the time I started turning a batch of ideas into the book you're now reading. On this April morning, I decided to work from home. I woke up early, already thinking about trying to drink coffee before fitting in a workout. During said workout, my mind divided its time counting down the minutes until the pain ended and counting up the number of emails and tasks that awaited me when I logged in. When I got home from my workout (a three-minute walk from door to door), I showered, spending far too much time during the shower wondering if the exercise-induced sweating would stop by the time the shower ended, which only caused me to sweat even more. Out of the shower, I quickly scanned the emails that had come in overnight. With my mind now partly occupied by work and partly occupied by complaining to myself about how it's so hot and I'll never stop sweating, I took a few minutes to meditate and read. But my mind was already onto the day's to-do list. The mental whirlwind had begun. Already I was worried about fitting everything in.

Whether it was a Tuesday in the hectic environment of the Senate or a Thursday in the peaceful surroundings of my own apartment, one common thread ran through all of these routine activities: *fitting everything in.* (Actually, there was another common thread: sweating.) Too often, the parameters of every activity we undertake are dictated by the other things we want to do (or have been told to do) and how much time we have to do them. We spend our days desperately trying to fit everything in. And we spend most of our activities trying to fit in even more sub-activities, all while trying to anticipate what's coming next and building increasingly unrealistic expectations of what we can accomplish. During all this fitting in, what's the easiest and, thus, the first item on the calendar that we sacrifice? Blank space. Empty space. Uncommitted space. Time when we could go for a walk, think, journal, talk to a friend, be bored (and possibly inspired), or open up a blank document and start typing whatever comes to mind. Time we *need* to process what's going on in our lives.

Instead, what we get is the foggy knock-off version of headspace that Georgetown University computer science professor Cal Newport describes as a "state of distracted hyperconnectedness."[21] It's an epidemic, and if you're anything like me, the underlying illness has infected you slowly and almost completely, without your even realizing it (since, you know, you don't have time to stop and think about it).

A couple of years before I began writing this book, I jotted down what felt, at the time, like a random passing thought: "Seek out time w/o deadline to think, ponder, brainstorm...no deadline, no looming task/ pressure, nothing to check off, no specific deliverable." Sometime later, I wrote another one: "Seek stillness – calmness – deep thought. Going to have to improve – > setting aside time for deep thought & reading (uninterrupted)." As best as I can interpret these scribbles, in between tasks and meetings and endless things to do, I was receiving flickering signals from my brain that I needed time to pause to try to make sense of it all. It's these flickering fragments of ideas that can turn into insights and, ever so often, passion projects. These are the weird fragments of ideas that require time and space to develop subconsciously before occasionally congealing briefly, fleetingly, in the conscious mind—if we make space for them. The unexpected thoughts that somehow passed through my conscious mind were some of the insights that led to this book, floating pieces of ideas that would've remained buried in the depths of my subconscious had I not given them the time and space to emerge.

I don't remember exactly what prompted those notes, but they surely came at a time when I wasn't frantically trying to cross work tasks off an endless to-do list before fitting in the reading I felt I should do before fitting in the workout I wanted to do. They came because I had a chance to step back from the relentless dash of busyness and getting things done. Some fortunate series of events had allowed me to temporarily set aside the constant sense of "running out of time to get everything done" in favor of just seeing and experiencing my thoughts as they arose.

Who knows—I may have found this stillness in a brief moment of accomplishment. Maybe it was one of those days when work was already finished, when I'd completed everything I needed to do *and* everything I wanted to do, and there was still time left. Perhaps it was late on a particularly productive Friday afternoon heading into a three-day weekend. Or, perhaps it came to me while lying in bed thinking to myself, as the British comedian James Acaster would say, "No more jobs!" to be done that day.

Imagine, though, if I were to make a conscious effort to cultivate this sense of stillness on a regular basis, rather than unexpectedly stumbling upon it late on a Friday afternoon or right before bed?

Rushing
Think how rare it is not to feel rushed

No matter the activity—working out, shopping for groceries, watching a short video, having lunch with a friend, reading a book—think how rare it is *not* to feel the pull of "everything else." Think how rare it is not to feel the sense of guilt that there's something else waiting for you, something that needs to get done, something else you're supposed to be doing. Think how rare it is to sit down to face a challenging assignment or something you want not just to check off but to do *well*, without being aware of the ticking clock, without thinking that you only have 30 minutes to get it done before the next call, meeting, or obligation. I originally titled this book *Finding Stillness* because my search for fulfillment led me to wonder why I sought out these rare moments. I kept thinking: Will there ever come a point when it feels like the world has paused long enough for me to catch up? Will I ever have time just to think? There's another way to think about these questions, though. If such a time came, would I even notice it? What if it's already here?

As with any other activity that matters to you, you can *choose* to make time for thinking, and you can give yourself permission to take this time. You can forgive yourself for not using every waking moment to get things done. You can cultivate and then actually embrace having time to think, rather than feeling guilty because you don't feel you're using each minute "productively." Finding stillness is, in part, about being present and aware in the moment. If you're always counting down the minutes until you have to do something else, you're not really here. Constantly thinking about what else you need to do adds an unnecessary layer of anxiety to the mind (*What if I don't get everything done?*) and infects the time you have with others, preventing you from being present for them. While your mind is whirring in some purgatory between your to-do list and the future, you're missing countless opportunities right in front of you to find moments of stillness, contentment, and human connection.

Consider, for example, the feeling you get when you're talking with someone and you feel your phone vibrate in your pocket. Instantly part of your attention shifts to wondering who has contacted you and whether you need to do something in response, even though what you really *need* to do is stay present with the human being already in front of you. Or compare your commute when you're running late—stressed, anxious, resentful, brain racing and constantly calculating and recalculating how long it'll take to get to your destination—to when you have the time to read, listen to a podcast, chat with a stranger, or just think without worrying about the time. Stillness is about providing the space and security for your brain to operate at its best. It's about calming those ego-driven background anxieties and enabling what you care most about to find a home in your consciousness. Stillness is about turning off all of the brain's false alarms (*Shouldn't I check this? Shouldn't I be doing that? Should I go to that event? How long will this take? What will they think if I don't do that?*) long enough to focus your attention on what's in front of you, whether that's a person you care about or a project you're working on.

It's the type of *work* I do during this focused, present, unrushed time—reading, writing, meditating, learning—that most fulfills me. Even tasks or chores that I don't particularly enjoy are more manageable and satisfying when I don't feel rushed to complete them and can focus instead on doing them well. It's the type of *fun* I have during that time— hiking with my partner Erin, eating dinner with my grandparents, going to the gym with my brother Chris, hanging with our friends and family—that most fulfills me. When I'm in the zone, focused on what's in front of me without worrying about needing to be somewhere or do something else. When I can put my phone on airplane mode and throw it in a backpack with no second thoughts or urges to check emails or get something done. When there's nowhere else I want or feel compelled to be. When I can say with confidence, as Ulysses S. Grant once remarked, "My time is all my own and there is nothing to hurry me."[22]

Stillness
Stillness is an empty calendar for the rest of the day

How often do you find moments of stillness? How often do you actively silence external stimuli? How often do you sit down to work without time pressures or to-do lists looming in the back of your mind? If you're like me, the answer to those questions is rarely, if ever. The lives we lead don't often accommodate these moments of stillness. Even when an opportunity for such a moment presents itself, it's quickly sacrificed when new obligations crop up. Clinical psychologist and meditation teacher Tara Brach observes, "Often the moment when we most need to pause is exactly when it feels most intolerable to do so."[23] When we most need a moment of stillness is when it feels most impractical to make time for one. When we most need to focus on what matters is when we're overwhelmed by things that don't. When we most need to track down the pause button and reboot our perspectives and priorities is when we don't even realize we've gone off course.

Moments of stillness aren't just for thinking about big ideas or taking on big challenges. They are just as important for brainstorming a thoughtful birthday gift, making sense out of your financial situation, or composing a meaningful note to a friend you haven't been in touch with in a while. The point isn't necessarily what you think about but rather that you do that thinking consciously, intentionally, and regularly. Consider how Ta-Nehisi Coates describes his struggle to write his 2017 cover story, "My President Was Black," for *The Atlantic*.[24] Compared to other times in his career when he had more time on his hands than he knew what to do with, Coates writes, "The challenge here was not in the interviewing [for the piece] but in finding that quiet space I'd occupied to write all of my previous pieces. I needed to find some way to withdraw from the world, to ignore every critique of my writing I'd (mistakenly) read, and to not forget my own voice."[25] We all struggle to hold onto our own voice—who we are and what matters most to us—in the midst of this crazy and hectic world that constantly demands our time and attention. We all struggle to find a way to withdraw from the world, even for a moment. But those moments of stillness, of clarity, of awareness are vital. We need this time to think. Why don't we prioritize it?

If you wait for thinking time to present itself, you're likely to wait a long time. If you can only find stillness when all of your afternoon calls happen to be canceled on the same day or when you finally go careening into a Friday evening, then you're doing yourself a disservice by placing your mental well-being at the mercy of your schedule, which is often defined by what other people need from you. Cultivating time to be still almost always requires a conscious effort. For me, that conscious effort is one of those weird paradoxes of life: I *know* this is good for me. I *know* I'll benefit from this. I *know* a little bit of thinking time can make my day a lot more fulfilling. But instead I'm stumbling through each day, my time and attention dominated by little tasks and obligations, with a constant, stressful monologue of "what's next?" running in the background.

Perhaps there's a lesson to be learned from former Secretary of State George Shultz, who practiced what *New York Times* columnist David Leonhardt describes as a "Shultz Hour."[26] As Secretary of State for Ronald Reagan, Leonhardt writes, Shultz "liked to carve out one hour each week for quiet reflection. He sat down in his office with a pad of paper and pen, closed the door and told his secretary to interrupt him only if" his wife or his boss (the president) called. Shultz tells Leonhardt that "his hour of solitude was the only way he could find time to think about the strategic aspects of his job. Otherwise, he would be constantly pulled into moment-to-moment tactical issues, never able to focus on larger questions of the national interest. And the only way to do great work, in any field, is to find time to consider the larger questions." While most of us aren't America's highest-ranking diplomat, nearly all of us allow ourselves to be "constantly pulled into moment-to-moment tactical issues," responding to whatever flashes on our screens and leaving our time, attention, and focus to the mercy of our surroundings.

Another approach to making time for stillness is what my dad, Steve Lowenstein, calls "Tuesdays to write." My dad long recognized the difficulties he and his colleagues at the University of Colorado School of Medicine faced as they tried to balance commitments to teaching, supporting their families, practicing medicine, writing, and publishing. In January 2009, inspired by the uninterrupted (and often unconnected) simplicity of working in a hotel room or on an airplane, he wrote an article urging faculty members to "protect a few extra hours each week— hours that can be used for writing, study, self-renewal, or the 'quiet pursuit of knowledge.'"[27] At the top of his list of recommendations is to schedule "blocks of time for writing. ... Then, protect this time: it is now unavailable for walk-in visits, phone calls, or rogue meetings." If setting aside four uninterrupted hours one day each week to write or think strikes you as implausible or unrealistic, my dad suggests considering whether you really have any other choice. "Should you postpone your writing until the day when you magically have more time?" He notes that reserving a weekly block of time comes with an added benefit. If that time has already been set aside on your calendar, you'll be less overwhelmed by spending time on other responsibilities today because you know that another Tuesday to write (or a Shultz Hour) is right around the corner.[28]

A third way to carve out deliberate thinking time in the middle of a busy day is to pursue what Cal Newport calls "productive meditation." This is not meditation in the traditional sense, although it has some of the same characteristics, namely, an intentional focus on a single topic or challenge, and a conscious effort to return to that topic or challenge when the mind inevitably wanders. (We'll get into actual meditation in the next chapter.) For a productive meditation, Newport suggests, "take a period in which you're occupied physically but not mentally...and focus your attention on a single well-defined professional problem."[29] By way of example, he suggests a walk in the middle of the day. Not a walk where you check your phone constantly or call a friend or listen to a podcast, but a walk where you intentionally think about a specific challenge, and consciously bring your mind back to that problem when you get distracted.

"Productive meditation" is really just another way of proactively creating mental space. Imagine the challenges you could work through or the ideas you could come up with, or even just the complicated emotions you could process a bit better, if you, to paraphrase Newport, "develop an ability to carefully work through thoughts during the many hours" you spend walking or commuting or standing in line or just lying in bed.[30] Newport also notes an added benefit of productive meditation: It's a chance to hone the ability to concentrate. Even if your intentional thinking doesn't yield brilliant, earth-shaking insights during every commute, you can practice being present and sitting with your thoughts.

Intentionality
Make a conscious, intentional effort to pause and think

Life moves quickly, and most of it is out of our control. We can't wait for stillness to magically present itself, because it won't. Whether it's a Shultz Hour or a Tuesday to write or a productive meditation, we have to create these moments. We have to protect them. And we have to pause from time to time to appreciate finding them where we can. As Ryan Holiday argues, "It's not simply a matter of saying, *Oh, I'll live in the present.* You have to *work* at it."[31]

Stillness doesn't require a specific day or a weekend or a vacation or a special occasion. No matter your schedule, with proactive and intentional effort there are plenty of ways to find a brief dose of it in the middle of every hectic day. Sometimes, it's as simple as sitting down for a few minutes with a pen and a blank notepad, or switching the phone to airplane mode and opening a new document in a notes app, to brain-dump the little things that have been bouncing around in your head, drawing down your mental and emotional reserves and creating that lingering feeling of being overwhelmed and forgetting something. The Stoic philosopher Marcus Aurelius remarked, "People find pleasure in different ways. I find it in keeping my mind clear."[32] A short, intentional mental cleanse can clear the mind, recalibrate the brain, and bring a little more peace and perspective to each day. Like a powerful medicine, stillness is highly concentrated. It doesn't take a huge dose to make you feel a lot better.

"Creating stillness" means different things to different people. For me, stillness is an early morning of unrushed work when I can write without worrying about the clock or the looming email inbox. It's sitting on a bus at the end of a long day without feeling compelled to check my phone or watch the clock or get something done before I reach my destination. It's stepping out of a chaotic open-plan office or a noisy happy hour to take a short walk and engage in some mental processing. Other times, stillness has nothing to do with quiet surroundings, and everything to do with a quiet mind that's fully engaged in the present moment. It's walking home from a tough workout class with Erin on a Saturday morning knowing we have a day ahead that's free of commitments or obligations. It's an unplanned night of creative energy when I focus on writing for two straight hours without worrying about what else I should be doing. It's an unexpectedly fun catch-up over drinks that begins with to-do lists and unfinished tasks on my mind but ends with me forgetting to look at my phone for hours. It's a long dinner with friends or family without anywhere to be afterwards, or anything to do while I'm there, except be present.

Stillness is the moment when you don't need anything else and your thoughts aren't anywhere else. The moment when, as Tara Brach describes it, "we have stepped outside the normal rush and into the openness and clarity of a 'time out of time.'"³³ Like a number of ideas in this book, this may sound a bit selfish. But cultivating stillness is about being fully present for others as much as it is about finding fulfillment for yourself. If you can find calmness and stillness in any situation, you can be there more fully for those who need you.

How do *I* find these moments? In many ways, that question is the driving force behind the ideas in this book. I find stillness by including items like "make time to think" and "take walk" on my to-do list, so that I'm reminded every day that life is more than a series of burden-some obligations. I find it by scheduling blocks of time for deep work, and by trying to write and meditate first thing every morning. I find it by uninstalling apps and deleting social media accounts, so I'm better able to resist the compulsion to spend time online. I find it by recognizing that stillness and stimulus rarely coexist, so I disable technology traps that steal my attention, like smartphone notifications and email alerts. I find it by consuming more of the content I find fulfilling and less of the political news that stresses me out. I find it by taking concrete steps to reject my addiction to busyness, like refusing to check work email on the weekends. I find it by catching myself before I say "yes" to something based solely on FOMO, the fear of missing out. I find it, somewhat unexpectedly, when I take time to reflect on mortality. I find it when I realize I'm needlessly judging people around me, or needlessly judging myself, and make a conscious choice to practice forgiveness instead.

I don't do all of these things all of the time. When I do manage to do them, I don't do them perfectly. Each approach to stillness is a work in progress. But the goal isn't a life of perpetual stillness, which is surely impossible anyway. The goal is to find a little stillness each day. A little more today than yesterday, if I can, and a little more tomorrow than today. Even the simple act of *thinking* about these tools and techniques helps me to reframe how I go about my days so that stillness sits higher on my list of priorities than it used to.

But what if you're not even thinking about doing these things? What if stillness isn't yet on your radar? What if you don't even realize that you've been going through day after day, morning to night, without setting aside more than a passing moment to think, to brainstorm, to ideate, to gather your thoughts, to process the world?

Stillness starts with awareness.

2

Build awareness

> *"The truth is that meditation does not eradicate mental and emotional turmoil. Rather, it cultivates the space and gentleness that allow us intimacy with our experiences so that we can relate quite differently to our cascade of emotions and thoughts. That different relationship is where freedom lies."*
>
> Sharon Salzberg[34]

Meditation

Awareness is a practice

It's a rainy Tuesday morning in London, like a lot of Tuesday mornings, and a lot of other days of the week, too. Today, I wake up early(ish), only hitting the snooze button once. I check that the alarm on my phone is actually off, and not still in snooze mode. Otherwise, I don't look at my phone, which remains on "Do not disturb." I throw on a hoodie, shuffle into the kitchen, and start brewing coffee. While the coffeemaker does its thing, I sit in the blue living room chair, with the heating pad on my back because I have the lumbar ailments of an octogenarian. I put in my headphones and open my phone's Headspace app.* Before I have

---

* There are plenty of great meditation apps, devices, websites, and services. I mention Headspace only because it's the one I usually use. (I also use the timer function on the Insight Timer – Meditation app.) I haven't tried most of the other apps, for no particular reason other than that Headspace works for me, so I haven't needed to go looking for alternatives.

a chance to start thinking about all the busyness and running around and to-do-ing and fro-ing that the forthcoming day will bring, I tap "play" on a 30-minute unguided or semi-guided meditation. And so begins another iteration of a habit that's transformed my life more significantly and more subtly than anything else in recent memory.

I practice a very simple form of meditation. I don't recall the Buddhist name of my preferred practice, but I file it under basic mindfulness. For 30 minutes (sometimes less, occasionally more), I sit. I start by scanning my body from head to toe, sometimes naming each body part as I go to help me focus on it. Next, I turn my attention to my breath. I watch thoughts coming and going, and I try to focus on the sensation of breathing. With each breath, I picture accompanying numbers (in – one, out – two, in – three, out – four, and so on), counting up to eight before I start the count again. When I realize that I've gotten lost in thought, which happens approximately every single breath, I say to myself, "Thinking, thinking," return my focus to the breath, and start counting again.

I continue this pattern until the timer on my phone sounds. Sometimes when I meditate, my mind is calm, and I can focus on the feeling of breathing and not become distracted by random thoughts for five, or even ten, breaths, before getting carried away. Other times, my mind is all over the place, and I spend the entire session thinking about this book, or an upcoming work task, or some disagreement Erin and I had, or an awkward comment I made during a meeting the day before, or what I'm doing with my life, or any number of other things, usually all mixed together. Many of my best days begin with meditation. But despite my good intentions, I sometimes don't meditate first thing in the morning, or in my usual chair at home. Sometimes I meditate while walking, or lying down on the floor, or sitting on a train. Sometimes I forget until right before bed. Sometimes I fall asleep meditating. Sometimes, I don't meditate for as long as I'd like.

I didn't start my meditation practice at 30 minutes a day; only recently have I begun to do half-hour sessions consistently. For the first year, I didn't even think of meditating for more than 10 minutes. Then I began dabbling with 15 minutes, every now and then. Slowly, 15-minute sessions became the norm, so I experimented with 20. The pattern continued. As I write this, 20 minutes usually feels pretty easy. Thirty is my new norm, and I'm now starting to explore 45-minute sits. The point is that almost every aspect of how I meditate is subject to daily change and longer-term evolution.

In fact, since 2016, when I started meditating regularly, only four aspects of my practice have remained constant. First, I meditate every day, even if only for a minute while standing in the bathroom stall of a restaurant because I forgot or didn't have time earlier in the day. Second, I have never found inner peace, everlasting bliss, or zen-like calmness, and I never expect to. Third, my mind wanders nearly every second of every meditation. That's not hyperbole—I consider it an enormous accomplishment if I make it through a full eight breaths before I get lost in thought. I can literally be visualizing the words, "My mind will not wander," and before I know it, I'm thinking about whether I should do laundry this morning or if it would make more sense to wait until tomorrow. The fourth consistent aspect of my practice is that I've never regretted meditating. No matter how burdensome or pointless or distracting or silly it may feel, no matter how excruciatingly bored or anxious I get during some sessions, I'm always grateful when I've done it.

Awareness

Awareness changes everything

What is the awareness I'm seeking with all this meditating, and why does it matter? For me, awareness is the recognition that I'm not really in control of my thoughts or my emotions. It's the understanding that while I might like to *think* that my behavior is always intentional and my decisions are always rational, they're not. It's the sudden realization in the middle of an argument that anger and judgment have taken over. It's the moment of clarity during a family dinner that the phone vibrating in my pocket or the work task looming in my mind can wait. It's the conscious acknowledgment that thoughts and emotions and distractions are perpetually hijacking my interpretation of everything I'm doing and everything happening around me, whether I'm planning my day or working on my relationship or trying to better understand the people in my life. It's the practice of coming back to the present moment when past regrets or future anxieties steal my attention. Awareness is a bit more clarity about the world happening around me. It's a bit more appreciation for the joys, and a bit more acceptance of the pain, that come with living. In ways small and large, quotidian and consequential, shallow and deep, awareness is about reasserting the agency we can while recognizing how little agency we actually have.

Let's bring this back down to earth. Over the years, as I explored the internet literature of self-improvement, personal growth, productivity, life-hacking, and mental well-being, I repeatedly encountered one activity: meditation. Many of the high-performing people I read about made meditation a core part of their daily routines. For a long time, though, my own nonexistent practice didn't extend beyond occasionally reading about other people extolling the virtues of meditation. Why didn't I try meditation when I first read about it? Perhaps it was because the image of an orange-robed monk sitting silently in a mountainous monastery, having renounced all material possessions, meditating on peace for all creatures, didn't really resonate with me. Or, perhaps, for the same reason I still haven't developed a reliable journaling habit, despite recognizing how easy it could be and how valuable it might be to my mental and emotional health, and adding it to a decade's worth of New Year's resolutions: I simply didn't do it.

Late in the summer of 2016, I downloaded the Headspace app (not for the first time) and decided to give it a go, starting with just 10 minutes. That first time, I lay flat on a yoga mat. It was a weekday, I was wearing jeans, and the sun was still up, so the Senate must have been out of session (otherwise I would never have been dressed so casually or home so early).** I don't remember feeling much after those first 10 minutes, other than the mildly pleasant feeling one experiences shortly after committing to a new habit but before encountering the challenges of sticking to that habit. My main reaction was surprise that I didn't fall asleep. Yet for whatever reason (perhaps subconsciously anticipating future presidential election outcomes), this September 2016 session of Headspace was the first instance of what has become a daily mindfulness meditation practice. It's now one of the most important things I do each day. As Robert Wright observes, "What begins as a modest pursuit— a way to relieve stress or anxiety, cool anger, or dial down self-loathing just a notch—can lead to profound realizations about the nature of things, and commensurately profound feelings of freedom and happiness."[35] I have become a true believer and, perhaps somewhat annoyingly to those around me, one of those people who talks and writes about the virtues of meditation.

Before I continue, let me be clear about two things. First, there's more to building awareness than meditating. Second, no matter how much I hype it here, meditation has not transformed me into a new, morally superior, eternally-at-peace person who's permanently calm and open to the world. Not even close. But it has had a significant, noticeable effect on how I process emotions, how I feel about myself and those around me, how I experience each day, and how I view the world. As the writer and meditation teacher Sharon Salzberg observes, the impact of a daily practice "likely won't show results in the formal period we dedicate to meditation each day." Over time, though, it "will show in our lives, which of course is where it counts."[36]

◆

** The Senate being "out of session" means that most senators have returned to their home states, so most DC-based staffers are dressed more casually, far less busy, and working more humane hours. It's probably no coincidence that I made time to start a consistent meditation practice when I wasn't as exhausted and as busy as when the Senate was in session.

I first encountered meditation in a relatable way when I read Dan Harris's half-memoir, half-meditation treatise, *10% Happier*, in which the ABC News anchor (and fellow alum of Maine's Colby College) chronicles his own journey from meditation skeptic to evangelist.[37] The book's title comes from his conclusion that meditation hasn't transformed him into a new person or completely revolutionized his worldview. But on balance it has, he believes, made him 10 percent happier than before.*** Harris defines mindfulness as "the ability to recognize what is happening in your mind right now—anger, jealousy, sadness, the pain of a stubbed toe, whatever—without getting carried away by it." The "entire endeavor" of meditation, he writes, "revolves around moments of mindfulness, interrupted by periods of distraction, then gently catching yourself and returning to the breath."[38] Focus on the breath (or anything intentional), witness thoughts as they come and go, notice when you get distracted, and consciously return to the object of focus. Find awareness, lose awareness. Find awareness, lose awareness. Over and over and over again. It's that simple.

It can be helpful to point out what meditation is not. It's not about turning off the mind. It's not about achieving a state of blissful and ever-present nothingness. It's not about stopping or fixing passing thoughts or feelings, even the uncomfortable ones. It's not about healing all grudges or preventing new ones from forming. It's not about neutralizing anger or judgment or sadness. It's not about building a beautiful new emotional house for you to shelter in.

Meditation simply helps you notice your thoughts and try not to get sucked into them. And, when you inevitably do get sucked in, it's

---

*** I first came across *10% Happier* long before I applied any of its lessons to my own life. As with most of the books I read, I highlighted some passages in my Kindle, assuming I would remember all of it despite all evidence to the contrary, and went about my life, not returning to meditation for a couple more years. Only in hindsight have I realized how the notion of becoming 10 percent happier is an ingenious and refreshingly realistic way to describe meditation's potential impact. It's also a powerful way to think about habit formation in general, including a lot of the lessons in this book. If we could get 10 percent more fit, eat 10 percent healthier, or get 10 percent more work done, of course we'd do it.

about recognizing that fact more quickly, acknowledging those thoughts without blame, and letting them go. As Harris puts it, "thinking without awareness can be a harsh master."[39] For most of us, the master's grip on our minds and behavior is stronger than we realize. Mindfulness is about cultivating awareness of how often we're carried away by our thoughts and emotions, and in doing so, lessening that tendency just a little.

What's transformed the way I think about meditation is a particular way Harris (and presumably many others) describe it. Meditation is an exercise for the mind. A "bicep curl for your brain," Harris calls it.[40] It sounds so simple and obvious, but it's worth emphasizing: "The brain, the organ of experience, through which our entire lives are led, can be trained."[41] *The brain can be trained.* We know physical fitness is important, so we try to eat healthily and exercise our bodies every day. Why not give mental and emotional fitness the same level of commitment? You can treat the brain like any other muscle that can be strengthened with time and effort. Meditation is called a practice because, as with physical fitness, there's no end point. Success isn't measured by crossing some threshold beyond which you achieve perpetual bliss. There is no such threshold; you succeed every time you practice. You succeed every time you notice your thoughts wandering, recognize them, and return to your breath or object of focus. "The moment when we notice ourselves veering away from the present moment is the most important," Sharon Salzberg writes. "We see where we've become lost and begin again."[42] Noticing when you become distracted isn't a sign of failure. It's a sign of success.

Noting
Noting is unexpectedly powerful and liberating

The more bicep curls for the brain I've done and the greater the sense of awareness I've built, the more I've been able to appreciate the volume and complexity of thoughts and emotions bombarding my mind. *All. The. Time.* Just when I think I may finally have conquered them with a spark of awareness, I'm gone again, lost in thought, without even realizing it. This is where the concept of what Tara Brach calls "mental noting" comes in. Essentially, noting is about saying to yourself what you're thinking or experiencing to become more aware of it. By identifying your passing thoughts and emotions, you gain a bit of an opportunity not to get lost in them. When the mind wanders during meditation, for example, and "thoughts carry your attention away," Brach suggests, "gently note, 'Thinking, thinking,' and then reconnect."[43] After noting the thought, you simply return your focus to where it was before. The technique is widely applicable. Recognizing a craving can become "craving, craving." Realizing you're getting carried away in planning your day might be "planning, planning." Noticing unnecessary judgment of a colleague at work, or a stranger standing on the wrong side of the escalator, could prompt "judging, judging."

The power of noting lies in its ability to create a tiny foothold of awareness. Saying "thinking, thinking" might translate to, "Well, there my mind goes again, off on some tangent. I recognize it, and I choose not to let it take me away." The exact words or phrases hold no specific power. What matters is the conscious and intentional act of noting. Implicit in this recognition is a sense of self-forgiveness for getting carried away by the thought or emotion, and for recognizing that these mental drifts and impulses come with being human. The passing thoughts that seize control of your mind aren't your fault, so there's no reason to punish yourself for them. But there's also no reason to be controlled by them.

Noting works for a simple reason: As humans, we can only think one thought at a time. You may think you're thinking about multiple things at once but, like the illusion of multitasking, you're not. Author Susan Cain writes, "Scientists now know that the brain is incapable of paying attention to two things at the same time. What looks like multitasking is really switching back and forth between multiple tasks."[44] When you think you're thinking multiple thoughts, your brain is really just shifting its focus from one thing to another, endlessly and pointlessly. That's exhausting, but the fact that you can only think one thing at a time is also an opportunity. Say someone cuts you off in traffic. You can be angry and honk and throw your hands up in righteous disbelief (which is, as Erin will tell you with a sigh, one of my go-to moves). Or you can think, "That's anger I'm feeling." But your brain can't be angry and also think "That's my anger!" at the same time. It's a subtle distinction. By recognizing a passing thought and noting it, you replace the thought with awareness of the thought. That brings you closer to escaping the thought's grip.

Cultivating awareness when an unpleasant emotion or feeling strikes, or when thoughts come flying into your brain unprovoked and unannounced, is a way of neutralizing their power. It's a way of reminding yourself that you control the response. It's like being in a scary situation or outside your comfort zone—hiking a knife-edge ridge, say, or preparing to give a big speech—and choosing to crack a joke. Done tactfully, it doesn't minimize or trivialize the seriousness of the situation. Nor does it resolve anything. But it reminds you that you can choose, and have chosen, how to respond to the situation. It provides you with a little more awareness and a little more control, and thus a little more freedom from being blindly led by your emotions. Count me among the skeptics who've been pleasantly surprised by how powerful noting can be. (Many meditation instructors, including Tara Brach, describe this process using the acronym RAIN: recognize, allow, investigate, nurture awareness, i.e., let go.)

Control
Take back control (of the mind)

Meditation is one of the tools I depend on most to cultivate a greater sense of awareness in the world. So, a few years into a regular meditation practice, what do I have to show for it? As I've mentioned, even at my calmest, stillest, most focused, and least distracted, it's hard for me to make it more than a breath or two without my mind wandering or getting lost in thought. That's both normal and completely unsurprising. Think about how long, and how intensely, the human brain has been trained *not* to focus only on one single thing. Then consider the thousands of years of evolution that have trained us *not* to pay attention to things like breathing or walking, but instead to be hyper-alert to perceived threats and fears. Then add in the distractions of the current digital age, and it's no wonder that even a few mindful breaths can seem impossible.

It took a long time for us to build up impatience, and it will take a long time for us to build up patience. The evolutionary wiring that reacts instinctively to distractions didn't develop overnight, so of course it will take a long time to hone a sense of awareness and focus that will help us to resist those distractions. It's a meditation *practice*, after all. Rather than thinking of getting lost in these thoughts as failure, I try to look at it as a chance to practice. When I notice out-of-control mental planning, for instance, like my habit of composing emails or reorganizing to-do lists in my head, I frame bringing the mind back to the breath as an exercise, as another step on the long road to better mental fitness. This reframing lessens the pressure of perfection, and each repetition of that endless exercise makes the brain a tiny bit stronger. The volume of distractions and wandering thoughts to which I succumb every time can still leave me feeling like a failure. But then again, a few years ago if someone had told me to sit in a chair and follow my breath for 30 minutes, I would've been bored out of my mind and highly agitated thinking about all the other things I should be doing with that time. That's some sort of progress, at least.

The skeptical reader may still be thinking, "Uhh, I guess it's cool that you can sit still for 30 minutes a day. So what?" Fair question. To paraphrase the Brexiteers, those hard-core advocates for the UK's departure from the European Union, the point is to take back control. Take back control from your runaway thoughts and emotions. Take back control from the passing impulses that hijack your mind and put your reactions on autopilot. Take back control from the endless mental planning of schedules and hypothesizing of pointless things. Take back control from the future- and goal-obsessed mentalities that lead so many of us to spend so much of our lives striving to shape the future that we forget to exist in the present.

Brexit aside, when it comes to individual awareness, the first step in taking back control is to recognize that you never had much control in the first place. You may *think* you're in control, but science says pretty unequivocally that that narrative is mostly a comforting illusion. The journalist Robert Wright observes, "This is a matter of nearly unanimous agreement among psychologists: the conscious self is not some all-powerful executive authority." Wright's analogy for the human brain appeals to me for obvious reasons. The conscious mind, he suggests, is "less like a president than like the speaker of the U.S. House of Representatives, who presides over votes and announces the outcome but doesn't control the votes. Of course, the speaker of the House may do some behind-the-scenes nudging and so exert some influence over the votes. And we can't rule out the possibility that the conscious mind gets to do some nudging here and there."[45] But running the show? Nope. As much as we like to think we're in control, we're not.

What does it mean for me to recognize that I'm not in control? Today, after a few years of daily meditation, there's no doubt I'm the same person I was a few years ago. There's no doubt I'm living the same life. But there's also no doubt I'm more aware of that life as it goes by. I'm more aware of just how little control I have over which thoughts pop into my head at any given moment. I'm more aware of emotions coming and going, and just how quickly my mind can wander even at the very moment I'm trying not to let it wander. I'm more attuned to my relentless inner monologue, which is a propaganda broadcast of criticisms, to-dos, distractions, ambitions, unnecessary plans, and random thoughts that come and go throughout nearly every waking moment. I'm more likely to recognize a tendency to plan and re-plan my day, or even the next few minutes, over and over in my head, or fixate on something relatively trivial, endlessly replaying hypothetical scenarios. (Should I shower at home or at work? Should I work out and then meditate, or meditate then work out? Should I check my email now? How about now? How about now?)

Because I've committed time and effort to a regular awareness practice, I'm quicker to recognize my mind playing the top 40 greatest hits of insecurities and regrets and judgments on repeat, and quicker to realize just how paralyzing and exhausting that can be. These days, when Erin and I are in the middle of a disagreement, I'm more likely to recognize my inclination to avoid conflict or, when the conflict ship has sailed, to try to fix everything right away. When I leave a meeting, I'm more likely to catch myself before immediately reaching to check my phone or press play on a podcast and forget everything that's been discussed over the past hour. When I'm sitting at the kitchen table with my grandparents, I'm more likely to notice my mind drifting to work responsibilities, making me anxious and distracted and removing me from the room. When I feel sad and wistful after my parents head back to the airport after visiting us in London, I'm more likely to sit with that feeling and embrace what it means, rather than bury it. Thanks to my awareness practice, I'm more likely to notice when my mind is obsessing over something and trying to control the uncontrollable, which distracts me from the challenges and injustices that deserve real attention and effort.

These days, I'm more inclined to recognize the creeping onslaught of Resistance (a counterproductive force we'll discuss in the next chapter), meet it head-on, and make a conscious choice to shelve my procrastination-enabling distractions. I'm better at noticing an impulsive mental recoiling from things that are hard, scary, or uncomfortable. These are often things that I really care about (like writing), but about which my brain misleadingly says, "This will be unpleasant, so you just need to get it over with." I'm more cognizant of my tendency to make plans to do things while resisting actually doing them. I'm more likely to cut myself some slack when I get distracted or come up short on the goals I've set myself. Perhaps most importantly, I'm more capable of recognizing when I've been unwittingly taken hostage by thoughts or emotions, even though I've convinced myself that I'm fully in control.

I'm more likely to do all these things, but I'm never *guaranteed* to do them. Not every time. Not even close. Each meditation is about coming back to the breath, distraction after distraction. And meditation as a whole, like life, is about coming back to the practice, day after day after day.

Space
Build buffers, not walls

As we'll discuss in chapter eight, in my teens and early twenties I prided myself on building an impenetrable emotional wall to shield me from vulnerability, rejection, and life's scary and difficult emotions. I thought I was building a fortress. All I was really doing, it turns out, was burying these feelings in the backyard. I was building the wrong thing. To paraphrase legions of Democratic politicians in the Trump era, what I needed to do was build buffers, not walls.

There's immense power in knowing that it's possible to build what Sharon Salzberg calls "space between our actual experiences and the reflexive stories we tend to tell about them." [46] Unlike walls, buffers don't isolate. They simply create a little extra space to operate, a little more room to maneuver. Putting a buffer between yourself and your thoughts doesn't close you off from other people. It doesn't isolate you from the world. It doesn't free you from the obligation to confront injustice or the responsibility to intervene in the face of wrongdoing. Counterintuitively, insulating yourself with a small buffer of self-awareness can actually empower you to face the world more openly and authentically.

The fact is, though, there will always be some separation between you and the world, whether you acknowledge it or not. Will you use that space to open up to the world? Or will you build a protective barrier to hide behind? If you choose openness, you can use this space to control how you respond to any situation. Marcus Aurelius suggested simply, "Choose not to be harmed—and you won't feel harmed. Don't feel harmed—and you haven't been." [47] Awareness frees you to explore your thoughts with a little more clarity, and choose your responses with a little more intentionality, than you might otherwise. Robert Wright calls it "the basic irony of mindfulness meditation: getting close enough to feelings to take a good look at them winds up giving you a kind of critical distance from them."[48]

As my dad read an early draft of this manuscript, he was reminded of an article published in a medical journal by University of South Carolina pediatrician Amy-Lee Bredlau, in which the author confronts a devastating aspect of her profession. When a terrible disease takes the life of a young patient, she wonders, "Where do you put the pain?"[49] It can't all stay inside, she reasons. No human could contain all of that. Nor is it possible to grieve uncontrollably for every child she treats; she'd never be able to do her job or support the families of her patients. "In the end," she writes, "I let the pain wash through me, and I let it leave... I don't put the pain anywhere. I let it wash through me and go wherever it goes."[50] She doesn't avoid it, but she doesn't wallow in it, either. She simply recognizes it, acknowledges it, and sits with it. Bredlau knows she doesn't get to choose her emotions. But she has enough of a buffer between herself and those emotions that she can choose how she responds to them. Making that choice starts with an awareness that the choice is even there. That gives her a little extra agency.

Almost everything happening in any given moment is out of our control. The one thing we might be able to control is our response. Yet most of us try to control the uncontrollable while willfully yielding what little authority we have to passing emotions or impulses. Why is that? We're not resigned to being life's passive bystanders, blindfolded and dragged around by these impulses and emotions. You can choose not to let your well-being be dictated by outside events or forces. You can choose to experience the uncomfortable emotions inherent to life and, as Amy-Lee Bredlau puts it, let them wash through you. "Because awareness is as present in our lives as the air we breathe," suggests Yongey Mingyur Rinpoche, "we can access it anywhere, anytime."[51] When you think about the world this way, every moment becomes a chance to find awareness. This is true even for the little things. Sitting in traffic. Doing a tough workout. Getting irritated by a work project. Being annoyed by a noisy commuter in the quiet car (a borderline unforgivable sin). Reading an infuriating news story. Without awareness, it's easy to get caught up in the emotions of these situations, yielding control of your time, attention, and well-being to someone or something else. With some space between you and the world—space that's always there, if you choose to see it—you can recognize the uncontrollability of life and do your best to select how you respond.

These days, I still get frustrated and angry and sad and moody (just ask Erin). I still feel insecure and anxious and stressed about things over which I have no control. I still feel all the unpleasant emotions popular culture wrongly implies meditation will "cure." The difference is that I'm now better at recognizing these feelings, looking at them semi-objectively, and letting them go more quickly. That lessens their grip and makes their impact more manageable. I'm more likely to recognize different thought patterns, like the one that tells me it's more important to clean out my inbox than have beers with a friend (as if emails were a measure of worth, and as if the inbox won't fill up again tomorrow). I'm more equipped to notice when I'm counting down, with futility, until the end of something—a painful commute, a boring meeting, a bumpy flight—thereby prolonging the suffering. I'm more likely to notice the feeling that tells me I must solve a conflict immediately to avoid the discomfort of sitting with it, rather than confront the underlying issue or let a painful moment wash through me. Building a sense of awareness has simply made it a little easier to pause, note these tendencies, let them pass, and not judge myself for feeling or thinking them in the first place.

Suffering
Everyday life is full of suffering, much of it self-imposed

In addition to writing bestselling books of incredible complexity, author and historian Yuval Noah Harari is an exceptionally committed meditator who goes on a two-month silent retreat every year.[52] This means that what he writes about comes both from professional study and personal experience. "According to Buddhism," Harari observes, "the root of suffering is neither the feeling of pain nor of sadness nor even of meaninglessness. Rather, the real root of suffering is this never-ending and pointless pursuit of ephemeral feelings, which causes us to be in a constant state of tension, restlessness and dissatisfaction."[53] For some, these ephemeral feelings might be immediate physical or emotional pleasures. Perhaps they're the sense that if only you check more things off your to-do list or gain access to more senior-level meetings or get a raise, you'll be satisfied. Or maybe they're the feeling that the only thing missing in your life is more sleep, or stronger fitness, or greater professional success, or the perfect romantic partner, or more time to do more work. Whatever our pursuits are, they leave us incapable of contentment because their requirements can never be met. Obsessively chasing after them is a form of self-imposed suffering, to which we needlessly subject ourselves day after day.

(To be clear, there are different types of suffering. At any given moment, human beings around the world are encountering and living with horrific physical, mental, and emotional pain. Countless people are burdened with traumatic experiences and memories. To some degree, each one of us, to paraphrase the famous saying, may be fighting a great battle that no one else knows about—illness, addiction, depression, loss. There's a vast amount of pain in the world, and much of it is a universe away from the moment-to-moment "everyday" suffering that I'm describing here. What I'm referring to is the relentless, often imperceptible, often self-imposed ways that we make our own lives more difficult. *This* is the suffering that you, as an individual, can control. The world's pain is not zero-sum, and you can attack everyday suffering without drawing comparisons or losing sight of the great injustices in the world.)

"We live so much of our lives pushed forward by these 'if only' thoughts, and yet the itch remains," Dan Harris writes. "The pursuit of happiness becomes the source of our unhappiness."[54] Many of us realize

—at least objectively—that any long-term goal of satisfaction, meaning, or fulfillment won't come from the next pay raise, promotion, possession, or professional achievement. We know this intellectually. We tell it to friends and loved ones who we see chasing things that we know won't bring *them* fulfillment. Yet we ourselves still pursue and strive relentlessly. This postponement of fulfillment in pursuit of the impossible is a crutch—and a comfortable and flattering one at that. As Tara Brach describes it, "Living in the future creates the illusion that we are managing our life and steels us against personal failure."[55]

Enter meditation, or any other awareness practice. It doesn't solve the relentless striving. What it does is help you to see that you're often driven and controlled by irrational pursuits and itches. The awareness that can emerge through meditation allows you just a little more control to determine whether you really want to dedicate all your time and attention to chasing, seeking, and striving, and whether the inevitable suffering that results is worth it. Like mental noting, learning to be aware of the routine suffering of everyday life dampens that suffering. Even more importantly, it helps you to confront, with awareness and acknowledgment, the profound human suffering in the world, rather than running away from it when it threatens to overwhelm you.

Striving isn't the only form of everyday suffering we impose on ourselves. Judging is another. I'm constantly controlled by feelings of judgment: Judgment of myself. Judgment of others. Judgment of situations. Judgment of systems. Judgment of humanity as a whole. These feelings are often wrapped tightly around how I feel about my life at a given moment. When I've just accomplished a difficult task or spent a couple hours writing, I'm likely to be less judgmental. But if I'm stressed or defeated or irritated or even just running late, watch out you who dares to almost run into me because you're walking and texting, or you who misreads my email, or you who speaks too loudly on the phone while I'm trying to read—my silent mental wrath is coming for you. Judging someone, Yongey Mingyur Rinpoche observes, "provides a toehold to climb up from and allows you to temporarily enjoy the illusion that you are better than someone else." That's because, he says, "It's never just: They are bad. It is also: Therefore, I am good."[56]

The fleeting sense of self-righteousness that comes with judging others doesn't translate into feeling good. That doesn't mean we're bad people; it just means we're human. But it also means we waste a lot of brain space and emotional energy trying to find ways to feel superior to those around us. Constantly finding yourself irritated by things outside of your control is exhausting and futile. Interrupting these compulsive spirals of negative thoughts is a means of taking back control from the all-consuming forces of self-righteous indignation and superiority. Awareness doesn't stop judgment, but it does help you recognize it, interrupt it, and replace it with something a little less draining. When you catch yourself judging someone, you can choose, for instance, to give them the benefit of the doubt—or simply let your judgment go. Forget all the good that decision might do for the person you're judging. Just think of the relief you'll feel. That relief, that freedom, is the power of awareness.

Freedom
Meditation is about awareness, and awareness is about freedom

Over the past few years, my brief meditation journey has coincided not just with switching careers and moving across the Atlantic with Erin, but also with an unexpected presidential election outcome that completely transformed my view of my own country and my responsibilities in the world. The move has also coincided (though perhaps not coincidentally) with finding a deeper, more sustained sense of fulfillment in my day-to-day existence. Throughout all this upheaval and growth, meditation hasn't fixed anything, but it has served as a foundation for transforming, bit by bit, how I interact with the world. "The wisdom of seeing that everything passes is liberating," Tara Brach writes. "Observing desire without acting on it enlarges our freedom to choose how we live."[57]

Meditation has served as the jumping-off point for building awareness of emotions that try to take me hostage. It's helped me recognize the allure of FOMO, the emptiness of social media, and the pull of activities I do because they're easy or because I think I'm expected to do them, not because I enjoy or learn anything from them. It's also empowered me to go through each day slightly less reactive and slightly more fulfilled, an almost imperceptible transformation on a daily scale that can have a monumental impact over a lifetime. As someone constantly thinking about the future ("what's next?") with a tendency to normalize my successes and not forgive my shortcomings, meditation has helped me recognize these feelings, note them, and accept them simply as empty thoughts that will always be coming and going.

Meditation is for the good times, too. I often find myself in a reflective mood during difficult times—"Why am I sad?" or "I don't like this. How can I fix it?" But I'm less reflective when things are going well, when I'm coasting along in a happy daze. Building awareness and honing an ability to step out of the hectic rush forward helps unlock the joy and happiness that I otherwise sail right through. It helps me appreciate the moments when I *am* fulfilled, satisfied, and content, rather than constantly wondering what comes next or when the moment will end. Meditation, like anything that brings us into the present, helps me appreciate moments of happiness for what they are, *while* they are.

One final note. This chapter isn't an instruction manual for meditation. It is just my experience. Even though I've spent the past few years practicing meditation and reading and listening to a lot of meditation-related content, and even though you've just read a couple thousand words of my thoughts about it, I would not describe myself as even an amateur meditator. I'm so far from expertise that it feels deeply presumptuous to write any of this. It's not false humility or self-deprecation to say I'm not equipped to teach anyone how to meditate—it's simply a fact. I am *wholly* unqualified.

But I'm sharing this anyway because spending a few minutes each day practicing meditation has flicked an internal switch of awareness that's transformed how I experience my life. Cultivating a sliver of awareness through meditation has helped me become a bit more appreciative of the joys, and a bit better at sitting with the chaos and pain, that are inherent to life. It's also brought my mind closer to a place where kindness, generosity, openness, forgiveness, and understanding come a little easier than they used to. I make more space for those feelings, and that makes me feel better—with, one hopes, some positive side effects for those around me.

What better way to reframe each day than simply to be a little more aware of it?

3

Make work a craft

"Your work is craft, and if you hone your ability and apply it with respect and care, then like the skilled wheelwright you can generate meaning in the daily efforts of your professional life."

Cal Newport[58]

Presence

The commitments of modern life conspire to distract us

In my early 20s, first as a student running the Colby College radio station and then as a young professional working on Capitol Hill, I trained myself to judge my productive output by standards familiar to many: emails sent, inboxes emptied, to-dos checked off, meetings and calls scheduled, contacts established, calendars filled, weekends worked, hours not slept. Similar metrics applied to some of the other side hustles I took on, like organizing an annual world tour for a ski film company and, later, building a political networking organization with my friend Shad. No one sat me down and told me my professional worth depended on these factors. I simply adopted them through observation and office osmosis. Everyone else seemed to be busy all the time, so I should be, too. And if I managed to be more busy than everyone else…well, then who knew what I might be able to achieve? Even my personal goals, from eating better to reading more books to undertaking my own self-education in politics and world affairs, were measured in outputs in which *more* almost always meant *better—more* successful, *more* valuable, *more* accomplished, and so forth.

I kept myself frantically busy with activities and commitments. I reasoned that the more items I had to juggle and the busier they made me—the longer they took and the more exhausted I was by them—the harder I was working and, therefore, the more important and worthwhile I was. I believed the relentless busyness of my life guaranteed me access to some special club of busy people. These were the people with whom I made eye contact early in the morning at the office or late at night on the Metro and thought, "You look tired. I look tired. We must be busy with important and significant things for which we'll someday be respected and remembered!"

We'll talk more about the busyness addiction and the productivity obsession in chapter five, but here's the key takeaway for now: During these years, I was almost never fully present for anything I did. Take graduate school. For a couple years during that busy period, I spent my days working on Capitol Hill and my nights studying for a master's degree at George Washington University. At the office, between committee hearings and meetings with health care advocacy groups, I was thinking about what I needed to do for school that night. Meanwhile, during evening classes, as well as trying to stay awake, silence the perpetual grumbling of my empty stomach, and pay attention to obscure theories of public administration, I was catching up on work emails and thinking about the tasks I hadn't completed that day. I was so unfocused and disengaged from the program that I was basically a nonexistent member of my cohort. (At a class get-together a year or so after graduation, I failed to recognize many of my former classmates. When I asked someone who all these strangers were, she exclaimed, "Those were *our classmates*," understandably bewildered that I didn't register any of their faces or names.)

Instead of focusing on what was happening in front of me, I was always thinking about what was coming next, what still needed to be done, and, for some incomprehensible reason, what other commitments I could add to my already-overflowing plate. I rarely felt fulfilled at school, at work, or in the spare moments I had to see a friend or work on a side project because my head was never entirely there. I was obsessed with everything *except* the present moment. Life was happening right in front of me, and all I could think about were my to-do lists and future accomplishments.

Many of my responsibilities during those years—learning about public policy issues, drafting legislation, writing articles, understanding those arcane public administration theories, researching grad school papers—demanded deep focus and sustained concentration, at least if I wanted to do them well (which, one would hope, was the whole point of doing them). But focus and concentration were in short supply. Rather than making time for the big, meaningful stuff, I measured my accomplishments and progress in the LinkedIn connections I made and the lines on the school syllabus I crossed off. Instead of diving into important-but-challenging tasks in front of me, I would flit between the little stuff, constantly distracted and obsessed with checking items off my many lists. I was mired in busyness, but was I doing anything of value? Was I learning anything? Was I choosing to do these things for any reason other than juggling too many responsibilities made me feel important?

Mostly, I was stressed, exhausted, oblivious, and distracted, forever wondering why the finish line for all these tasks and responsibilities never felt as if it were getting any closer. That I was a card-carrying member of the busy people club was increasingly my only consolation.

Deep Work
Work deep. Single task. Be present

This book is about reframing your days to make your life more fulfilling. Many of us spend a significant portion of our days working on different things in different capacities—jobs, careers, passion projects, studies, fitness, family, social life, causes, commitments. So, it follows that we should try to make these kinds of "work" more fulfilling. (One semantic point before we continue: To me, "work" represents any activity in which I invest my time, energy, attention, and care. It's not restricted to "things I get paid for" or "things I have to do." But if "work" has negative connotations for you, feel free to mentally replace it with something else, such as "activities" or "how I spend my time.")

When it comes to work, no single book has had a greater impact on the way I understand the quest to make the time I spend on it more fulfilling than Cal Newport's *Deep Work: Rules for Focused Success in a Distracted World.** I urge everyone to read *Deep Work* in its entirety, but its premise is simple: The type of work necessary to create meaningful output often requires deep, sustained, uninterrupted concentration. What constitutes meaningful output could be anything, from writing a book to reading history to learning a language to carving a piece of wood. It could simply be undertaking administrative tasks you've been assigned, but with more focus and fewer distractions. Regardless of the activity, the type of mental engagement required is characterized by long periods of presence and intense focus on a single task.

A key premise of Newport's "Deep Work Hypothesis" is that, today, human beings are perpetually distracted. Many of us spend so much time in "frenetic shallowness," Newport argues, that we *"permanently* reduce [our] capacity to perform deep work."[59] This reality owes something, at least in part, to a concept he cites called "attention residue," or the notion that "when you switch from some Task A to another Task B, your attention doesn't immediately follow—a *residue* of your attention remains stuck thinking about the original task." As Newport writes, "the constant *switching* from low-stimuli/high-value activities to high-stimuli/low-value activities, at the slightest hint of boredom or cognitive challenge…teaches your mind to never tolerate an absence of novelty."[60] By attempting to multitask, you deplete your ability to focus on what's in front of you and train your brain to crave constant stimulation. This observation will ring true for anyone who's found themselves without

---

*   There's probably no book I've recommended more in the last few years, except perhaps Bryan Stevenson's *Just Mercy: A Story of Justice and Redemption.*

access to their cell phone for even a few minutes. How frequently do you feel a hint of boredom and instinctively reach for a dose of distraction? How often do you begin to work on something that you've been putting off and, upon running into the first challenge, automatically open Instagram to escape the challenge rather than work through it? We're not always conscious of it. Technology-enhanced life has cultivated a finely tuned, deeply embedded inability to concentrate.

The antidote, according to Newport, is deep work. He defines deep work as "professional activities performed in a state of distraction-free concentration that push your cognitive capabilities to their limit." Put another way, deep work is "the batching of hard but important intellectual work into long, uninterrupted stretches."[61] From these definitions, Newport's intended audience seems clear: professional employees, usually white-collar office workers, whose responsibilities require both a great deal of mental energy (writing, coding, researching, analyzing) and a lot of distracting tasks (emails, calls, meetings, emails, social media, emails, more emails). It's a call to action for knowledge workers who spend much of their time in front of computer screens and who want to make sure they're not automated out of the job market in ten years. That covers a lot of people, including me and many people I know, but it's still a relatively narrow audience.

That narrowness is a shame, because I think the principles behind deep work are about more than job security for knowledge workers. The type of effort and focus deep work demands is about more than being a valuable commodity on LinkedIn. Working deeply can make *any* type of work more fulfilling. Newport argues that human beings derive immense satisfaction from applying sustained focus to single activities. "The act of going deep," Newport writes, citing compelling psychology research as well as his own experience, "orders the consciousness in a way that makes life worthwhile."[62] No matter how you define "work," you can choose to reframe today's tasks, responsibilities, and obligations—whatever you have to do, for whatever reason—as activities that you'll undertake with all of your attention and focus. Instead of seeing a given task as one of a never-ending series of begrudging obligations, you can see each item as something to take pride in and focus intently on. In other words, by working deeply you can begin to see your work as a *craft*.

Shallow Work

The world doesn't make it easy to work deep

The opposite of deep work is what Newport calls "shallow work."[63] For many of us, our days are consumed by shallow work. In part, that's because deep work is hard. When you're staring at a blank screen that you're responsible for transforming into a detailed report, for instance, it's much easier to decide to respond to a WhatsApp message from a friend that's been lurking unanswered for a couple days. Or check Instagram. Or submit a timesheet. Or follow up with that person you never got back to about that thing. Or clean out the fridge. Or get some coffee. Or sort of do all these things at once in different tabs on different devices while listening to a podcast in the background.

But it's not only easily accessible distractions or a lack of willpower that leave your days inundated with shallow work. It's also an issue of incentives. Much of modern society equates shallow work with productivity and worth, while undervaluing what can be produced through long-term, sustained concentration. Because that's what the world around us does, that's what we internalize and, in turn, that's how we operate. We train ourselves to automatically denote a busy day of semi-distracted multitasking as a "productive" day, no matter whether we've actually "produced" anything.

I was no exception to this pattern until I stumbled into a role that forced me to prioritize deep work: writing speeches in the U.S. Senate. It was only as a speechwriter that I realized that the type of work I was avoiding, in part because it didn't fit with my traditional productivity metrics, was actually the type of work I found most fulfilling. My deep work awakening (i.e., discovering that there was a more fulfilling way to work than frenzied juggling while being perpetually distracted) was helped by the fact that I first read *Deep Work* while in that job. As life-altering books often do, Newport's book put into words and made me aware of what I had slowly been coming to realize as a speechwriter: The activities and vocations that matter most to us are often simultaneously right in front of us and impossible for us to see. *How* we're working is often just as important as *what* we're working on.

Writing is one of the crafts that politics depends on but rarely makes time for, particularly in the modern media era. An entire day or more can be interrupted by a legitimate breaking news event or, just as likely, by a single erratic tweet or faux scandal. Politics today often revolves around a catchy line or "hot take" on Twitter. An entire "crisis" can erupt and be resolved online in a matter of hours, known only to the political staffers, journalists, and pundits who participated in it. In this world, particularly if one is working for the party out of power, one's time can easily be consumed by reacting to external events rather than working proactively. Even if most voters won't read an entire op-ed column or watch an entire speech—another reality of today's media environment—preparing articles and speeches nonetheless requires deep research, uninterrupted time, and sustained concentration. None of these requirements describe the work environment of Capitol Hill, which reflects the reactive and short-term media ecosystem it's shaped by, as well as the fact that everyone has too much to do and not enough time to do it.

Before becoming a speechwriter for Senator Chris Coons of Delaware, I'd written some speeches, columns, reports, and other items requiring sustained bouts of single-tasked focus. But it was only when I wrote for someone who spoke frequently and who took his speaking engagements seriously that I was required to write with enough frequency and concentration that "write speech" could no longer be a box I checked off as part of the job. It *was* the job. If I wanted to do the job well (or just keep the job), I had to accept that there would be no end to this particular responsibility. Senator Coons would always have more speaking obligations, so I would *always* have to write. And he would always want his speeches to improve, so I would always have to improve. That meant two things: I had to learn to see writing as a craft, rather than a task. And I had to find ways to conduct deep work in a shallow-work environment.

As a speechwriter, part of you—the ego, largely—hopes that the person you write for will say what you've written word-for-word. It feels nice when that happens. But what's even better is to write for someone who only goes public with the good stuff and tosses the rest. Someone who challenges you, critiques your work thoughtfully, and throws out the so-so parts while honing the parts that work. Someone who shares your vision for continual improvement and impact. I was fortunate to find myself writing for someone who fit that description. Soon after starting as a speechwriter, I quickly came to realize that there would be no end point. No finish line. If I couldn't learn to embrace and find fulfillment in the *process*—in this case, the process of writing and rewriting—I'd never succeed in the job. Nor would I enjoy it.

The more I wrote for Senator Coons, the more this reality became clear. I became more familiar with his voice. I began to anticipate the messages he sought to convey to different audiences. I learned about the stories he liked to tell and the policy issues he cared about, all of which allowed me to spend less time writing basic talking points and more time developing themes, coming up with rhetorical twists, and identifying new communications opportunities. I started to see my job as something more than a series of obligations. Instead of asking myself, "What's next after I finish these talking points?" or "How can I get this done as quickly as possible?" I began to step back and think, "How can I make this speech more impactful? Who can I call? What internet rabbit hole can I explore in search of the perfect quote? Instead of finishing this just to have it finished, why don't I sit with the draft for an hour and see what comes to mind?"

As my view of the role shifted, I began to notice an evolution in my own emotional well-being. At the end of each day, the difference between feeling happy, fulfilled exhaustion, and drained, zombie-like exhaustion, was the depth of the work I had done that day. While a day honing a long, difficult speech left me feeling satisfied and accomplished, a day switching incessantly between email, Twitter, cable news, and my to-do list left me unsatisfied and unfulfilled. A satisfying day was characterized by uninterrupted hours of challenging writing and rewriting, leaving me with a feeling of having created something, not a day bouncing in and out of meetings while I shuffled tasks and emails around on my phone. Winifred Gallagher writes that "the skillful management of attention is the *sine qua non* of the good life and the key to improving virtually every aspect of your experience."[64] A sense of fulfilled exhaustion, I came to realize, reflected time spent with depth and focus. *That* would be my metric for fulfilling work.

Political speechwriting may be a unique role, but the fundamental evolution of how I saw my job, from a series of tasks to a craft, is hardly limited to writing or to politics. No matter your personal or professional circumstances, life on its default settings can easily thrust you into a constant state of shallowness, leaving you exhausted, overwhelmed, and unfulfilled. You have to take proactive steps to work deep because, as Cal Newport suggests simply, "a deep life is a good life."[65] A day characterized by lengthy, intentional bouts of sustained concentration can be deeply fulfilling. Again, that can be true regardless of what you're working on. "Work" doesn't have to be inherently meaningful or creative to benefit from focus and depth. Almost any activity of any kind, even just responding to emails, can be done with deliberation, care, and single-tasked focus. In other words, as a craft.

Singletasking

"One thing at a time. Most important thing first. Start now." [66]

Many psychologists and journalists have studied and opined on "decision fatigue," the possibly real and possibly manufactured idea that we have a finite amount of willpower and decision-making strength on any given day. As with several other well-known psychology studies, the research supporting this concept (which is also known as "ego depletion"[67]) is facing increasing scrutiny for its inability to be replicated.[68]

But the notion of decision fatigue still resonates. Even President Obama made it part of his mental framework. "You'll see I wear only gray or blue suits," the "decider-in-chief" famously said in 2012. "I'm trying to pare down decisions. I don't want to make decisions about what I'm eating or wearing. Because I have too many other decisions to make. ... You need to focus your decision-making energy. You need to routinize yourself. You can't be going through the day distracted by trivia."[69]

Regardless of the concept's scientific validity (which is not my usual standard, for the record), the lifestyle validity of decision fatigue is not in question. Few things drain my reserves of focus and creativity more quickly than making decisions and repeatedly switching between tasks. I picture my brain as a computer that's been charging (i.e., sleeping) all night. In the morning, once my computer-brain has been booted up with coffee, it runs like new. All the work and knowledge from the day before is there, saved (and backed up endlessly), but no other processes are running in the background, needlessly draining the battery. I'm not yet thinking about the news, the errands I need to run, or the work meeting I have scheduled for later in the day. I'm not sending, reading, or responding to messages. I'm not yet watching the clock, mentally counting down the time until I have to turn my attention elsewhere. In my computer-brain, there aren't yet any updates downloading. No alerts or to-do list reminders or calendar notifications are popping up on the screen. There are no lingering browser windows with countless tabs, each reminding me of a passing thought or search query that remains unfinished. The first file I open (perhaps a Word document of the latest iteration of this book) loads quickly and crisply. Although I know my computer-brain's performance will wax and wane over the course of the day, for now it is uncluttered, recharged, and focused.

That's how I think about the working mind. As far as I know, there's no scientific basis for this analogy. But, like "decision fatigue," whether this idea of a computer-brain is scientifically supported or just anecdotally appropriate, its consequences ring true for me. The type of deep, focused, fulfilling work I enjoy most is incompatible with multitasking. Switching tasks, starting new ones, and managing multiple attention targets will always leave something running in the background. (This is Cal Newport's concept of "attention residue.") If you spend a lot of time and energy moving through small, inconsequential decisions throughout the day, you're not going to have the mental strength for the big decisions. If you waste attention and energy on shallow tasks, you'll have little attention or energy left for the big stuff that you really care about. And if you don't make time to focus on the big stuff—the stuff that matters most to you—you're less likely to create fulfilling days.

Cutting back on the nonstop decision-making and pseudo-multitasking that dominates our lives doesn't only benefit knowledge workers or people working on creative projects. Focusing and being present can make even the most mundane activity more enjoyable and fulfilling. If your job is to respond to customer service inquiries, you can focus on that, not that *and* Instagram *and* the news. If your job is taking care of your children, you can focus on that (or them), not on child care *and* scrolling through Facebook *and* making a phone call. If your job in this moment is to pay your bills, try to focus on that, not that *and* your overflowing email inbox *and* the webinar playing in a corner of the screen *and* a Skype message from a colleague flashing on the toolbar.

Focus on the task in front of you. When you finish that task for the day, you truly finish for the day. In your computer-brain, you save the work and close the program before opening the next one. Maybe you even restart the computer by going for a walk after installing some updates that you've been postponing for a couple of days. No multitasking, no switching back-and-forth, no unnecessary decisions, no lingering guilt about having picked the easy task yet again. The formula for making your work a little more fulfilling is pretty simple. As the blog Lifehacker put it in 2010: "One thing at a time. Most important thing first. Start now."[70]

When and How

Know thyself (or at least know when and how thyself likes to work)

When it comes to work, we spend a lot of time thinking about the *whats*. What we have to do. What we want to do. What responsibilities we want to take on. What we might want to do next. What skills we want to learn. What connections we want to make. These *whats* are often long-term goals, and while it's important to aim for a little progress on them most days, realizing them in their entirety is often beyond our control, at least right now. Yet we spend far less time thinking about the daily aspects of our work that we can control: *how* we work and *when* we work. Tweaking the routine *hows* and *whens* of your work can make it significantly more fulfilling.

Start with *when*. Daniel H. Pink wrote an entire book exploring when human beings operate best. He argues that energy, focus, and attention aren't entirely functions of willpower, determination, or diligence. Sometimes what distinguishes a disciplined hour from a distracted one is pure physiology. Combining his own experience with human behavior research, Pink concludes that "all of us experience the day in three stages—a peak, a trough, and a rebound."[71] For three-quarters of us, Pink finds, our energy and focus peak in the morning, slump early in the afternoon, and rebound (to some extent) later in the day.[72] Individual systems vary, of course, but identifying how your physiology affects you—knowing your own peaks, troughs, and rebounds—will allow you to shape your days in the most effective way possible. If you naturally have better focus in the morning, for instance, why make your life more difficult by scheduling a bunch of calls in the morning and trying to write in the afternoon when your energy and focus are ebbing? When you work best during the day also matters because our lives are divided into days. The day, Pink writes, "is perhaps the most important way we divide, configure, and evaluate our time."[73] That makes the day the ideal canvas for trying to nudge your life in a more satisfying direction.

It also makes how you feel at the end of the day a helpful metric for knowing whether you're building the kind of life you desire. No matter what we do, most of us feel tired at the end of most days. But there are different kinds of tired. There's the "What exactly did I do with all my time today? Did I really just spend eight hours responding to messages other people sent me? I haven't moved all day, but I'm exhausted!" kind of tired. And there's another kind of tired that I call "contented exhaustion," the kind I began to feel after a day of writing speeches. In my case, contented exhaustion follows a day of focus and presence, of pushing through tough stuff and making my brain work, of embracing challenges and tackling big goals instead of succumbing to distraction and shallow work. For me, and I suspect for many of us, it's this second type of tired that signifies a fulfilling day.

That brings us from the *when* of work to the *how*. When you come home feeling contentedly exhausted—fulfilled by the work you did that day— how did you work? Was it a day when you were in back-to-back-to-back-to-back meetings and calls, sneaking a few emails in between (or during)? Or was it a day when you tuned out everything to write an article, code a program, or edit a video? Was it a day when you managed a large group of people, guiding a team toward success? Or was it a day when you were only responsible for your own output?

For most of us, our days don't consist of picking one extreme or the other. Reality is more complicated than that. But the core question is: In your ideal world, how do you work best? What way of working do you find most enjoyable and fulfilling? What leaves you contentedly exhausted at the end of the day? In a now-legendary blog post, venture capitalist Paul Graham describes two general ways of structuring a workday: a maker's schedule and a manager's schedule.[74] A manager's schedule, Graham writes, is "embodied in the traditional appointment book, with each day cut into one hour intervals."[75] Graham refers to the manager's schedule as the schedule of bosses, "powerful people," and those who "command." But I'd say that the manager's schedule has become the schedule for quite a few of us non-commanding non-bosses too. You may not have meetings or calls every hour, and the meetings and calls you have may not be that critical, but throughout each day you've got at least a few commitments of varying importance lined up, likely arranged around a more senior person's schedule.

For some people, operating on a manager's schedule brings fulfillment. They thrive on coordinating and participating in calls and plans and meetings, on managing people, on working in teams. "A great manager is essentially an organizational engineer," investor and Bridgewater founder Ray Dalio observes. "Great managers are not philosophers, entertainers, doers, or artists. They are engineers. They see their organizations as machines."[76] Managers derive great satisfaction from building and fine-tuning those machines, and someone who thrives on a manager's schedule might find enjoyment and fulfillment in fitting many different meetings and conversations into each day.

Not everyone does, though. That brings us to the maker's schedule, in which large blocks of time, ideally entire days, are set aside for making: writing, coding, designing, editing, crafting, thinking. As Graham writes, "there's another way of using time that's common among people who make things, like programmers and writers. They generally prefer to use time in units of half a day at least. You can't write or program well in units of an hour. That's barely enough time to get started."[77]

This distinction isn't just about the type of work being done. It's also about the type of person doing the work. Someone whose job doesn't entail any making or creating might still work better with a maker's schedule, for example. Some of the maker-manager distinctions mirror differences between extroverts and introverts. Author Susan Cain has demonstrated how Western society, and many workplaces within it, has been designed to reward managerial behavior while overlooking, or even penalizing, those who operate best with a maker's schedule. From open office plans, which supposedly encourage idea-sharing and teamwork but can make focus and deep work nearly impossible, to the corporate obsession with team-oriented work and meetings, many of the institutions in which we spend our days are designed by and for managers, not makers.[78]

Few of us are in a position to change these organizations and institutional behaviors, at least not overnight. But if we learn to recognize how deeply these default ways of working are embedded, we might be able to respond to them more effectively. Just as your physiology can determine *when* you work best, your personality can determine *how* you work best. Gaining an understanding of whether your ideal schedule is a maker's schedule or a manager's one, or whether you're a stronger introvert or extrovert, can help you better structure your days so they're slightly more aligned with who you are and how and when you prefer to operate. You probably can't revolutionize your workplace or exercise complete control over your day-to-day schedule, but even making little tweaks so that you're working with the grain instead of against it can make a big difference. Cain writes that "research from a field known as 'person-environment fit' shows that people flourish when, in the words of psychologist Brian Little, they're 'engaged in occupations, roles or settings that are concordant with their personalities.'"[79] What small steps can you take to better align how and when you work with who you are?

I'm continually surprised at the subtle ways these societal biases creep into our individual worldviews, altering how we evaluate our work and redirecting our trajectories from what we want to be doing to what we think we're supposed to be doing. For instance, I long assumed that a manager's schedule reflected success and importance. The busier one's schedule or the more people one had reporting to them, the more productive (and thus worthwhile) one was. While deep work and creative undertakings were nice ideas, I assumed they should fit between calls and meetings, not the other way around. An empty calendar wasn't an opportunity to focus without interruption or distraction; it was a timeslot that I failed to fill with calls, meetings, and other indicators of workplace value. Similarly, I thought that not managing people was a glaring shortcoming in my professional experience that I would someday have to rectify. For years, I listed the vague goal of "managing people" as a professional aspiration, not because I actually wanted to lead and oversee a team but because I thought I was expected to. I thought a maker's schedule was a luxury, while a manager's schedule was a necessity.

As I moved between different political jobs and then out of politics altogether, I kept trying to force myself into a managerial mindset. However, as I honed my awareness practice and began to reflect on the type of work that left me frazzled at the end of the day and the type that left me contentedly exhausted, I finally admitted something to myself: I don't want to manage people or organizations. My ideal way of working involves as few meetings and calls as possible. If I can help it, I don't want my time to be determined by someone else's schedule. For some, meetings and management are fulfilling. For me, they're part of what Cal Newport calls "the cacophony of voices attempting to convince knowledge workers to spend more time engaged in shallow activities."[80]

The more I've explored these ideas and experimented with them in my own workdays, the more I've come to question many of the tenets of the modern office environment. These are the "That's just the way things are!" rules: Busy is good, the more frantic the better, and if you're not frantically busy, you're not working hard enough. Multitasking and constant connectedness are inevitable, even desirable. All human beings must work in high-performing teams, while at the same time cultivating a sense of individual territoriality to be defended whenever anyone comes near their turf. Success, status, commitment, and worth are measured by being available 24/7, physically present at a desk during working hours, sending emails around the clock, opining on discussions just for the sake of having an opinion, and considering our responsibilities mainly to be responding to what others ask us to do. (And that doesn't even begin to consider countless other workplace biases, both implicit and explicit, from gender and accessibility to racial, cultural, and socioeconomic barriers.) We simply accept many of these precepts, perhaps because when we're new we don't know any better, and by the time we should know better we've been indoctrinated. These ways of thinking, which have become as good as gospel for many organizations, seep into our personal lives. Over time, they pervade how we see and understand the world. What can we do instead?

The notion of fulfilling work means different things to different people. Many people don't have the ability to work from home or turn off email notifications for hours at a time. But anyone can hone an awareness of the type of work and the ways of working they find most fulfilling. Within the limitations of your circumstances, you can do what's possible to tip more of your days in that direction. Even if you can't create your ideal work environment overnight, simply identifying it and seeing how it's impacted by your personality and your physiology can be clarifying and liberating. It doesn't matter whether your preferred day leans toward a maker's or a manager's schedule. One type of day isn't inherently superior to another. It all depends on how you're wired and what you're working on. Even if you wanted to, it's not always possible to avoid the "cacophony of voices" that Newport describes, whether in an office or in life in general. No matter how strong your preferences are or how perfect your job may be, no one can spend every day doing *only* the type of work they prefer.

But we often have more agency than we think. These days, for example, I seek as much deep, creative work as possible, while still accepting that some days won't allow for working deep at all. Some days I'll get caught in the shallow end of calls and distractions, and that's ok. Equally importantly, I recognize that other people—colleagues, friends, strangers—have entirely different ways of working, and sometimes I have to adapt. That's ok too. You don't have to revolutionize your schedule right now. If you can learn *when* and *how* you operate best during the day, you can begin to shift your days in a slightly more rewarding direction. That shift may seem small, but it's far from insignificant. Fulfilling moments make more fulfilling days, and more fulfilling days make a more fulfilling life.

Resistance

The Resistance is real

Whether maker or manager, early riser or night owl, practitioner of shallow work or seeker of the deep, identifying how and when you work best can make your days more fulfilling. But this recognition is just the first step. After all, developing a better understanding of your physiology and personality doesn't actually *do* any work. (Remember, "work" in this context refers to anything you're laboring to achieve, not just what you get paid to do or what someone says you have to do.) There's often another factor that challenges motivation, enables procrastination, and stands between thinking about and doing work. This factor is a cruel, insidious force that the author Steven Pressfield has deemed *Resistance*.[81] Resistance is that powerful, imposing, and often overwhelming feeling that arises when you want to work on something but don't, won't, or can't. This force is present in each of us, at least to some degree. Between us and what Pressfield calls the "unlived life within us"—the book you want to write, the music you want to record, the skill you want to learn, the promotion you want to apply for, the goal you want to accomplish—is Resistance.[82]

What Pressfield's description does so brilliantly is put a name to something so many of us struggle with but are unable to identify. In most cases, Resistance isn't an actual person, rule, or tangible impediment to forward motion. It isn't even a single feeling or emotion, such as fear or laziness, or an excuse, like having too much other stuff to do. Resistance is what prompts you to create the excuse. It's a constellation of internal forces conspiring against you. It's a self-imposed barrier to your own progress. It's a relentless presence that, for whatever reason, keeps you from working on the things that you care most about. When it comes to writing, for instance, "It's not the writing part that's hard," Pressfield says. "What's hard is sitting down to write."[83] The same could be true for any passion project or side hustle that you care deeply about, or even any difficult task you need to do but simply can't bring yourself to act on. The barrier between you and starting is Resistance.

The more you can recognize Resistance, the greater your capacity to neutralize its grip, and the better equipped you are to benefit from what this strange force is trying to tell you. That's because Resistance can serve as a gauge for the work you care most about. "The more important a call or action is to our soul's evolution," Pressfield writes, "the more Resistance we will feel toward pursuing it."[84] Resistance, Pressfield says, "will unfailingly point to true North—meaning that calling or action it most wants to stop us from doing."[85] How do I know when a particular activity is going to yield satisfaction or fulfillment? How do I know when I really care about doing something? I know, for instance, that spending a couple of hours working intensely on a political column leaves me feeling good. Yet, when I sit down to write, I constantly feel compelled to check my email or start the laundry or tidy the apartment first—anything to keep from writing. Counterintuitively, that's one way I know that writing matters to me. That's the illuminating power of Resistance.

You don't really have to understand Resistance, but you do have to figure out ways to overcome it. And to overcome it, you first have to be aware of it. When I encounter Resistance, as I did when writing this paragraph (and, indeed, most of the paragraphs before and after it), I try to approach it mindfully. Step back. Identify it. Observe it from a distance, making a mental note that perhaps I feel this way because the work is important to me. (I might even use the noting technique we discussed in chapter two, saying to myself, "Resistance, resistance.") Then I can make a conscious decision to ignore it, and start to write. As my mind seeks out new reasons *not* to start writing, I'll think, "You can do 150 words, even as a stream of consciousness," which makes Resistance seem much less insurmountable. Or, when avoiding a workout, I'll say to myself, "You can do 15 minutes," which feels less daunting, even though I know 15 minutes will probably turn into a normal-length workout.

"The more Resistance you experience," Pressfield observes, "the more important your unmanifested art/project/enterprise is to you—

and the more gratification you will feel when you finally do it."[86] In its confounding and contradictory way, Resistance is both the force that has kept me motivated to write this book and the force that has kept me from writing it more quickly. Not everything you're avoiding is a secret passion project, of course. But some things are. As I discovered with speechwriting, Resistance tells you that the work you find most challenging to start and most difficult to complete might actually be the work you find most fulfilling. When you encounter Resistance, you can take the urge to procrastinate and instead reframe it as a signal that you might have something deeper to explore.

Craft
No matter the work, you can fulfillment in it

The toy maker LEGO nearly collapsed in the early 2000s. In a book chronicling the company's struggles and subsequent revitalization, David Robertson and Bill Breen describe how LEGO conducted countless focus groups to better understand the types of toys that engaged children. Among their observations was that children are driven by "the notion of mastery."[87] In other words, as Robertson and Breen write, "whether it was flipping skateboarding tricks or obsessing over the design and history of warplanes, kids demonstrated an innate desire to dig into a discipline and conquer it."[88] Putting aside the fact that no one who's actually ridden a skateboard would dare utter the phrase "flipping skateboarding tricks," Robertson and Breen capture a core human yearning to master a craft that endures well beyond childhood. The authors frame this example as an instance of kids building social capital among their peers, but viewed more broadly, it's also an example of human beings building fulfilling lives. For whatever reason, we are wired to enjoy mastering a craft. It's satisfying and rewarding to take on new challenges, develop expertise, and push our brains in search of mastery.

Mastery doesn't mean perfection. When it comes to LEGOs, it's not really about the finished product but the act of building and creating. In your case, it's not about attaining a certain job title or status. It's about working and striving for noticeable, tangible improvements, even if that's in how efficiently you stock a shelf or how clearly and succinctly you write a memo. That process starts by choosing to view your work not as something to check off or get done, but something to focus on and experience in the present.

Like all of the ideas in this book, pursuing deep work is an aspiration, not an expectation. It's impossible to spend every waking moment engaged in profound and meaningful activities. It's unrealistic to expect every workplace to conform to all of your personal preferences. Like aiming for perpetual happiness, asking yourself to never fall prey to Resistance or to consistently resist the lure of distractions is a futile and counterproductive expectation.

But you can try to reframe how you see your work, regardless of what that work entails. You can find satisfaction in your day-to-day responsibilities by doing them as intentionally and with as much focus as possible. Your work might be writing, managing people, or running. It might be painting, sweeping floors, or teaching. It might be a Saturday's worth of errands. You could be spending your time stuck in traffic or waiting for a doctor's appointment or applying for jobs or buying groceries. No matter what you're doing—even something as simple as emptying your inbox—you can reshape how you view this work by looking at it as a craft, rather than a series of burdensome tasks.

And you can take pride in what you're doing. As writer Joshua Wolf Shenk recounts, during the Civil War, a Union general asked President Abraham Lincoln for command of a larger regiment. The general was leading a mere 3,000 men, Shenk writes, and "felt humiliated."[89] But Lincoln declined his request, imparting some sage advice. "Act well your part," Lincoln told the general. "There all the honor lies."[90] The point is not that you should simply accept your lot in life or stay in your lane. It's not that you shouldn't be ambitious or pursue work that you find more enjoyable and fulfilling. Rather, it's that, *at this moment*, whatever your work is, however mundane or meaningless it may feel, there is honor and dignity in doing it with focus, care, and pride. Lincoln's comment reminds us that we each have the power to look at our work from a different perspective—as a craft, say, rather than simply a series of obligations.

Finish Lines
There will always be more work to do

I spent a decade working under the assumption that I'd eventually reach a finish line, some mythical point at which I'd run out of burdensome obligations to complete. If I just responded to enough emails or completed enough seemingly pointless tasks, someday I'd get to a point where I could focus on doing work *well*, rather than seeing it just as something I had to get done so I could get to the next thing. In the meantime, if I had to sacrifice spending time with family or reading a meaningful book along the way, or if I did most of my work in a distracted, half-focused fog, so be it. Eventually, I was sure, I'd get to a point where I could pay attention to what was in front of me. But not yet.

That unspecified future finish line can manifest in countless ways. When you complete a final exam. When you graduate. When you hit send on a difficult email. When you meet the perfect partner. When you find a new job. When you get a promotion. When you get the boss's approval. When you get invited to a more senior-level meeting. When you get healthy. When you have kids. When the kids are older. When the kids move out of the house. When you pay off your student loans. When you finally finish writing a book about building more fulfilling days. When you retire. These infinite possibilities all have one thing in common: They aren't actual finish lines. They're goals worth striving for and celebrating, yes, but they aren't the end of anything.

There will *always* be more work to do. You can see that fact as a burden, in which case you'll spend most of your life slogging through things you don't want to do as you chase a nonexistent finish line. Or you can reframe it. You can choose to accept as inevitable, as part of life, that obligations will always come your way. You can choose to see work as an opportunity to focus, to be present, and to improve. Whatever you encounter, you can reframe it as an opportunity to master a craft, rather than see it as a bunch of obstacles standing between you and future happiness.

"The satisfaction of success doesn't come from achieving your goals, but from struggling well," suggests investor Ray Dalio. "The happiest people discover their own nature and match their life to it."[91] They focus on what they can control, such as living in the present or mastering a craft or working deeply, and do their best with that. They have big goals and strive aggressively toward them, but they don't try to shape the unshapeable. They're not preoccupied by the unpredictable future. They're not paralyzed by the unchangeable past.

It's easy for a billionaire investor like Dalio, or for a powerful political leader like Lincoln, to suggest we focus on what's in front of us, right? Perhaps. But there's often more to the story. Take Lincoln. Before ascending to the presidency, he suffered from debilitating depression, exacerbated by personal heartbreaks and a series of painful political defeats. By the time he told the Union general that honor lay in acting his part well, Lincoln was speaking as a human being well-versed in the struggles and suffering of life. He gave this advice because he followed it himself. Throughout his life Lincoln "repeatedly returned to a sense of purpose," Joshua Wolf Shenk writes. "From this purpose, he put his head down to work at the mundane tasks of his job. And with his head down, he glanced up, often enough, at the chance to affect something meaningful and lasting."[92]

By reframing your work—indeed, your life as a whole—as a craft to be honed, rather than a series of tasks to be completed, you can make it more fulfilling. "The most important thing about art is to work," Steven Pressfield says. "Nothing else matters except sitting down every day and trying."[93] No matter who or where you are, no matter the line of work you're in or what you're trying to accomplish, sitting down every day and trying is a pretty reasonable goal. Take it from Harry S. Truman, who found himself president of the United States following the death of Franklin Roosevelt (during World War II, no less). Reflecting on the immense, almost unimageable, burden that suddenly rested on his shoulders, "I felt there must be a million men better qualified than I, to take up the Presidential task," Truman said in his farewell address. "But the work was mine to do, and I had to do it. And I have tried to give it everything that was in me."[94] Whatever work is yours to do today, you can, like Truman, do the best you can with what you have before you in the moment. You can do that over and over again, day-in and day-out, making a little progress and learning a little more about yourself each time. *There* all the honor lies.

4

Consume content intentionally

> "In an information-rich world, the wealth of information means a dearth of something else: a scarcity of whatever it is that information consumes. What information consumes is rather obvious: it consumes the attention of its recipients. Hence a wealth of information creates a poverty of attention and a need to allocate that attention efficiently among the overabundance of information sources that might consume it."
>
> Herbert Simon[95]

Social Media

Take control of social media

It's hard not to sound preachy and self-righteous when it comes to shunning social media, but here goes. I'm not on Facebook. I've given up on Snapchat. I almost never check Instagram. I rarely go on Twitter, an effort that gets easier with time but for which progress is constantly threatened by breaking news and elections. There are probably dozens of other social media sites and apps I've never heard of. (What is this "TikTok" people keep talking about?) My rationale for abstaining from them is simple, and it's *not* because I get no positive return from using them. It's that the negative impacts far outweigh the positive.

I joined Facebook as a freshman at Colby in 2005, shortly after the site opened to all college students. (I remember honing my Myspace page the summer before college and being told by friends in no uncertain terms that I should switch my online presence to TheFacebook.com.) As Facebook grew and expanded, I became a regular user, eagerly checking to see who had posted pictures of me and who had written on my wall. This was before Facebook had a news feed, chat feature, or smartphone app, but its hooks were already pretty strong. Without giving it much thought, I accepted Facebook, with its accompanying emotional ups and downs and the time and attention it required, as part of my college experience.

By the time I graduated, it had become an unquestioned part of my life. I took a year off from Facebook in 2012, but then signed up with a different email account for (as I slyly convinced myself) the purpose of networking in Colorado politics. I tried to be selective about adding friends and focus on building a limited profile to serve my career ambitions, but even then Facebook's algorithms were so powerful that people from previous networks found me and showed up as recommended friends in my new domain. Before I knew it, I had a new Facebook account that was essentially the same as the old one. In addition to the same connections and the same news feeds, both accounts were similar in the categories of "generally leaving me irritated and unfocused" and "adding little value to my life."

I continued to convince myself that I needed Facebook because otherwise I might miss out on something, which is a conviction the company works hard to cultivate. In an effort to make the site less irritating and time-consuming, I started removing friends or hiding them from the news feed. It wasn't long before the only thing I was doing on Facebook was reducing the number of people I interacted with on it. That raised a more fundamental question: If the only thing I was doing on a social networking site was eliminating the number of people with whom I was socially networking, what, exactly, was the point? So, in 2014, I closed my account for the second time. It's amazing how little I've missed it since.

When it comes to deciding whether to use social media tools like Facebook, asking yourself, "Do I get anything from it—*anything* at all?" isn't particularly helpful. The answer to that question will *always* be yes. If that's your decision-making framework, you will either a) always be able to justify using these sites, or b) stop using them but remain desperately gripped by FOMO (the fear of missing out) because you're focused entirely on all the benefits you're missing. A far more useful (and realistic) way to assess a site or service is to ask yourself, "On balance, does it leave me better off?" This framing implicitly accepts that there are both positives and negatives. Instead of zooming in on what you're missing, it helps you to zoom out and see the bigger picture—namely, not what you're missing on Facebook but what you're missing everywhere else in your life. In other words, how does using these sites impact your day-to-day experience? That's a far more important perspective if the ultimate goal is creating more fulfilling days.

As I've weaned myself off social media, I've become increasingly convinced that no matter the app or service or website, no matter how strong its pull, it's very possible to get to a place where you just don't feel compelled to check it at all. But getting there in a sustainable way has required me to recognize that ditching social media isn't all positive. It's *not* without trade-offs. I miss friends' engagement announcements and cute baby pictures and funny videos. There are probably networking opportunities I've lost out on that might have helped me get my feet under me in a new country. Given the fact that I'm only inconsistently decent at keeping up with friends and family by email and text, not being on social media deprives me of an easy way to stay in touch with people I care about. Selfishly, I'm sure that tireless engagement and self-promotion on social media would help bring my writing to new audiences, particularly given the extent to which Twitter drives the modern political discourse.

But at what cost? For all the value of social media services—and some of that value, though not the shareholder kind, is real—the benefits are exceeded by enormous personal costs. A frayed attention span. An inability to concentrate. A constant feeling of "mental hyperventilation, caught in tiny loops that seem to lead nowhere," as the writer Craig Mod describes it.[96] An enormous amount of time lost, privacy sacrificed, and valuable data transferred to wealthy tech executives and venture capitalists (and foreign governments). The lingering knowledge that soothing distractions, with all their immediacy, are just a tap away. The compulsion to "pull to refresh" for a little slot machine-esque dopamine hit. The constant imposition of social insecurity derived from relentlessly comparing yourself to what your e-acquaintances want you to think they're doing. (And that's all before the enormous societal and cultural costs, which are mostly beyond the scope of this book.)

The utility of social media, like a lot of what's lurking on the internet and emanating from our always-on technology, is far exceeded by its cost. Yet it takes little effort to convince ourselves that these costs are worth it. It's what Cal Newport calls the "any-benefit approach to network tool selection," in which you tell yourself that "you're justified in using a network tool if you can identify *any* possible benefit to its use, or *anything* you might possibly miss out on if you don't use it."[97] Not only does this approach guarantee you'll find a reason not to quit social media, but, as Newport adds, it "ignores all the negatives that come along with the tools in question." Instead, it plays right into what America's messianic tech oligopolies want you to do: trade your data, privacy, attention, and time—not to mention huge swathes of the economic system and even election outcomes—for a few quick hits of distraction.

The question isn't whether there are any benefits. It's whether the benefits exceed the costs. For me—and, I suspect, for many of us—I'm convinced an honest assessment yields a clear *no*.

In the years that I've been writing this book, I've been pleased to observe a growing awareness of the detrimental impacts of tech companies on society and of their constant distractions on our brains. Even Kanye West, whose career and family have benefited tremendously from social media, seems to agree. In May 2018, he tweeted, "Look at your phone as [a] tool, not an obligation. Would you walk around with a hammer in your pocket? You would pick up a hammer when you needed it. You would never be addicted or obligated to it. Use your phone like a hammer.

Only pick it up when you need it."[98] (To which another user promptly responded, "I tried your advice. The nail barely budged and now I need a new screen." Sometimes the internet gets it just right.[99])

Other than that tweet, I haven't followed Kanye much recently, but for the past few years I have kept an eye on the work of Tristan Harris, a former Google "design ethicist" and "product philosopher" who's one of the leaders of the social movement against social media.[100] After spending the early part of his career in the tech world, Harris got fed up with the attention-monopolizing and data-mining tendencies of Silicon Valley and formed the Center for Humane Technology (formerly Time Well Spent) to help people reclaim their time and attention from technology companies that spend vast sums of money and hire some of the smartest engineers in the world specifically to take this time and attention and monetize it. "The problem," as Harris puts it, "is the hijacking of the human mind: systems that are better and better at steering what people are paying attention to, and better and better at steering what people do with their time than ever before."[101]

The team at the Center for Humane Technology offers a series of recommendations for individual users to (re)take control of their attention from their phones: Turn off notifications except from human beings.[102] Open apps by searching for them, rather than swiping to find them, to make the process more deliberate and to interrupt the boredom-distraction cycle. Delete social media apps to control the time spent on them when bored (or, go further and delete the accounts entirely). Turn the phone screen to grayscale.*[103] As with most of the ideas in this book, minimizing notifications or following any of these other suggestions will not, by itself, alter your life in a fundamental way. Turning your phone to grayscale will not singlehandedly solve technology addiction or rebuild a frayed attention span. But it's a small step that can have a significant impact as part of a larger effort to reframe how you see and experience

---

* It's remarkable how quickly your brain gets used to grayscale, and after it does, how quickly the colors of your phone become jarring and difficult to tolerate.

each day. Even if these recommendations don't strike you as plausible, they'll at least make you think and, hopefully, *re*think your relationship with technology.

None of this is to say that all tech companies are inherently bad or that all notifications are harmful or that all social media is manipulative and unworthy of your time. Nor is it to say that spending time on them is somehow wrong or sinful. When used intentionally, smartphones and the internet can improve your quality of life in countless ways, both big and small. Carrying around a supercomputer in your pocket or purse is unbelievably useful and empowering. Moreover, it's unrealistic to expect everyone, everywhere to suddenly delete their social media accounts or to stop visiting their favorite sites en masse. Sometimes, mindlessly scrolling through Instagram or taking a break to play some FarmVille is exactly what you need to zone out for a few minutes.

My argument for taking control of social media is simply an argument for reflecting on how you use these services, gauging whether they truly make your days more fulfilling, and tweaking how you interact with them to put you back in control. It's also an argument for thinking about the alternatives. Instead of spending hours mindlessly reading about what others want you to think they're doing, for instance, you can make a conscious choice to do something. That something doesn't have to be social—it could be educational or creative. It could even be inactive. Watching a good movie, taking a nap, or staring out the window are probably more passive activities than scrolling through Facebook. But, at least in my experience, the impact on emotional and mental health couldn't be more different.

Twenty-first century life is overflowing with news, content, videos, hot takes, listicles, ads, and other ingeniously stimulating and distracting stimuli and distractions. Social media services and their powerful algorithms can make it feel nearly impossible to live without these things. But you don't actually *need* them. Nor do you need to disconnect entirely. You can try doing just a bit less. You can try making a few tweaks here and there, on a semi-regular basis, to put you back in control and to give you the power to select the services that add value to your life.

If the question you're asking is whether social media brings you any value at all, the answer will almost always be yes. But if the question is whether it adds more value than it takes away, the answer will almost always be no. When it comes to building more fulfilling days, sometimes all you have to do is reframe the question.

Tech

Take control of tech

The argument that you can (re)take control of your technology to build more fulfilling days is about more than social media. It's also notifications, tabs, and clickbait. It's temptations, distractions, noise, and stimuli. My growing aversion to all these inputs comes from a desire to spend my time and attention in ways that I find more fulfilling. It's impossible to do that all the time, but I want to aim to do so more often than not. I want to be in control of my attention. I don't want an app or a developer or a social insecurity taking me away from the life happening in front of me right now.

I've managed to achieve some control over this state of chaos by making my personal email inbox my incoming information hub. Almost every piece of electronic content I receive goes to one place. News alerts. Correspondence with family and friends. Blog posts I want to read. Updates from authors whose work I want to follow. Political newsletters. Other newsletters. Articles curated by Nuzzel (a useful tool that emails links to stories being discussed by people you follow on Twitter, so you don't actually have to open Twitter). Life stuff I have to deal with. All of it goes to my inbox. If something going to my inbox doesn't add value *and* isn't necessary for me to review, I either unsubscribe or create a filter that sends it straight to my archive, where I can easily search for it if needed. Out of sight, out of mind. Out of inbox, out of to-do list.

Yes, this system takes some work, although less than you might think since I don't spend any time organizing or labeling anything.** Sure, the system opens me up to some distractions. For example, when I want to see if I've received an email from a friend, I'm liable to get sucked into a breaking news story. Yes, it feeds my to-do list obsession by reminding me of things I have to respond to when I just want to make sure my credit card payment went through. But, for me, these shortcomings are outweighed by the simplicity of having a single place for incoming information. I can't check Facebook. I don't need to go to Twitter or CNN for news. I don't feel compelled to check multiple sites or services to make sure I haven't missed or forgotten something. It's all in one place. I control what goes there. And by turning off *all* new message notifications and not keeping the email app or browser tab open, I control when I see it.

This system offers mental benefits, too. In my mind, I disassociate my personal email inbox from deep work, so I know that opening Gmail equals news, tasks, distractions, and shallow work (mixed with some gems from friends and family). If I don't open email, I'm less likely to get distracted by small tasks and alerts. Fulfilling work happens outside of the inbox. Creating this structure on my phone and in my mind doesn't make sustained focus easy, but it does make it a little easier. It simplifies my life, helps me separate what matters from what doesn't, and gives me just a bit of control over the tsunami of stimuli that so many of us subject ourselves to every day.

That brings us to notifications. Someone uploaded photos of you. Someone tagged you. Someone liked your post. Someone loves your photo. You haven't logged in recently—better see what you're missing! Guess what your friends are up to? Look at all the new updates they posted! Look at how angry everyone is! Shouldn't you be outraged too? Why aren't you more outraged? Look at how much fun everyone else is

---

** In case you're curious… I use Gmail mainly because of its easy and thorough "archive" and "search" functions. I don't use folders. I just archive everything and search the archive when I need something.

having! What's wrong with you? You could have as much fun as they are if you give us your data and click on our ads! Don't log out—you're going to get left behind!

Just as meditation can help you take back control from emotions and thoughts that hijack your brain, turning off smartphone and desktop notifications helps you take back control from the distractions that hijack your attention and turn technological tools into addictions. Notifications are rarely designed to bring you fulfillment or to inform you of things you care about. These relentless updates aren't designed to add value to your life. They're designed to add value to their companies' share prices and valuations. They're designed to divert your time and attention away from whatever you're saying, reading, or doing, and redirect it to your pocket-sized data-collecting and advertisement-propagating machine. They're designed to build a dependency on connectivity and an addiction to short-term stimuli, all of which keeps us tapping and clicking for more.

Managing technology would be a lot easier if *all* notifications were evil—because then we'd simply turn them all off. But in some cases, notifications can make our days a little more fulfilling. Take group text messages, which can provide an amazing, and amazingly simple, way for people to connect. Like any communication tool, they can be overwhelming, but if limited to people you actually want to correspond with, they're hard to beat. I find it incredible, for example, that I, in London, can have an ongoing dialogue with my brother in Oakland, our friend Ben in Houston, and our friend Brian who, during our most recent chat, was somewhere in Peru. Writer Jia Tolentino describes group text messages one of "the most straightforwardly beloved digital technologies" because they "push against the attention economy's worst characteristics." As Tolentino puts it, "Group texts are effectively the last noncommercialized social spaces on many millennials' phones."[104]

This technology, in this type of situation, regularly puts a smile on my face (which is not a bad metric for measuring fulfillment). There are plenty of other worthy notifications, such as alarms and calendar reminders, old-fashioned phone calls, and tailored and intentional alerts, like a heads-up that a flight I need to buy has dropped in price. Mostly, however, notifications are engineered by some of the smartest programming minds in the world to tempt us, distract us, hook us, and make us curious and insecure. According to *The Guardian*, Loughborough University professor Tom Jackson has calculated that "it takes an average of 64 seconds to recover your train of thought after interruption by email. So people who check their email every five minutes waste 8.5 hours a week figuring out what they were doing moments before."[105] Given the fact that mobile notifications come in many more flavors than email and follow us around day and night, surely their impact is just as detrimental, if not more.

If you want to have any hope of controlling your attention, instead of yielding it to a manipulative and profit-seeking tech company, you can make everything on your devices as deliberate as possible. For me, that means no news alerts. No email push notifications. No social media apps telling me I haven't logged in for a while or my friends miss me. Yes, to text messages and iMessages and WhatsApp messages. Yes, to phone calls from a few key people, filtered by the iPhone's "Do not disturb" feature (which I almost always keep on).*** Yes, to functional notifications that respond to requests I've created. Yes, to things that bring me value or help me spend more time doing things that make my days more fulfilling, such as reminders from Headspace to meditate or a "Smile" notification.

You don't have to eliminate notifications entirely. Some people might choose to do that—and good for them—but for most of us, our days can be made substantially more focused and fulfilled by simply cutting back on notifications and using them more intentionally. In my experience, it's at those moments when I'm feeling most overwhelmed by incoming information, when it is abundantly clear that I can't possibly process everything I want to process, that I'm able to ruthlessly unsubscribe and

*** One downside of this approach is that I'm not as responsive to emails and texts from friends and family as I'd like to be. Even if a message would only take me 30 seconds to respond, it might sit unread for days. Why? I haven't figured it out, nor have I discovered a workaround yet.

turn off unnecessary notifications. The next time you feel like that, head straight to your notification settings, make some assertive changes, and see what happens.

News
Take control of news

I n the late 2000s, with a liberal arts degree in a field I ultimately had no interest in pursuing, I, like many millennials, entered the world of work as the global economy slowly began to recover from the Great Recession. Having spent four years in college studying math and computer science, and much of my free time DJing and running the Colby College radio station, I emerged into the post-Great Recession world feeling distinctly unprepared to understand the post-Great Recession world— and distinctly unfamiliar with the pre-Great Recession world. That led me to *The Economist*, which, prior to the summer of 2009, I had never read. Since my goal was to learn about the rest of the world, reading *The Economist* seemed like something I should do.

In many ways, what comes off as a statement of braggadocio among Davos-going elites is actually a powerful equalizer, a tool for bringing news and ideas from every corner of the globe to every other corner of the globe. A decade on, I've certainly learned a lot about the world from reading *The Economist*. However, the most important things I've gained from reading a chunk of this weekly "newspaper" (as it calls itself) every day has less to do with the content or perspective and more to do with the way it's presented. The fact that *The Economist* is packaged and delivered only once a week has helped me to rebuild my attention and break free of the day-to-day palace intrigue and political minutia that can easily soak up every minute of every day. Meanwhile, the fact that it's written from a global perspective has broadened my understanding of the scale, complexity, and mystery of the world. Our own lives and daily struggles can be all-consuming. Reading about a political protest in a small country I've never heard of is a helpful and humbling reminder of the lives and struggles of others. Most people in the world don't have time for the stories that obsess us today, and if we're honest, we probably don't have much time in our lives for theirs. But it helps at least to be aware that there's more to the world than our usual media diet might suggest.

Reading *The Economist* has convinced me that there's a way to consume better news, and a way to consume news better. "Better news" isn't limited to any one publication. For you, it might be the *Financial Times*, *The New York Review of Books*, *The Atlantic*, *The Guardian*, or— a personal favorite, even though I'm perennially a half-dozen issues behind—*The New Yorker*. It might be the same publication you always read, but delivered to your door in a plastic bag or to your e-reader in a single daily or weekly edition, ideally without hyperlinks and without the capacity to send you breaking news alerts. It might be a daily podcast or a weekly TV program. Whatever it is, it'll probably cover Donald Trump— it would be pretty irresponsible not to, unfortunately—but it won't *only* cover Donald Trump. It might also cover Indonesian election results, Malawian mobile phone use, or Japanese financial forecasts.

Don't get me wrong: I still inhale coverage of the American political horse race. I can't get enough of the "who's up" and "who's down" news-of-the-moment epitomized by outlets like Politico and Axios, the agenda-setting political "conversation" on Twitter, and the permanent *BREAKING NEWS* chyron on CNN. I consume this stuff constantly. Not only because I find it endlessly fascinating, but because I care about it, and I believe we all have a responsibility to be informed citizens. Even if we weren't living through particularly extraordinary times, that would be true. But the fact that I can't get enough of it is precisely why I need to set limits on how much I consume. That doesn't mean turning it off forever. It doesn't mean giving up on interesting stories or juicy *can-you-believe-it?!* headlines. It just means doing all of that a little less.

Building self-imposed barriers around my news intake has made my days substantially less anxiety-prone and noticeably more fulfilling, without any decrease in how "up to speed" I feel about the events of the moment. In fact, waiting until a story has had time to develop has probably improved my knowledge of the facts and sharpened my understanding of their significance. These self-imposed barriers haven't required any dramatic changes. I've simply tweaked the *what* and the *when* of how I consume media. These days, the *what* is a little less of the breathless drama and outrage that will be forgotten or supplanted by more breathless drama and outrage tomorrow, and a little more of the publications that require more work to process. It's a little less skimming of endless headlines in quick succession, and a little more diving deeply into a smaller number of stories. It's a little less of the latest dopamine-inducing and emotionally charged gossip from the Trump White House, and a little more of the stuff that ultimately leaves more substance in its wake.

The *when* of my media consumption is as simple: It's just a little more structured and contained than it used to be. For instance, other than reading a few articles from the latest edition of *The Economist*, which I usually do each morning, I try to avoid the day's political news until the afternoon, when I've completed my heavy thinking and deep work for the day. I know this arrangement isn't doable for everyone. Living in the UK, five hours ahead of the politics and news emanating from Washington and New York, helps. Not working in politics helps even more. (One of the most exhausting aspects of life in politics is that the news is your job, so it's impossible to ever really disconnect.) Not living in the United States helps, too. Despite having become, like all Americans living abroad, an ambassador for explaining why we put Donald Trump in the Oval Office, I've found that conversations in the UK are less restricted to "The president said *what*?!?" and more likely to move on to the craziness and drama of their own politics.

These self-imposed boundaries might not work for you. But think about what little tweaks you could make each day to improve your news intake. Could it be avoiding Twitter or Instagram until the afternoon (or the weekend, or forever)? Could it be turning off breaking news notifications on your phone? Could it be not consuming political news before 12 pm, or after 8 pm, or both? Could it be spending half an hour reading a book most mornings or nights? Could it be limiting your political intake to podcasts or specific TV shows? (My parents, for example, watch PBS's *Washington Week* every Friday night because the program's sober discussion is free of the outrage, arguing, and talking over each other that dominates almost all other political television.) Could it be adding a global publication like the *Financial Times*—the journalistic outlet of choice for Erin, who has the master's degree in journalism—to your rotation? Could it be subscribing to a print publication, and only reading that?

There's no perfect solution. Nor is there anything you *have* to read or consume every single day. We'll all go careening over our self-imposed news guardrails from time to time, of course. There are no hard-and-fast rules (except to be hypervigilant for the slippery slope of conspiracies). Your media diet will change over time. But it's remarkable how clarifying, invigorating, and—yes—fulfilling it can be to begin building boundaries on *what* news you consume and *when* you consume it. You need far less of it than you think.

Books

Spend more time reading books

No matter how useful the news, or how effectively you alter the *what* and *when* of how you consume it, you can only consume so much of it. That brings me to something else I started doing after college: reading books that hadn't been assigned to me by someone else. There are already countless blog posts, articles, and (of course) books that extol the virtues of reading in this short-term, social media-centric world. I won't rehash them here. Suffice it to say, reading a book almost always leaves me feeling sustained and renewed, and failing to read for an extended period of time leaves me feeling adrift and unmoored. There's something refreshing and invigorating about consuming a coherent, in-depth, well-thought-out argument or idea, and about doing so in an immersive way, staying focused on a single topic for more than a few minutes. Books remind us that ideas and stories are far more complex and nuanced than even the most in-depth newspaper article could ever be. And reading them seems to require just the right amount of work to trigger a sense of fulfillment and accomplishment, without requiring so much effort that it feels like work.

Despite its many benefits, reading books isn't something that happens automatically for me. I have to make a conscious effort to create time to read, and I have to make an even greater effort to use that time to read a book instead of opening yet another political email newsletter. I have to recognize that it will take time for my mind to settle. I have to trust that after 10-15 minutes of reading a book, the urge to seek out more political hot takes will subside, much as it takes time for the mind to quiet down at the beginning of a meditation session. Focusing intentionally on reading, and bringing my attention back to the text in front of me when my mind inevitably wanders, has helped me rewire my brain to focus better on single tasks (which itself makes reading easier and more enjoyable). That's a pretty positive cycle.

In an interview with Tim Ferriss, entrepreneur and investor Naval Ravikant says, "The genuine love for reading itself, when cultivated, is a superpower."[106] What he's referring to, I think, is not just that there's an unbelievable amount of knowledge available to us in the form of books. It's also that, when it comes to processing the world, reading can be incredibly liberating. I'm convinced that one of the most magical moments a person can experience is encountering a piece of writing, whether a single sentence or an entire book, that captures something you've been thinking or feeling but haven't quite been able to articulate. Finding the right phrase or idea at the right time doesn't just convey information. It brings clarity to the world and offers a better understanding of how we fit into it.

In his White House memoir, President Obama's longtime aide Ben Rhodes recounts a conversation he had with the then-president about the power of storytelling. In May 2016, as the president's motorcade traveled through Hanoi, Vietnam, Obama urged Rhodes not to shy away from using stories to make the case for the administration's policies and decisions. "The notion that there's something wrong with storytelling—I mean, that's our job," Obama says to him. "To tell a really good story about who we are."[107] Obama's comment gets to the heart of human evolution. Yuval Noah Harari argues that what sets human beings apart from other species, and what has enabled us to build societies and civilizations, is our ability to cooperate with each other. Key to that cooperation is storytelling. In Harari's telling, money is a story. Religion is a story. Nations are stories. Race is a story.[108] These are all socially-constructed concepts that, at their worst, manufacture divisions, hierarchies, and combustible notions of "us" and "them." At their best, though, shared values and ideas give our communities structure and enable us to build complex societies greater than the sum of their parts. Stories teach us about each other—and ourselves.

Today, we have countless ways to share information and exchange ideas. But for most of human history, there was just one: storytelling. Harari describes the Sumerians, an ancient Mesopotamian people who, sometime around 3500 B.C., developed a new way to communicate. In doing so, Harari writes, the Sumerians "released their social order from the limitations of the human brain, opening the way for the appearance of cities, kingdoms and empires." What was this secret to unlocking mass cooperation? "The data-processing system invented by the Sumerians," Harari explains, "is called 'writing.'" More than five millennia later, we're still using it. "With the appearance of writing," Harari communicates to readers using the Sumerians' invention, we start "to hear history through the ears of its protagonists."[109] The historian Joseph J. Ellis has described it similarly. "Reading history is like expanding your memory further back in time," Ellis writes. "The more history you learn, the larger the memory bank you can draw on when life takes a turn for which you are otherwise unprepared."[110] Through stories we learn, we grow, we collaborate, we empathize, and we better understand ourselves and where we might fit in the world. Perhaps that's why reading books can trigger such feelings of fulfillment.

Like a runaway conspiracy theory on Breitbart, that brings us back to Barack Obama and Ben Rhodes. What the president suggests to Rhodes about storytelling in politics is just as true for you as an individual.

Each time you read or hear about someone else's experience, you can hold up a mirror to your own life. You can listen for echoes of your own experiences and look for reflections of your own struggles. Seeing traces of your story in someone else's can be a profoundly powerful means of learning, understanding, and processing. Subconsciously or not, you can ask yourself, "What about this person's story applies to my life? Can I learn something from her? What would I have done in his situation? What do I want to do in my own situation?"

The content I consume is heavily biased toward nonfiction. There's obviously a lot to be gained from fact-based content. I love learning about history through the lens of biography, for instance. I love reading long-form investigative articles to better understand the world around me. But the idea that stories help us understand what it means to be human seems even more true for novels. President Obama, for one, has made a compelling case for reading fiction. "When I think about how I understand my role as citizen, setting aside being president, and the most important set of understandings that I bring to that position of citizen," he said in 2015, "the most important stuff I've learned I think I've learned from novels. It has to do with empathy. It has to do with being comfortable with the notion that the world is complicated and full of grays, but there's still truth there to be found, and that you have to strive for that and work for that. And the notion that it's possible to connect with some[one] else even though they're very different from you."[111]

Similarly, David Brooks has written about how the journalist and activist Dorothy Day learned about the world around her through reading fiction. "It's hard now to recapture how seriously people took novel reading then," Brooks observes. Day, for instance, "read as if her whole life depended upon it." Brooks also notes that the English writer Samuel Johnson "believed that literature could be a serious force for moral improvement." Why? "Literature gives not only new information but new experiences. It can broaden the range of awareness and be an occasion for evaluation. Literature can also instruct through pleasure." Yet today,

Brooks writes, "the cognitive sciences have replaced literature as the way many people attempt to understand their own minds."[112] Is there space to rectify that—to expand my emotional and empathetic understanding—through the fictional lives of others, whether novels, films, TV shows, or plays? There must be.

Overload

You can't consume it all

You can consume better content. You can consume content better. But—and this is a critical, if unfortunate, "but"—you can't consume it all. I'm sometimes overwhelmed by the volume of media I want to consume. There's too much interesting stuff out there. Sometimes, in fact, I'm so overwhelmed that I can't decide what to read, watch, or listen to, and I just default to political news, which is always easily accessible and doesn't require any effort. In other words, I become paralyzed by choice and end up choosing nothing. It's a good problem to have, sure, but why not fix it if you can?

Here's what I try to remind myself: Even if I spent every minute of every day reading and processing only the most important and highest-quality books ever written, I'd have no time to do anything else, let alone put any of that new knowledge to use. Nor would I even make a dent in consuming all the content that the millions of existing books have on offer. Nor would that scratch the surface of all the other amazing content available to human beings today: Podcasts. Audiobooks. Music. Musicals. Documentaries. TV shows. Movies. Long-form articles. End-of-the-year lists of the best books of the year. We live in a golden age of content and access to content. Companies like Disney, HBO, and Netflix spent more than $100 billion on new material in 2019, meaning that "roughly as much cash…is being invested in content as it is in America's oil industry," *The Economist* notes.[113] Even eliminating 99.99 percent of the "worst" content, whatever that means, would leave far more than any person could hope to process in a lifetime.

The point of taking the desire to ingest interesting information to its illogical extreme is to point out that it's impossible to consume it all. You have to resist the urge to try to process books or podcasts or movies like tasks to be completed, which implies you might someday "finish." Rather than trying to consume more, you can try to consume more deeply and more deliberately. Rather than continuing to add books to your "to read" list or movies to your "to watch" list, you can make your days more fulfilling by just reading or watching one of them. Rather than consuming as much content as you can as quickly as you can (my default mode of operating), and rather than seeing the completion of a book or podcast as the goal, you'll enjoy it all a lot more, and probably get more from it, if you give up the false hope of finishing it all and instead focus on being present while you're reading, listening, or watching the thing in front of you.

Whether it's reading an engrossing novel, listening to a compelling podcast, stumbling across an eye-opening documentary, or getting lost in a biography, consuming meaningful content that stands the test of time can help you build more fulfilling days. "Meaningful content" is the stuff that pushes you to learn and grow. The stuff that alters your perspective and articulates the lingering thoughts or ideas you haven't been able to put into words. The stuff that helps focus your mind only on what's in front of you, exciting and inspiring you while also giving your batteries time to recharge. Yes, staying informed about current events is important. Yes, we all need time to relax or zone out with shallow stuff. But could we do just a little less of that? If we rebalance our intake so it leans slightly more in the direction of meaningful content, we can (literally, in this case) reframe how we see and experience the world.

Writing
Write to make sense of the world

Consuming content, whether an Instagram post, magazine article, or TV show, requires the involvement of at least one other person: the person who created it. That means, by definition, you aren't fully in control of it. That's often the point, of course. I don't go to Vox to find a long article about something I already know; I go there to learn something new. I can't try to write *all* the time because if I did I would never have time to find new things to write about.

With that said, if your aim is to make your days more fulfilling in part by focusing more on what you can control, why not dabble in some creating yourself? Since I'm conveying the information you're currently consuming, and doing so through writing, let's start with this "traditional" creative pursuit. Even now, having spent much of my life writing in some form or another, having worked as a speechwriter, and having now (at least by the time you read this) written at least one book, I continue to be pleasantly surprised by how clarifying and fulfilling the process of writing is.

I am far—far—from the first writer to make this observation. Abraham Lincoln, for one, took to heart not just the power of the written word, but the power of actually writing the words. As historian Joshua Wolf Shenk recounts, while the sixteenth president "often spoke extemporaneously over the course of his career, most of the great works of his mature years were composed on the page. Going through many drafts, he worked out his thoughts by writing and rewriting."[114] More recently, Ta-Nehisi Coates has written movingly about his own growth as a writer. Coates says he views writing as a way of understanding and communicating with the world. "Writing is always some form of interpretation," he notes, "some form of translating the specificity of one's roots or expertise or even one's own mind into language that can be absorbed and assimilated into the consciousness of a broader audience."[115]

Writing can be many things, from a mechanism to influence public opinion to a way to earn a living to, as Coates puts it, a technique to transmit personal experience into the public discourse. In these instances, writing is a means to an end. But sometimes the act of writing is both the means *and* the end. Sometimes it's just a tool to make sense of the thoughts and ideas bouncing around in your brain. A tool to process the endless complexities of life. A tool to bring some order to your questions and doubts, anxieties and inclinations, by distilling them on the page. Writing, as Daniel H. Pink writes (naturally), "is an act of discovering what you think and what you believe."[116] Writing empowers you to transform mental fragments into coherent philosophies, and to communicate them to yourself and the world. It also helps make that world more manageable. As Nina Riggs says in her powerful memoir, "We contain things and give shape to things in order to be less afraid of them. Yes. The crafted idea does this. It's why I write."[117]

In an age when typing more than a text message or tweet can seem daunting, it's easy to forget how fulfilling—or simply relieving—it can be to transfer what's inside (the mind) to the outside (the page in front of you). It's liberating to finally articulate on paper the fleeting strands of a thought or notion that has been ricocheting around in your head, consciously or not, for who knows how long. Paul Kalanithi captures this idea beautifully and succinctly in describing why he began penning his memoir. "Now I felt that to understand my own direct experiences, I would have to translate them back into language," Kalanithi writes. "Hemingway described his process in similar terms: acquiring rich experiences, then retreating to cogitate and write about them. I needed words to go forward."[118] If mental clarity is what you're after, there's often nothing better than writing to help track down a bit of it.

In 1884, nearing the end of his life and in dire need of income, the former U.S. president Ulysses S. Grant was convinced to write a series of articles that would eventually become his memoir. As historian Ron Chernow describes it, Grant originally found the process uninspiring. But, guided by a talented editor, he began to find joy and, presumably, some peace of mind in the task before him. "Why, I am positively enjoying the work," he remarked. "I am keeping at it every night and day, and Sundays."[119] Over time, Chernow writes, Grant "experienced the pride of authorship, pleasure of craftsmanship, and delight of reliving past triumphs."[120]

Like Grant, and like countless other writers, it took a long time for me to see writing not as an obligation but instead as an opportunity. An opportunity to make sense of the world. An opportunity to process my thoughts and experiences. An opportunity to figure out what I think about things. An opportunity to hone a craft. An opportunity to explore new ideas. An opportunity to share what I've learned. An opportunity to create. Even if it doesn't change any minds or pass any bills or reach any audience besides me, the craft of writing helps me take the raw materials of life and transform them into something marginally more coherent. Even if the only outcome of what I write, read, and share is a little more clarity about my own experience, that goal is undoubtedly worthwhile, and the process itself is enormously fulfilling.[121]

Creating

Create opportunities to create

Clearly, writing is useful to me. A day that involves writing, even if it's only a few minutes to process the thoughts bouncing around in my brain, is a more fulfilling day than one that doesn't. But the satisfaction that comes with creating something doesn't just emerge from writing, or even from stereotypically creative pursuits. We all have countless opportunities to create as we go about our days. Send a detailed and carefully proofread email to a friend that you crafted not while distracted on the subway in between meetings, but in a quiet space with single-tasked focus and care. Post an Instagram story in which the goal is the presentation of the narrative, not the likes or comments. Compile a playlist on Spotify that tells a story. Cook a meal from scratch and present it in a thoughtful way. Instead of racing through a work presentation or conference call unprepared and distracted, practice, polish, and perfect your part to remove the "ums" and "ahs." Transform your to-do lists into art using a technique like bullet journaling. The satisfaction that comes from creating is in the word itself: Something wasn't there, and now it is. And that happened because you created it.

You could spend every minute of every day consuming content and responding to incoming information, requests, and stimuli. Much of this consumption happens without your realizing it, but creativity doesn't happen like that. We rarely program our days to make space for creative endeavors. Fortunately, you don't have to work in an art studio or spend a month at a writing retreat to make space to create. You can simply look for small moments each day to turn your full attention and focus to the act of creation. Often these opportunities are already on your calendar or to-do list. You could see responsibilities such as writing a difficult memo or updating your resume as tasks to be begrudgingly checked off the to-do list. Or you might choose to reframe them as opportunities to communicate a message about yourself in a clear, concise, and thoughtful way.

What opportunities to create are already sitting right in front of you? What burdens might you reframe, even slightly, as satisfying pursuits? Writing is my creative tool, but yours might be different. Or, you might not have a tool at all. You don't need one. Your days are already full of small, usually forgettable, tasks that are also opportunities to do a little creating. These types of obligations will never come to an end, so you might as well try to hone some techniques for making the process of completing them a little more satisfying.

In a world dominated by incoming stuff, carving out some space to create some outgoing stuff can be hugely fulfilling. Even if you never share what you've created with anyone else, you can distill meaning and satisfaction from the process, often by doing nothing more than reframing how you view it. That squeezes more meaning out of each day. Just as importantly, it puts you back in control.

5

Resist the productivity obsession

"People who have learned to answer e-mails on Sunday evenings also need to learn how to go to the movies on Monday afternoons."

Ricardo Semler[122]

Productivity

Busyness does not equal productivity

One week last summer, I experienced two very different days. On Monday, I worked from home. I woke up early, meditated, made coffee, hung out with Erin while she got ready for work, and spent a few satisfying minutes muttering to myself about how much it had rained recently. I then read uninterrupted for two hours, followed by two more uninterrupted hours writing an article about the social purpose of the corporation. By the time midday rolled around, and my colleagues in the U.S. started to wake up and log on, I'd accomplished what I needed to accomplish before beginning a series of conference calls.

Tuesday started similarly to Monday, with the same meditating, coffee making, hanging with Erin, and muttering to myself about how hot and sunny it had been recently and why-oh-why don't apartments in the UK have air conditioning? At that point, the two mornings diverged, as I raced out of the apartment, rode a sweaty rush-hour train to the office, and began a morning's worth of back-to-back meetings and phone calls. As I scrambled from one 30-minute increment on my Outlook calendar to the next, emails, texts, to-dos, and other stuff piled up in the background, though I had little energy or enthusiasm for any of them by the time the onslaught of meetings, calls, and discussions about action items and next steps ended.

It's pretty clear from the tone of these descriptions which type of morning I prefer. What these descriptions don't tell you is anything about which type of morning was more "productive," "worthwhile," or "valuable" for my employer—or for me. Based on these descriptions alone, I might've enjoyed Monday morning but spent it wasting company time, while Tuesday morning fit my job responsibilities precisely. Or, Monday morning might have been far more useful for the job I was hired to do, while the frantic Tuesday morning really just meant that I spent my time chatting with coworkers instead of doing actual work. Without knowing the answers to a few follow-up questions, there's no way to say which morning was more "productive" or "worthwhile." Among those questions: On Monday, what was I writing? What was I reading? On Tuesday, what were the meetings and calls about? What role did I play in them? On either day, did it matter where I was working? Did it matter what I was working on?

It's certainly possible that Monday, with all that reading and writing, was, in fact, more "productive" for what I needed to do to be a good employee, not to mention for what I care about and the type of work I enjoy doing. But modern work culture almost always assumes that Tuesday was the more productive morning, simply because I was busier. (To refer to our maker-manager discussion from chapter three, managers' schedules are generally seen as more "productive" than those of makers.) On Monday morning, I sat at home in shorts and a t-shirt, with my email set to "Work offline" and my phone on "Do not disturb" so I could focus on what I was doing. Did that mean that I must have been lazy and ignoring all of my urgent responsibilities? On Tuesday morning, I sat in an office, facing a packed calendar, running frantically to the bathroom and the coffee machine in between calls and meetings, hopelessly multitasking, while emails and other requests piled up. Did that mean I must have been working on urgent, important, high-value tasks?

These types of cultural assumptions impact more than just how modern workplaces, and society at large, are organized. They also seep into our individual, day-to-day experiences, and into how these experiences make us feel about ourselves. Even if we know, intellectually at least, that Monday morning might have been more "productive," the expectation that busy-equals-productive and productive-equals-good means we feel accomplished and valuable for having sat for hours in potentially pointless meetings, and guilty and slacking for having spent the same number of hours crafting, creating, and expanding our brains.

We are desperate to feel productive. But because we don't have a good way to measure productivity, we use busyness instead. Eventually, we get addicted to the feeling of busyness itself.

The Con
Productivity is a metric for machines, not people

M ost human beings seek meaningful and fulfilling lives. Most machines, on the other hand, exist to produce things. Generally, the more things they produce, the more valuable they are. Human beings are not machines (biologically, at least). None of this is particularly controversial. So why do we, as non-machine humans, evaluate our worth using the same metrics we use to evaluate machines? Whether as employees, students, parents, creators, peers, or simply as individuals, society has trained us to judge the value of how we spend our time using the same metric we use for assembly lines: Was I productive?

I've long been obsessed with my own productivity, and I *constantly* stoke this obsession. I commend myself for days that I feel have been productive, and I beat myself up for days that I feel weren't as productive as they could (or should) have been. Both consciously and subconsciously, I regularly assess my day-to-day routines to see where and how I might be able to make myself more productive. On a given day, how can I complete more tasks, in less time, to achieve more things, to be more productive? What tips, tricks, and hacks can I employ to do more, get more done, achieve more? *How can I produce more?* Our value as individuals, this notion teaches us, hinges on how much value our labor produces. Therefore, if we optimize our lives to enable us to produce more, we will be more valuable and, thus, happier. This is the human productivity con, and it's one of the great scams of modern life.

Even setting aside the fact that human beings aren't machines, the obsession with productivity suffers from two fatal flaws. The first is how to define "productivity." Unlike machines, we don't always know how to measure individual productivity well, so we often use a proxy measure: being busy. As a result, rather than assessing the quality of our work, we measure our productivity in units of busyness—how many emails we sent, how many meetings we had, how many hours we spent in the office, how few hours we slept. Yet busyness, as demonstrated by the Monday morning versus Tuesday morning anecdote, has precisely zero bearing on whether we have or have not done anything valuable.

The second flaw with the productivity con is the more important of the two, at least for this book: Neither productivity nor its busyness proxy generate fulfillment. There are plenty of people who are busy and productive and leading fulfilling lives, but the first two states of being don't automatically lead to the third. In fact, they often stand in its way. Our modern-day obsession with busyness and productivity leaves us consumed with *doing more now* because we promise ourselves that we'll get to *do less later*. In the meantime, we reassure ourselves that the achievements we rack up along the way will make us happier and more fulfilled. They rarely do, of course. Plus, as we discussed earlier, the mythical "later" (when we finally get to "do less") never arrives.

To be clear, the goal of producing things is not the problem. As a writer, I want to produce sentences that add up to coherent ideas and arguments, and I want what I produce to be valuable and impactful to readers. As an employee, I want to produce work that serves my company and my colleagues. As a spouse, I want to contribute to producing a committed and supportive relationship. As an individual, I want to produce a clean apartment, a healthy lifestyle, and strong connections with friends and family. As a human being, I want to co-produce meaningful interactions with interesting people. (Swap in the word "create" for "produce" in the preceding paragraph, and you'll notice that the tone changes completely.)

These acts of production, one hopes, are measured by their quality and not their quantity, by their value and not their volume. How can you make sure that's the case? Can you reframe how you evaluate your day so that your core metric—your measure of whether you're "producing" a fulfilling day—is quality and value, not quantity and volume?

Resisting our obsession with busyness and productivity requires the acknowledgment of three truths. First, many of us are addicted to busyness. Second, busyness is not a useful proxy for productivity. And, third, productivity—as in, producing *more*—is a tool *for* life, not the purpose *of* life. It's a means to achieving your goals, not the goal itself. Let's take a closer look at each truth in turn.

Busyness

We're addicted to busyness

I n 2014, journalist Kate Murphy reported on a pretty depressing study. It concluded, in so many words, that we're terrified of spending time without incoming stimuli. "In 11 experiments involving more than 700 people," the research found, "the majority of participants reported that they found it unpleasant to be alone in a room with their thoughts for just 6 to 15 minutes." Murphy noted that nearly two-thirds of the men surveyed "began self-administering electric shocks when left alone to think."[123] It's true we're uncomfortable with being bored. But a more honest interpretation might suggest that we're terrified of confronting the doubts lurking in the crevices of our minds, which are easy to ignore when we're inundated by distractions and busyness.

For most of my working life, I made no distinction between busyness and value, between working on things that kept me busy and working on things that I really cared about. For me, the metaphorical electric shocks—the self-imposed pain to avoid being with my thoughts—

manifest in an over-scheduled calendar, an impossibly long to-do list, and an unwillingness to carve out any time or space to think. Being busy was a measure of working hard. Any free time, any hint of boredom or downtime, was an inefficiency to be eliminated. Busyness was a confirmation of my own significance and worth. And it was a shield from being alone with my thoughts, which might have forced me to confront unpleasant or even painful questions, such as what the purpose of all this frantic busyness really was.

"Staying occupied," Tara Brach writes, "is a socially sanctioned way of remaining distant from our pain."[124] Without entirely realizing it, I was obsessed with staying occupied because it enabled me to bury uncomfortable inadequacies and vulnerabilities. Because it was socially sanctioned, it made me feel part of something bigger (the "busy and important people" club) and gave me a sense of status. It helped me avoid more challenging work and relieved me of the responsibility of confronting my own uncertainties and insecurities. With more than a hint of self-righteousness, I would justify to myself the barriers I put up: "I mean, I *wish* I could make time to get closer to my friends or make an effort to explore my own emotional insecurities, but I'm just too busy. Maybe next month!"

Modern life does a pretty good job of training us to feel this way. In a striking essay, Tim Kreider reflects on self-proclaimed "busy people" and the culture that's created them (us). "They're busy because of their own ambition or drive or anxiety, because they are addicted to busyness and dread what they might have to face in its absence," Kreider writes. "I can't help but wonder whether all this histrionic exhaustion isn't a way of covering up the fact that most of what we do doesn't matter. … This busyness serves as a kind of existential reassurance, a hedge against emptiness: Obviously your life cannot possibly be silly or trivial or meaningless if you are so *busy*, completely booked, in demand every hour of the day."[125]

Kreider's observations echo the explanation of busyness that writer Scott H. Young offered in an email newsletter in early 2018. "I believe busyness is a much more dangerous state than sloth or laziness," Young asserts. Both conditions prevent us from growing personally and professionally, he says, but "the difference is that our culture lauds busyness and sneers at laziness." Society tells us that "it would be better to be seen as busy, at all times, so as to signal how important you are." But the outcomes are essentially the same. "Busyness and laziness have the same impact: you're not in control," Young says. "Your schedule and all the responsibilities you've stacked up are dictating your time."[126] Busy is also easy. Tim Ferriss writes that "being busy is a form of laziness—lazy thinking and indiscriminate action. Being busy is most often used as a guise for avoiding...critically important but uncomfortable actions."[127] It can also be a consequence of being unable to say "no" to requests or opportunities, or to requests disguised as opportunities. For some, in fact, it's the only way they know how to operate because they never learned to how *not* to be busy.

As these observations suggest, we can find plenty of explanations for our collective addiction to busyness. It's a distraction from pain. A hedge against anxiety. A form of laziness. A signal of importance. A reflection of ego. An inability to say "no." The only lifestyle we've ever known. Seven definitions that all, in essence, reflect a similar point: Busyness is a crutch, insulating you from your fears and insecurities and keeping you from doing what matters most. How busy or stressed or overwhelmed you feel, or how packed your calendar is, or how long your to-do list grows, or how many nights and weekends you have to work, might be useful metrics for many things, from poor time management to simply trying to do too much. But they're not metrics for "producing" the things you care about. They're not metrics for measuring a life fulfilled.

"It's a skill to know how to deploy your time successfully at any activity," Yale Law School professor Daniel Markovits suggests. Contrary to what societal norms imply, the list of activities that require skill includes more than just professional responsibilities. It also includes leisure. It includes being bored. It includes *not* working all the time. Eighty-hour weeks may be a skill of professional elites—a skill the market seems to value highly—but "it's also a skill to deploy your time successfully at non-productive things. To know how to have a hobby. To know how to have a drawn-out Sunday afternoon casually with family or friends," Markovits says. "It's not just that elites are addicted to the work," he adds. "It's that they don't have the skill at the other thing."[128]

Breaking the busyness addiction doesn't mean liquidating your possessions and moving into a tiny home so you can grow your own crops and meditate six hours a day in isolation. It doesn't even mean not being busy. It just means learning to live without the rush of misguided adrenaline that comes from racing from task to task or meeting to meeting in a frantic hurry. It means recognizing the compulsion to be busy for the sake of being busy. It means cultivating awareness of how you spend your time, why you're so compelled to say "yes" to everything asked of you, and whether you're equating self-worth with work. Breaking the busyness addiction means accepting that when you make decisions that leave you *less* busy, you might well encounter withdrawal symptoms as you learn to judge your value in different ways. Like learning any new skill or changing any behavior, it means investing time and effort in *not* working, even if you may have been training all your life to work. It means accepting that many people around you are also wired to see not being busy as laziness, weakness, or inadequacy, so you may encounter skepticism, doubt, scorn, or even rejection from others as you proceed along this journey. "It is not enough to be industrious; so are the ants," Henry David Thoreau wrote. The question is, "what are you industrious about?"[129]

This brings us back to this chapter's Monday-versus-Tuesday opening anecdote, about which it's worth noting a few things. You may recall that Monday morning was filled with reading and writing, and Tuesday morning with meetings and frenzied busyness. It's true that not everyone always, or sometimes ever, has the choice between the two mornings I described. Moreover, the busyness and productivity obsession is generally characteristic of a particular subset of people, particularly those in high-paying and relatively comfortable jobs. Working tirelessly for minimum wage without benefits to cover the rent or pay for health insurance or put food on the table isn't busyness addiction—it's survival. And it's a symptom of a host of different (and more fundamental) failures of society, from unaffordable housing and child care, to broken and unequal educational systems, to rising income inequality and multi-generational wealth disparities. Many of these challenges stem from deeply institutionalized biases and unaddressed consequences of unchecked capitalism. It's true that being obsessed with busyness and productivity is, in many ways, a lucky problem to have. But that doesn't mean we shouldn't try to tackle it.

It's also true that many people would find a morning of reading and writing pointless and excruciating, and a morning of meetings fulfilling and invigorating. (We're all different, both in what we enjoy doing and in what we're expected to do.) It's true that these days, no matter who you are or what you do, you probably feel busy most of the time. It's true that plenty of busy people lead fulfilling lives. And it's true that everyone has days when they have a long list of things that must be done, and whether they make progress on that list is probably a decent measure of how "productive" they were that day. That's especially true when that list of tasks comes from, say, an employer or teacher.

Yet even when we acknowledge these caveats, I suspect more of us are addicted to busyness and obsessed with productivity because we internalize what society tells us: that they reflect a measure of our value to the world. Productivity and its busyness proxy give us a comforting, if illusory, sense of purpose. That's why our obsession with productivity is almost always about producing and working *more*, rather than producing and working *well*.

Over the course of a lifetime, how many of the activities that make your life fulfilling are actually measured by the number of things you produced? I'd argue that a more authentic measure of what I care most about—at least in terms of building a fulfilling life—is how much of my attention, effort, and heart I commit to them over a lifetime. They're measured, in other words, by how *well* I work on them, not necessarily how many of them I "produce" (whatever that means).

Unfortunately, "well" doesn't lend itself to easy measurement. "More"—more meetings, more calls, more tasks, more emails, more running around, more sacrifices of sleep and leisure and passion projects—is much easier to measure. It's also, conveniently, a tool that society has deemed acceptable.

Tools
Productivity is a tool for life, not the purpose of life

As any millennial will tell you, even though we're expected to be busy and productive all the time, we're also expected to live healthy, balanced, educated, social, self-aware, curious lives. These dueling expectations have created quite a market opportunity, from which has emerged an entire universe of time management books and productivity apps and life-hacking blogs that contain tantalizing promises of hyper-productivity. As a matter of fact, some of these sources *do* contain valuable tips and ideas. From waking up early to starting the workday with my most important task, I've incorporated some of the most common productivity refrains into my daily routine.

But despite their occasional usefulness, they also play a foundational role in the productivity con by implying that any one of us can *do it all* if we hack our lives *just right*. All we have to do, they assure us, is wake up early, drink yerba mate, take the right supplements, listen to audiobooks at triple speed, build and maintain a bubbly and slightly ironic social media presence (which is part of a rigorously cultivated personal brand), download the newest to-do list and calendar apps, and generally work harder, multitask better, and hack our lives more craftily than anyone else. Just look at the morning routines of these nine entrepreneurs! Just implement these 18 time-tested time-management hacks honed in the fires of the C-suite! Just listen to these productivity podcasts and do everything these guys do! (And don't forget to purchase the mattresses and subscribe to the food-delivery services they advertise!)

I've long been a time-manager and self-improver and life-hacker and, thus, a voracious consumer of these types of books, blogs, and podcasts. I've been absolutely convinced that if I can find the right way to be more productive and efficient, I'll unlock secret reserves of time and energy, leaving me in a magical place where I can slow down and live while still accomplishing everything I want to accomplish. In part, this obsessive search for life-hacks grew out of the forces of ambition, careerism, and fruitless planning that characterize politics. But more of it came from a conviction that permanent happiness awaited me just beyond a certain activity, achievement, or amount of time, and all I had to do to reach the threshold of a satisfying life was discover and implement the appropriate productivity regimen. This mentality, which seems endemic to Western culture today, leads to the relentless striving and searching for *more*.

Broadly, I traveled down four different paths as I sought the perfect combination of hacks that would enable me to do it all. These paths were hustle, efficiency, getting-things-done-ness, and minimalism. Each of these paths can be constructive when used to reframe how you view your work and how you spend your time. But when these paths become end goals instead of tools for the journey, all they do is feed the productivity con. Let's walk through them.

Hustle. In this specific productivity context, the "hustle" is the idea that you can out-work everyone, and there's no time for anything but work, professional development, and building your personal brand. It's a lonely way to live, but it's often the way that you're taught to operate. In a 2019 *New York Times* column whose headline rightly wonders, "Why are young people pretending to love work?" reporter Erin Griffith tries to make sense of "hustle culture." This modern phenomenon, she writes, "is obsessed with striving, relentlessly positive, devoid of humor, and—once you notice it—impossible to escape."[130] It's spawned entire organizations for which the purpose, as Griffith puts it, is to "glorify ambition not as a means to an end, but as a lifestyle." Implicit in such a mindset is the assumption that once you achieve a certain level of seniority, power, influence, or achievement, you'll be satisfied. If I earned that promotion, my thinking in politics went, or handled that policy area, or got that bill passed, or worked for that senator, or had that job title, or got invited to that high-level meeting, I wouldn't feel that same sense of gnawing insecurity that leads so many of us to look over the shoulder of the person we're talking to, to see if someone more important has entered the room.

This mentality can capture other aspects of our lives beyond work, from relationships to health. Any finish line defined by "If only..." is impossible to reach. But that's harder to see (and easier not to think about) if you convince yourself, with a tinge of self-righteousness, that all you have time for is work. You have to keep hustling. "I don't know what these other people are doing," you say to yourself, "but *I* have ambitions and goals, so *I* have to hustle. I'm willing to sacrifice things I enjoy doing because I'm going to be successful." Tucked in there sometimes is a sense of, *I'll show them.* Meanwhile, as the hustle becomes more intertwined with your identity, you become less comfortable doing anything other than hustling. "For congregants of the Cathedral of Perpetual Hustle," Griffith writes, "spending time on anything that's nonwork related has become a reason to feel guilty."[131]

These toxic notions, combined with the look-at-me power of social media, have created a huge online cache of what's sometimes called "hustle porn." These "hustle culture" posts are often fitness- or entrepreneurship-related, and organized with hashtags like #RiseAndGrind.[132] Sure, there's value in finding support on the internet when you need to do some hard work. But if you were wondering whether the definition of "hustle" has evolved from working hard to self-righteously proclaiming work-is-life as a status symbol—how hustling has changed from a tool to an identity—there's your answer. I hope we all find work we're passionate about. I hope we all find causes or efforts or ideas that fire us up. But hustling for hustling's sake is just exhausting. Burnout, not bliss, is far more likely to greet us along this path.

◆

Efficiency. Out of this notion of the hustle emerged a second obsession in my search for the secret to doing it all: efficiency. With this guiding principle, life should be lived as efficiently as possible so as to leave maximum time for work (read: busyness). Once inefficiencies are eliminated, happiness will emerge organically, in part by leaving maximum time for the busyness of the hustle, which is itself the point of life (see previous section, and repeat). Thus, an efficient life will allow you to more quickly reach a place of power and seniority (which will lead to happiness), even though that mythical place is perpetually and permanently out of reach.

In my early 20s, this mindset was characterized most literally, and perhaps most absurdly, by a daily experiment on my morning walk from my apartment to the DC Metro. As I began my commute to the fifth floor of the Cannon House Office Building, I walked from Massachusetts Avenue through Franklin Square Park. Instead of, I don't know, taking time to enjoy the park, as I walked I incessantly considered whether it made more sense to walk straight ahead and only turn to cross the street when I hit a red light, or whether it would be quicker and more efficient to zig-zag the whole way, crossing the street as soon as I could, even if reaching my destination didn't yet require me to cross. Who knows for how long my commute involved this ridiculous thought experiment, or what I ultimately concluded. The conclusion is not the point. The point is that it was a pointless exercise that focused exhaustingly on entirely trivial decisions. On a ten-minute walk to the subway, how much time could I possibly have saved by crossing the street at the most opportune moment? Thirty seconds? A minute, at most?

It's certainly worth finding some satisfaction in small moments of efficiency. A stressful commute transformed into a peaceful one by just barely catching the train is a moment worth savoring (and, for me, a lesson worth learning). But an obsession with efficiency can easily lead to absurdity, especially when what I really needed to do was to leave my apartment five minutes earlier so I wouldn't be late every day.

What the efficiency obsession also reflects is a constant search for ways to finish things as quickly as possible, instead of spending even a fraction of a second trying to find meaning or enjoyment in them. It's exhausting to spend your life counting down until the end of tasks or activities. But that's what you're training your mind for when you equate the "most efficient" way to do something with the "best" way to do it. This mentality also has a permanent effect on how you view the rest of your existence because long-term projects—the ones that are often most fulfilling over a lifetime—require steady progress over days, months, even years. They often lead to the development of expertise in a skill or issue area, a deeply rewarding process in itself. Yet an efficiency obsession can make long-term projects too excruciating to consider because they don't provide the immediate satisfaction of being checked off a list. It might even make them too daunting to begin in the first place, leading you to replace steady but immeasurable progress on a long-term goal with relentless to-do-list-friendly tasks that never add up to any total greater than the sum of their parts.

An efficiency obsession trains your brain to always look for a finish line by building a mindset in which everything is an obligation to be completed or something to do as quickly and with as little substantive investment as possible, "just to get it over with." An efficiency obsession, in other words, makes it nearly impossible to actually enjoy or be present for how you spend the overwhelming majority of your time.

Getting-things-done-ness. A third, and closely related, path along my search for the perfect life-hack was my obsession with "getting things done." (Call it "GTD," to use the popular online acronym that emerged from a book of a similar title.) This obsession with GTD stemmed from a conviction that the more things I got done, and the quicker I did them, the more worthwhile I would be (and the more time I would have later to do things I actually enjoyed). GTD-ness sits at the heart of the productivity con. Its driving forces are *how much* and *how fast*, not *how well*, *how important*, or *how fulfilling*.

As most readers have probably experienced, the tempting idea that there are hidden ways to do more, and to do so more quickly, creates some strange incentives. Take the classic to-do list shuffle. When I was in the throes of the productivity con and obsessed with getting things done, I could spend hours organizing and reorganizing tasks, thinking I was making myself more efficient so I could get more done. What I chose not to see was that organizing and reorganizing tasks, and then exporting them and re-importing them to a different app, before copying them all into a small notebook, before deciding I don't want to carry a notebook around and going back to the original app, having now wasted a weekend and returned to the starting line without doing anything of value, didn't actually do any of the things on that list. All it did was take up time I could have spent seeing a friend, reading a book, going for a run, volunteering, or lying on the floor and staring at a ceiling fan—doing literally anything else. Not surprisingly, spending a weekend shuffling to-do items wasn't a very fulfilling way to spend my time.

Instead of doing the work I needed to do or the activities I wanted to do, my GTD obsession offered a comforting reassurance that somewhere some magical productivity tool existed that would make work easy, and all I had to do was find it. According to that logic, my relentless to-do-listing today was an investment in productivity tomorrow, or some unspecified time in the future (when, of course, I'd be happy and fulfilled). In reality, the idea of "getting things done" was a distraction. The fetishizing of productivity and busyness fed my ego while giving me an excuse not to make meaningful progress on hard work or confront hard questions. Questions such as: If I've checked off 17 tasks in my new to-do list app, why do the tasks keep coming? And why, no matter how many tasks I complete, do I still feel a gnawing lack of fulfillment?

Just like relying solely on dietary supplements to get healthier instead of eating better and exercising more, obsessing over little GTD hacks is way easier than working or prioritizing. It feels great to convince yourself that you can do it all, and it will all be easy, if only you find the right tool to help you multitask and get things done. The problem isn't the way you work or how you choose to allocate your time. The real problem is that you haven't yet found the right blog post on "12 Ways to Supercharge Your Productivity Today."

But whether it's completing an assignment at work, paying taxes, dealing with a broken fridge, moving to a new apartment, doing laundry, or going grocery shopping, life never stops throwing little tasks at you, let alone big ones. You can never check every item off any list. No matter what you do, "the choices don't stop," as author and surgeon Atul Gawande writes. "Life is choices, and they are relentless. No sooner have you made one choice than another is upon you."[133] That doesn't mean you shouldn't get things done—that's a necessity—but it does mean setting boundaries. It means redefining productivity to reflect actual work on things you value, or at the very least deleting some items from those lists, rather than simply organizing and reorganizing them. It means accepting the obvious fact that you can't do it all, and that beyond a certain point productivity is a fantasy that's easier to chase than just doing the underlying work.

The endless to-do list always beckons because the fallacy of the finish-able to-do list, like that of the empty inbox, is so powerful. Instead of searching for *the* magical elixir, you just need to find *a* system that works well enough, and stick with it. If you're working, work (rather than reorganizing tasks and pushing them around). If you're not working, don't work (rather than floating in the space that's neither work nor rest). If you're procrastinating by watching Netflix, at least you know you're procrastinating. If you're procrastinating by organizing tasks beyond the point of diminishing returns or refreshing your email over and over, you're just hiding procrastination under the guise of productivity and busyness. That's not a recipe for a fulfilling day.

Today, I still like reading about organizational systems that sync across platforms and devices. In spite of everything I've just written, one of my guilty pleasures remains listening to podcasts by productivity and life-hacking gurus. I still like learning about the different ways people stay on top of their work and what their morning routines are. I still like seeing an empty inbox. But I'm learning to accept that I can appreciate these moments without equating them with productivity. I can strive to get things done without losing sight of why I'm trying to do them in the first place.

Minimalism. As my GTD obsession began to wane, I started experimenting with minimalism, the fourth path I hoped might lead me to the promised land of *doing it all.* The minimalism path was characterized by reducing the number of "things" in my life—items, ideas, responsibilities—to simplify my world. This technique sometimes took the form of eliminating possessions. (I spent many satisfying hours getting rid of old, mostly unread, copies of *The New Yorker* on Freecycle and donating finished books to the DC public library, for instance.) Other times, minimalism was about cutting down on commitments, reducing the number of decisions I needed to make, or eliminating toxic, often self-imposed, expectations.

Minimalism got me much closer to the desired destination than the previous three paths. After half a century of relentless corporate promises that more possessions and more wealth and more achievements will bring human beings eternal happiness, there's a growing understanding in society that less can be more. This trend has entered pop culture—a sure sign it's "arrived"—as reflected in films like Netflix's *Minimalism: A Documentary About the Important Things* and books such as Marie Kondo's *The Life-Changing Magic of Tidying Up.* It's easy to see why: None of us have the time, money, or space (physical or emotional) to have everything. Saying "no" is liberating and invigorating.

Many of the lessons in this book tie strongly into the minimalist ethos of simplifying and focusing on what you care most about. Much of what stands between you and a more fulfilling life is the stuff that a maximalist lifestyle creates: too many possessions, too many obligations, too many activities dictated by others' expectations rather than your own priorities or passions. In part, having too much stuff trains you to think the next purchase or promotion will bring you permanent happiness, and that the lack of said purchase or promotion will leave you in a state of impoverished depravity and yearning. (In reality, the purchases and promotions often leave us with all of the yearning and none of the happiness.)

It also takes a lot of effort and money to manage and maintain a giant house full of expensive, complicated things. It takes a lot of time and energy to manage a busy schedule full of commitments that you don't enjoy but that have found a home on your calendar because of your inability to say "no." It takes a lot of emotional energy, and demands giving up control of your well-being, to continually search for that perfect item or identity that you're sure will make you happy. Like many of the recommendations in this book, the minimalist path is not always an option, especially when it comes to professional commitments. But simplifying and saying "no" is an option a lot more often than you think, perhaps in some parts of your life more than others. These are all reasons for adopting a minimalist lifestyle that focuses on the people and activities that leave you fulfilled at the end of the day.

There's a catch, though, and this is the catch I was missing when I first stumbled across the concept. Minimalism *in itself* is not fulfillment. What minimalism unlocks is what really matters. Countless times over the past decade I've spent an evening purging clothes, doing a deep clean of an apartment, unfollowing people on Twitter, throwing things out, reevaluating how I spend my time, declining invitations. While I still find those activities liberating and satisfying, it's not the actual donating of clothes or deleting of an item on the to-do list that's fulfilling (although the feeling of generosity certainly is). The freedom and satisfaction comes from using that newly-available headspace to build a more fulfilling life. Minimalism itself is not what matters. Minimalism, I've finally come to understand, is a means to create space for what matters.

Delusions

Resist the delusion of productivity

P roductivity and fulfillment have a weird on-again, off-again relationship. The same is true for minimalism, efficiency, and hustle. They can be valuable, even critical, tools to aid your journey. They can help to unlock more time, attention, and focus for what you care about. But they're *means* to an end, not the ends themselves. A to-do list, for instance, is a means to accomplish a big project, but in most cases the list isn't the actual project. Clearing your schedule of unnecessary obligations is a means to make time for work that matters, but just declining a bunch of calendar invitations doesn't automatically accomplish anything. If you're saying "no" to social opportunities just so you can spend more time on social media, what are you really minimizing?

For years, I assumed that a lifestyle defined by productivity and getting things done would eventually leave me fulfilled. I assumed that what gave me more time to be busy would also make me a more worthy and valuable person. I assumed that what mattered was the mental drain that came from pushing around emails. Or being the person who said "yes" to things I didn't want or need to do simply because they filled up my calendar. Or being the person who woke up earliest and worked latest, or who had the fewest number of possessions in his apartment.

The intention of this chapter isn't to say you should never be busy, or that producing things should never matter, or that you should never seek out life-hacks or efficiencies here and there. What I'm saying is that you can move these modern-day obsessions from the metaphorical mantle above the fireplace to the slightly-less-metaphorical toolbox in the garage. You can stop seeing them as accomplishments and goals in and of themselves, and instead see them as tools for the journey.

Constant busyness is a tool for gauging whether you've taken on too much and might be unconsciously losing touch with what matters most to you. Hustle, efficiency, and minimalism, meanwhile, are tools to make space for the people and activities you care most about. At least in my experience (sample size: one), a busyness-addicted, productivity-obsessed day reflects a day in which too many of the things that bring me fulfillment have been bumped to second- or third-tier priorities. It reflects a day in which I haven't made time for what matters most to me.

◆

If you don't measure your life in busyness and productivity, though, how do you know if you're on the right track? There's no secret metric, but here's how I take stock at the end of each day. Looking back on the past 17-ish hours, did I find myself experiencing moments of stillness, moments when I wasn't worried about looming deadlines or an overflowing inbox? Did I ever lose track of time, like I do when I'm deep in a writing project or hanging out with friends or in the middle of an intense workout? Whether a friend, a colleague, or someone sleeping on the ground outside the subway station, did I see and hear people who needed to be seen and heard, rather than flying through the day caught up in my own mini-dramas and micro-problems? Am I feeling the sense of contented exhaustion that we discussed in chapter three (as opposed to the feeling of, "I've been awake for 17 hours and have no idea what I've done with all that time")? If the answer to these questions is generally yes, then I'm probably on the right track. If, on the other hand, I spent the day feeling stressed, judgmental, unmotivated, or distracted, I might just need to sleep it off and start fresh the next day.

But maybe I can do more than sleep it off. Maybe I need to sleep *more* and start the next day more rested and focused. Or, maybe I need to sleep *less* and wake up earlier the next morning to be sure I've set aside time for meditating, writing, or reading something meaningful. Maybe I just need to turn my brain off for a couple hours and sit with Erin to watch an episode, or three, of a TV show we love. Maybe I need to tweak tomorrow's calendar and to-do list a bit. Maybe I need to review the expectations I've set for myself and scale them back. Maybe I need to scan the commitments I've said "yes" to and see if I can postpone or eliminate them entirely.

Or, maybe tomorrow I need to switch off notifications and, as I often did on Capitol Hill, put my headphones in, with white noise playing in the background, so that I can focus. Maybe I need to make a conscious effort to go out for lunch tomorrow with a colleague, instead of stuffing down a sandwich while I sit in front of my computer and read agitating political news. Maybe I need to move the most important, most meaningful, and most time-sensitive things I want to get done to the top of my list, and start the next day by tackling those. Maybe I need to force myself out of my chair to go for a walk in the middle of the day to clear my head and remind myself that the planet will continue rotating even if I fail to respond immediately to every message I receive. Maybe I need to be more assertive about closing my work laptop at 5 pm and not opening it again until the following morning. Maybe I need to take intentional steps to put my own little world in context by seeking out the stories and experiences of other human beings dealing with different, often more profound, challenges.

These are all techniques I've employed, and continue to hone through trial and error, to fight my addiction to busyness and my obsession with productivity. I'm constantly seeking new ways to interrupt my own productivity-emptiness-guilt cycle. To remind myself, over and over again, that there is more to human existence than being productive. To take to heart that there are more fulfilling ways to live out my existence than being perpetually, frantically, exhaustingly busy. Your life is different, so the tools and tricks and techniques you use might be different. We're all busy. We all want to be productive. We will all have to continue to tweak and experiment to find ways to do what we need to do while nudging our lives in a more fulfilling direction. The point is not that you should be doing any specific activity, but rather to remain aware, as best you can, that diligently following the roads of busyness and productivity from when you wake up until after you fall asleep and dream about to-do lists might not get you where you want to go.

6

Make time for what matters

"The easiest way to increase happiness is to control your use of time. Can you find more time to do the things you enjoy doing?"

Daniel Kahneman[134]

Responsibilities

Redefine what you care about as a responsibility, not a reward

It's the end of the workday. I'm at a Starbucks in central London, where I've been powering through work miscellanea for the past hour. While wrapping up for the day, I've been observing the people around me. I always find it encouraging and reassuring to see people packing up for the day. Even if it's not actually the end of their day, seeing people pack their things like they're headed home is a good reminder that we (in this case, the other human beings at Starbucks) have made it through another day. It's an entirely manufactured sense of camaraderie, of course. I haven't spoken with anyone besides the barista, and for all I know, these coffee shop patron-strangers are headed to a second job, or a late-afternoon meeting they've been dreading, or a packed rush-hour commute across the city. But I like to think they're finished with work and are on their way to see a movie or hang out with their kids.

Anyway, it's that time of day. In 15 minutes, I'm meeting Erin near her office. With my work done for the day and my laptop shut, I've managed to carve out a few minutes free of incoming stimuli. It's a good time to take stock of the day. I pull up the to-do list on my phone, checking off the errands and other forgettable-but-necessary stuff I've done that day. Do laundry, drop off dry-cleaning, buy groceries, pay rent—*check, check, check, check*. Clean oven, pay credit card bill—*move to tomorrow*. But those to-dos, while momentarily satisfying to check off, aren't the only items on the list. Those items aren't why I wanted to find a quiet, distraction-free moment to open the app. I continue. Read *The Economist*—*check*. Meditate with Headspace—*check*. Take a walk—*check*. Call my parents—*do that tonight*. Write or do some reading for the book—*check*. Check in with Erin—*priority for tonight*. Work out—*missed it. Priority for tomorrow*. What's going on here?

I can anticipate the skepticism: "What are all these items doing on a to-do list? These lists are supposed to be for burdens and boring tasks. Chores. Things that make us more productive. Things we have to do. Things that stand in the way of stuff we care about, not the actual stuff we care about. How can you put important, meaningful activities on a to-do list—right next to laundry and rent? Come to think of it, that's pretty depressing! How does that not trivialize calling home or checking in with Erin? If meditation is so important to you that you've written an entire chapter about it, why do you even need to be reminded to meditate? I literally just read the chapter that said not to see things we care about as tasks to be checked off. Life isn't a to-do list!"

These are legitimate questions. And I fully agree—life is *not* a to-do list. Or, at least, it shouldn't be. But if we're being honest, most of the time most of us are going to treat it like one. Most of us are going to determine how we budget most of our time using things like to-do lists. So, we might as well put the things we care about on those lists, too—not just the stuff we think we have to do *before* we get to what really matters to us.

Spending time with Erin, family, and friends. Reading. Writing. Exercising. Traveling. Meditating. These are some of the aspects of my life that instill in me a sense of fulfillment, wholeness, and completion. The activities that force me into the present moment and create value in my life. The activities that give me energy and leave me with a feeling of contented exhaustion. The activities that give me the confidence and stability to be there for others. The activities I need to prioritize for a life fulfilled.

Yet I've long operated on a model that doesn't reflect these priorities. What gives me joy and fulfillment—the things I *want* to do, the things that are entirely in my control—are slotted around the things I *have* to do—the things rarely in my control that I often feel I'm supposed be doing. Instead of carving out time for a workout, I let work emails determine whether there's time to exercise. Instead of reading books that challenge and educate and inspire me, I let Twitter, political news, and email come first. Only once those are "finished" (whatever that means) will I allow time for reading. Instead of creating time for side hustles and passion projects, I postpone them or try to fit them into 15-minute increments at the end of a long day.

It almost goes without saying that what I value most—spending time with Erin and our families and friends—suffers because of my inability to make that time a priority, rather than a reward for having gotten everything else done first. The writer Ryan Holiday asks rhetorically, "If real self-improvement is what we're after, why do we leave our reading until those few minutes before we shut off the lights and go to bed?"[135] To paraphrase Holiday, if more fulfilling days are what you're after, why do you leave the activities that fulfill you until those few minutes in between obligations or at the end of the day? If a meaningful life is what you're after, why do you assume you have to save some of its most meaningful chapters for the very end?* Why, in other words, do I feel compelled to squeeze in reading or writing or meditation or exercise around news, emails, and errands, rather than the other way around? Why

---

* In *Truman*, his Pulitzer Prize-winning biography of Harry S. Truman, David McCullough tells the story of the thirty-third president coming across a framed poem that resonated with him. Truman recited it out loud: *"Every man's a would be sportsman, in the dreams of his intent, / A potential out-of-doors man when his thoughts are pleasure bent. / But he mostly puts the idea off, for the things that must be done, / And doesn't get his outing till his outing days are gone. / So in hurry, scurry, worry, work, his living days are spent / And he does his final camping in a low green tent."* McCullough describes the president's response: "'Hurry, scurry, worry, work!' Truman sighed. 'That's the way it is.'"[137]

have I been trained to feel that being seen as "online" or "available" or "not slacking" should dictate how I spend my time, rather than recognizing these thoughts as the insecurities and irrational cravings for acceptance they are? Why do I continue to say "yes" to things that I have no interest in and don't need to do?

I've increasingly come to recognize these backwards trade-offs in how I allocate my attention and time. My instincts are to make the activities I care about, the *want-to-dos*, rewards for completing the *have-to-dos*. But what if, on occasion, I flip that order upside-down? What if I make the *want-to-dos* responsibilities, not rewards? What if I make it my responsibility to prioritize fulfilling activities, such as meditation, because they make me a more thoughtful and less judgmental person? What if I make it my responsibility to spend more time with friends and family instead of with Outlook and YouTube? What if I reframe, even only slightly, my approach to each day so I think just a little bit more about the *want-to-dos*, and a little bit less about the *have-to-dos*?

Priorities

Put your priorities on your to-do list

My argument for putting the activities that matter most on a to-do list is for practical as much as philosophical reasons. Activities like taking a walk, calling my parents, and thinking are recurring entries on my list. (Yes, that third task just reads "Think," as in, "Be with your thoughts without any incoming stimuli.") It's not because I'm likely to forget any of these things. Nor is it because I believe I can do them once and then they're "done." Rather, it's because, as Daniel H. Pink puts it, "What gets scheduled gets done."[137] I want the things that matter most to me to get done. I want my priorities to happen.

You might assume that putting "Play with kids," "Read positive affirmation," or "Write in gratitude journal" on the to-do list or schedule trivializes them. You might think that doing so is a sign you're over-prescribing your life, trying to control the uncontrollable and fit your entire life into the model of work. To some degree, you might be right. It certainly can feel weird to put this stuff, the stuff that matters most, on a list alongside "Respond to emails," "File taxes," or "Call cable company." It might seem like I'm equating calling my parents, which is one of the most important and meaningful things I do every week, with calling my internet provider yet again to find out what's wrong with our service, which is one of the least fulfilling tasks imaginable. But the to-do list is what I depend on to make sure I do both what I need to and what I want to do. I invest my time and trust in the to-do list. Why not use it to keep the important stuff on my agenda, in addition to the unpleasantries and obligations that I have to tackle?

Putting the activities that most bring me fulfillment into the system I use to manage my days makes me prioritize the *want-to-dos* at least as much as the obligatory *have-to-dos*. It forces me to consider the trade-offs that come with, say, sacrificing time with a passion project to run an errand. This system elevates the fulfilling *want-to-dos* to their rightful place, so that activities like meditating, writing, and calling home get the time they deserve. It doesn't mean I succeed in doing everything I want to do every day. Any set of to-dos, whether groceries or life goals, requires flexibility to function. However, it does mean that I'm generally aware of whether I'm focusing on the big stuff over time. It's about prioritization, not productivity.

Dropbox co-founder Drew Houston describes to Tim Ferriss how he prioritizes his "rocks," the things that matter most to him. "Schedule specific blocks of time in advance for your rocks so you don't have to think about them," Houston urges. "Don't rely on wishful thinking (e.g., 'I'll get that workout in when I have some downtime'); if you can't see your rocks on your calendar, they might as well not exist. ... If you don't put those in first, no one will."[138] (This approach echoes my dad's reasoning for scheduling "Tuesdays to write," which we discussed in chapter one.) Houston's last observation is perhaps the most important: *If you don't put them first, no one will.* Whether you call them your rocks, priorities, goals, want-to-dos—it's on you to put them first.

◆

Still, you might wonder, if something's *truly* important to me, shouldn't it be easy to prioritize? Maybe for some, but I'm not confident that's how it works for most of us in our over-stimulated, oversubscribed world. I don't trust myself to always know what matters to me at the exact moment I need to know, especially in the middle of a hectic day. And even when I do know, I don't trust myself to act in accordance with that knowledge, like when I get out my phone to read a saved *New Yorker* article but end up instinctively tapping my way to political gossip on Twitter. Instead, I trust that the person (undistracted and self-aware Adam) who designed this to-do list system knows what I genuinely want to focus on better than the person (distracted and overwhelmed Adam) who's tired and not sure what to prioritize at a given moment.

If there's something that really matters to me, I make sure it gets added to my list so I remember to make time for it, rather than having lots of things I want to remember floating in and out of my consciousness all day. On a given day, if an activity I value isn't on my to-do list, I trust I've done it already or decided it's not a priority for that day. In other words, I let my list do the hard work of prioritizing for me, freeing me from the relentless decision-rehearsing, brain-wandering, nagging feeling of forgetting something that comes with trying to balance all the things I want to do in a given day. That makes my days more fulfilling.

Somewhat counterintuitively, building this structure into my days also leaves me with more mental bandwidth to embrace the unplanned and the unexpected. Because I have a high-level view of where I want the day to go, I'm more aware of the inevitable trade-offs in how I choose to spend my time. When an exciting but last-minute request comes in at work, for instance, or I get a call from a friend who's passing through town and wants to get a drink, I can say "yes" without worrying about missing something or not making time for my priorities, instead of saying "no" because I have the vague sense I'm too busy or don't have time. Call it intentional spontaneity.

There are caveats, of course. Anyone who's spent a day organizing and reorganizing a to-do list, only to find all the tasks shifted around but none of them were actually checked off, knows that systems don't do our work for us. Nor do systems prevent us from building unachievable lists packed with far more than we could possibly accomplish in a single day. Sometimes our jobs or other circumstances make these types of hard-and-fast rules impossible. For a technique like this to work, you have to learn to be flexible and comfortable missing things. No system enables anyone to do it all. Accepting that unfortunate reality is a prerequisite to *any* time management tactic.

But if you're being realistic about how much you *really* need to do in a given day, and how much time you *really* have to do it, it becomes abundantly clear that you'll only spend more time doing what matters to you if you choose to prioritize it. You can take small steps to reframe your most important activities as responsibilities, not rewards. Putting my personal priorities on my to-do list doesn't mean I'm doing everything I want to do every single day—far from it. But it means that, each day, I consciously try to make time for what matters most to me, in a way that combines flexibility, openness to disruption, and a guarantee of *some* fulfillment-generating activity. If I'm checking off most of my priorities most days of the week, I'm probably feeling pretty good and making progress on what I want to accomplish. And if I fall short and miss a day, or a week, that's ok. I'll get back to it tomorrow. (That's another benefit of recurring systems.) This way of thinking also supports long-term habit formation since one of the challenges of working toward long-term goals is the lack of a sense of progress or completion on a day-to-day timescale. When you put these ongoing, multi-day goals on your list, you get the added benefit of being able to check them off the list and get them out of your head each day, knowing they'll be back again tomorrow.

Framing

Work like you have young kids

Here's one (admittedly odd) way I balance life and work, which was inspired by observing the professional habits of some former colleagues in the U.S. Senate: Work like you're a parent of young kids.

This sounds pretty strange, especially coming from someone without children. But what I've observed is that families with kids don't have much time (or, I imagine, energy) for things that don't satisfy one of two conditions: 1) it *has* to be done, or 2) it provides them and their families with real, meaningful value. They *have* to prioritize. They have to work deliberately and efficiently when they're at work; they don't have the option of staying late to catch up on emails because they've spent the first three hours of the day on Twitter. They have to focus on what's most important and what matters. They have small humans counting on them being there at 5:30 pm.

The same is true at home. These theoretical parents of young children don't have time (or interest) in circulating project plans for the sake of circulating project plans. They don't have the time (or interest) in working relentlessly for the purpose of fooling themselves into a fleeting sense of accomplishment or productivity. Evenings? Weekends? Vacations? Holidays? They know what matters, and it isn't PowerPoint. Like any boundary, working with the urgency of having kids at home focuses the mind and closes off the impossible-yet-tantalizing possibility of doing it all. It makes it more difficult to justify obsessing over the small things that don't really matter in the long run. When we know we can't do it all, we *have* to choose.

To be very clear, this is *not* a call to action for working more efficiently or trying to sneak in extra tasks after your hypothetical (or real) children are asleep. It's a call to action for working less. Doing less. Prioritizing. Focusing on what's most important, and letting the rest go. This mental framework is about using your limited energy and attention to invest passionately in activities that you find fulfilling. I imagine raising a child is one of those activities, but there are plenty of other ways to nudge your brain and your schedule in a more meaningful direction. I've listed many of mine throughout this book: Spending time with friends and family. Working out. Meditating. Writing. Reading. I'm fortunate to have a flexible job and the means to prioritize many of these activities, but again, the point is that no matter your circumstances—even in the heat of a political campaign, for instance—you can tweak your priorities so what you care most about isn't the first thing you sacrifice by default.

I'm sure actual parents can find plenty of ways to quibble with this imperfect analogy, and I'm sure they're right. I have no idea what it's like to raise a child, which is why I'm not giving parenting advice. I'm simply urging you to organize your days more deliberately, spend your time more intentionally, and free yourself from the mythical idea that any of us can do it all. "Clarity about what matters provides clarity about what does not," Cal Newport writes.[139] If you choose to prioritize the small things, you inevitably run out of time for the big things.

If this child-rearing thought experiment isn't working for you, the writer Neil Pasricha suggests a complementary approach. (His suggestion is conveniently free of the awkward complexities that come with urging someone to pretend there are small children in their home.) It's what Pasricha calls "The Saturday Morning Test." When you're trying to identify the activities that bring you happiness, "What do you do on a Saturday morning when you have nothing to do?" Pasricha asks. "Your authentic self should go toward that."[140] Time is the most valuable resource you have. Why not invest it in fulfilling ways?

The next time you're tempted to check in on the office Slack channel over the weekend or to stay late to clean out the inbox yet again (as if it won't be full again in the morning), choose instead to work as if you have kids at home. Or as if it's Saturday morning and you have time, not a few minutes, but hours, potentially a day, and potentially the next day, of uninterrupted, unscheduled, uncommitted time, to do what you really care about. Or work as if you're on vacation, when you do only the most critical non-vacation stuff, and scrap the rest until you return to the real world.

Work Inflation
Embrace Parkinson's law

Work expands to fill the time allotted for it. This fundamental attribute of human behavior was first captured in *The Economist* in November 1955.[141] The column that introduced the world to this notion (known as Parkinson's law, after the writer C. Northcote Parkinson[142]), or at least put it into words for the first time, described a hypothetical "elderly lady of leisure" who spent an entire day crafting a postcard to her niece. This task "would occupy a busy man for three minutes all told," the piece observed. But because this lady of leisure could spend all day writing the note instead of having to fit it into three minutes, it took the whole day to accomplish.[143]

Setting aside the painfully gendered stereotype of the "busy man" and the "lady of leisure," this simple observation of a powerful truth has only become more relevant in an age of constant distractions fighting for our attention and tasks fighting for our time. Within reason, the more time you set aside for something, the more time that something will take. The less time you set aside for a project, the more efficiently you'll get it done. This unscientific law is the foundation of my unscientific observation about how coworkers with children seem to get their work done and still find time for the things that matter to them. They recognize the limits on their time, and they work within those limits. They focus on and commit to doing the most important stuff first.

This formula has worked particularly well for the software firm Basecamp. Company co-founders Jason Fried and David Heinemeier Hansson explain that Basecamp employees generally work a 40-hour week for much of the year, no matter what (except in summer, when they adopt a four-day, 32-hour-a-week schedule). "If you can't fit everything you want to do within 40 hours per week," they write, "you need to get better at picking what to do, not work longer hours."[144] Basecamp employees do what they need to do in the time they have. And with limited exceptions, if they aren't able to accomplish what they expected, they change their expectations, not their schedules.

Parkinson's law applies to more than office tasks. It could be finding an apartment, searching for a job, fitting in a workout, seeing friends and family, or really anything else. Human beings thrive under deadlines and can accomplish a lot more in a short space of time when there's a sense of urgency, whether real or artificial, external or self-imposed. (We'll explore this effect in a different way in chapter nine.) We can always do more than we think in less time than we think. And we have far more control over how we use that time than we think.

This observation comes with a critical caveat, however. Planning your days with Parkinson's law in mind can make it dangerously tempting to set your expectations even higher and cram in even more tasks and commitments just because you can. That would be a missed opportunity. Just because you *can* do more than you think doesn't mean you *should*. The power lies in leveraging Parkinson's law to make more time for the things that matter to you, not letting the less important stuff take up even more time or mental energy than it already does. Don't do more for the sake of doing more. Do more of what matters. (Perhaps the "elderly lady of leisure" who spent all day writing to her niece had it right.)

Fortunately, many societies already have a structure that empowers us to embrace Parkinson's law: It's called the weekend. Few things make me less effective during the week than thinking "I'll finish this project over the weekend." And few things make me moodier and more distracted by a vague sense of guilt or obligation over the weekend, not to mention fail to recharge me for the week ahead, than worrying about doing work that I could've done during the week (or could still do next week). As Parkinson's law suggests, if we allot two extra days for a task, that task will magically expand to require those two days. Make Saturdays and Sundays off-limits to everything *except* what matters most, and you'll probably get done in five days whatever you need to get done. And if you don't? Take two days off over the weekend, and then log in on Monday rested and ready to get back to work.

There's nothing particularly unique about the weekend, except that it's more socially acceptable not to work on Saturdays and Sundays (though it should be even more socially acceptable than it is). Whatever way you choose to do it, you can make an intentional effort to leverage the power of Parkinson's law to make more time for the things that matter to you. When specifically you find this time is less important than the fact that you make a conscious effort to find it sometime, somewhere, and with some regularity.

Two Selves

Beware the "tyranny of the remembering self"

The legendary psychologist and Nobel Prize winner Daniel Kahneman observes that our lives are essentially composed of two selves. There's the "experiencing self," which is how we feel in the middle of doing something. Then there's the "remembering self," which is how we feel about that activity afterwards—in other words, how we remember it.[145] As Kahneman points out, how we remember something often differs from how we felt as we experienced it.

When it comes to planning and decision-making, for example, the remembering self seems to be more in control than the experiencing self. How many times have you committed to something—a networking event, a workout class, drinks with an old acquaintance—only to ask yourself as soon as it starts, "Why did I say 'yes' to this yet again?" Why do we keep returning to activities that we don't enjoy? Why do we prioritize activities that don't give us a sense of fulfillment and bump the ones that do to the mythical "tomorrow?" There are plenty of answers to these questions, some more legitimate than others. You made a commitment. You have to (perhaps because it's the law—that's a good reason). You want to help someone out. You believe it's important. You like what the activity signals about you. You enjoy the idea of being the type of person who does that activity. You think it's good for you. You get the productive satisfaction of saying "yes" to a future commitment without having to actually do anything about it yet.

These are all real and, to differing degrees, valid reasons. But there may be another reason why you say "yes" to things that don't leave you fulfilled. That reason is that you remember things differently than how they felt as you experienced them. "The remembering self's neglect of duration, its exaggerated emphasis on peaks and ends, and its susceptibility to hindsight combine to yield distorted reflections of our actual experiences," Kahneman notes.[146] These shortcomings in perception and memory impact how we recall things and, thus, how we make future decisions. "I am my remembering self," Kahneman writes, in a reflection of all of us, "and the experiencing self, who does my living, is like a stranger to me."[147]

If you're determined to spend more of your days in genuinely fulfilling ways, you have to recognize and reckon with these two selves. Unlocking more time to do what matters means identifying the activities that bring you value as you experience them, not just in what they signal about you or how you remember them. Embracing the experiencing self, in other words. But it also means embracing the remembering self by choosing to push through uncomfortable activities that leave you contentedly exhausted afterwards. "For human beings, life is meaningful because it is a story. A story has a sense of a whole, and its arc is determined by the significant moments, the ones where something happens," Atul Gawande observes. "Unlike your experiencing self—which is absorbed in the moment—your remembering self is attempting to recognize not only the peaks of joy and valleys of misery but also how the story works out as a whole."[148]

Don't expect to get the remembering-experience balance exactly right. There probably isn't a "right" balance, anyway. But you can tweak how you choose to spend your time by building awareness of these two selves and by recognizing how their squabbling, or the dominance of one over the other, can lead you astray. "The central fact of our existence is that time is the ultimate finite resource," Kahneman writes, "but the remembering self ignores that reality."[149]

The next time you're considering a far-off request or volunteering to work on a non-urgent project over the weekend, take a moment to think about Kahneman's two selves. Do you *really* want to say "yes," or is doing so just the path of least resistance? Do you *really* need to work this weekend, or do you just like what that would signal about you? Do you *really* want to get a drink next month with that person whose presence you don't particularly enjoy, or is it just harder (and less satisfying) to say "no" now than it is to schedule it for some future Wednesday evening? Reflecting on the remembering and experiencing selves as you make decisions about how you spend your time and organize your days can help you tilt the balance slightly more in the direction of the things you care about. And a slight tilt today can lead to a dramatically different trajectory over a lifetime.

"Doing It All"

We can do more of what matters. But we can't do it all

In this chapter, I've suggested four ways of thinking that have helped me make more time for what I care about: including my priorities on my to-do list, building a work schedule as if I were a parent, embracing Parkinson's law, and recognizing the tensions between my remembering and experiencing selves. And it's true that reframing my days with these ideas in mind has helped me make them more fulfilling.

But the entire premise of this chapter requires some fine print. No one can spend every minute of every day engrossed in life's most fulfilling activities. When it comes to how we spend our time, simply existing in society demands a constant balancing act of the ideal and the practical, of what matters and what's mandatory. Work responsibilities *do* matter, even if we'd rather be working on a side hustle. Current events and political news *are* important for anyone hoping to be an engaged citizen, even if we'd rather read a meaningful (or not so meaningful) novel. Taxes, car insurance, health challenges, accidents, chores, lost wallets, and family emergencies are a reality for all of us at some point or other, even if we'd much rather be dealing with anything else.

No matter how much your work aligns with your passions, how in touch you are with your desires, or how efficient you are with your to-do lists, life will intrude upon even the best-laid plans and the most relentlessly culled schedules. Making time for what matters doesn't give anyone permission to neglect basic responsibilities and obligations. Holding oneself to a standard that requires perfect compliance with ideas such as "I only do things that matter to me" is a recipe for failure. Human beings control very little of the world around us. And even when we do have some control, we still get distracted, make mistakes, and fall short of our goals a lot of the time. Sometimes we need time to be bored or watch TV or play video games mindlessly. Sometimes— a lot of the time, presumably—we need to do things because we have to, or just because it's the right thing to do. Life is full of trade-offs.

More fundamentally, even if life weren't full of trade-offs, even if we were all lucky enough to be able to spend every minute of every day doing what matters most to us, no one could life-hack or time-manage their way to doing *everything* they want. Yet, as we discussed in the previous chapter, there's an entire online universe promising that each one of us can unlock secret reserves of time—enough time to *do it all*—if we simply work harder and multitask better and hack our lives more craftily than anyone else. As Basecamp founders Fried and Hansson write, these hacks "all reflect an obsession with trying to squeeze more time out of the day." But, they rightly note, "rearranging your daily patterns to find more time for work isn't the problem. Too much shit to do is the problem. The only way to get more done is to have less to do."[150] *The only way to get more done is to have less to do.*

The next time you're lucky enough to look at tomorrow's calendar and see a day without meetings, or when you find yourself with a few moments on the subway or waiting for a meal without any incoming stimuli, resist the instinctive temptation to fill that blank space with something that will give you a false sense of productivity or importance. Instead, fill that time with something that matters to you—or, perhaps, with nothing. After all, as Winnie the Pooh reminds us, "Doing nothing often leads to the very best of something."[151]

Self-Indulgence
There's a thin line between fulfillment and selfishness

There's another variable lurking in the fine print, too. It applies not just to this chapter but to the premise of the entire book. It's one thing to ask whether we *can* find more time to do what matters most to us. It's another to ask whether we *should*. People in our lives depend on us for all sorts of things, even if we don't always want to do those things. People around the world face enormous challenges, as does the planet itself. Without taking away from anyone's suffering or minimizing anyone's situation, if you're reading this book, there's a good chance you have enough disposable income to afford an e-reader and enough time to use it. Why should *we* have the luxury to reflect on our lives and spend time crafting our days to make them more fulfilling? Why aren't we using every spare moment to volunteer for a meaningful cause or serve others in some form or another?

In other words, how do you make time for what matters to you in a responsible way? How do you find a pragmatic balance between pursuing what you care most about and upholding the obligations of life—not just the daily to-do list and what you've been assigned, but your commitments to your spouse, your children, your parents, your friends and family, your colleagues, civic society, and those in need? There's something that feels inherently selfish about urging generally well-off people to spend more time pursuing passion projects. Who am I to tell an exhausted single parent working multiple jobs for minimum wage that what she *really* needs is not a raise but rather to spend more time doing what she cares about? Instead of writing this book from a comfortable apartment in London, shouldn't I be back in DC using my resources and connections to advocate and agitate for a stronger social safety net? For me, and for many of us, there are inherent tensions between what fulfills us and what we think we're supposed to be doing. Can we resolve them?

Sometimes, these tensions lurk even closer to home. The steps we take to build more fulfilling lives, and the routines and habits we construct along the way, impact the people around us. Those impacts are generally positive, but not exclusively. A commendable intention to spend time in more fulfilling ways, for instance, can easily turn into an obsession. It's easy for me to become overly focused on checking all the boxes that are important to me (meditation, writing, reading, and so on) every day. That takes a toll on others, too—not just in the time I spend on these goals and routines, but in my resulting irritation if they get interrupted. Perfection is an impossible standard, especially on the scale of a lifetime, but any successful self-improvement undertaking can make it tempting to pursue. Aspiring to "do it all" can easily tip us too far in the direction of self-obsession and away from the ultimate goal of self-awareness. In some instances, in fact, it's clearly selfish to focus on making more time for what matters to you. It these instances, it may indeed be hurtful, morally wrong, or emotionally damaging to pursue the recommendations in this book at the cost of other commitments.

The point of reframing how you see your day is to find tweaks that make each day a bit more fulfilling. The point is *not* to eliminate the trade-offs inherent to life or to enable you to focus entirely on yourself at the expense of other human beings. You have to approach this effort with an open mind, recognizing that perfection is impossible and forgiving yourself when you go too far or don't go far enough. You have to accept that you will come up short. Your routines will be interrupted. You will not be able to do it all. At the same time, though, it's impossible to operate at your best if you don't carve out *any* time for the people and activities that matter most to you. It's impossible to maintain the strength for the sacrifices and struggles required for our *collective* future if you don't take some time to build a fulfilling foundation for your *individual* future.

Getting the balance right is tricky. If you're running a large NGO that's improving the lives of millions around the world, but you're neglecting to spend time with your own children, are you getting the balance right? If you work for a large oil and gas company that's pumping carbon dioxide into the atmosphere and spreading disinformation about climate change, but you spend your weekends volunteering to clean up the park across the street from your house, are you getting the balance right? If you're so busy and overwhelmed organizing people to fight voter suppression that you don't take any time for yourself and snap at your loved ones and demean your employees, are you getting the balance right? If you decide to write a book about building more fulfilling days because you genuinely think it can help people reflect on their own lives, but you do so at the cost of thousands of hours that could've gone to making phone calls during the 2018 midterm elections, getting involved with a local mentoring program, or just spending more time with your partner, are you getting the balance right?

These aren't rhetorical questions. I don't know the answers, nor am I sure there are any. I don't have any way of resolving the tensions between what we want to do and what we have to do, between what fulfills us and what's expected of us, between our obligations to ourselves and our obligations to those around us. In many ways, navigating these tensions is the whole point of life. Whatever the case may be, feeling these tensions is a good thing. We *need* to feel them, especially if we're on this journey of building more fulfilling days, because these tensions serve to guide us. If we veer toward one extreme, they keep us from tipping too far in the direction of self-indulgence and self-obsession. If we veer toward the other extreme, feeling them can remind us to spend a little more time taking care of ourselves.

Resolving these tensions is impossible. Life is, and should be, a constant calibration and recalibration. The sooner you accept that, and the more often you remind yourself of it, the closer you'll come to finding a balance that works for you, and those around you, each and every day.[152]

7

Have a trajectory (not a plan)

"The secret to life is to put yourself in the right lighting. For some it's a Broadway spotlight; for others, a lamplit desk. Use your natural powers—of persistence, concentration, insight, and sensitivity—to do work you love and work that matters. Solve problems, make art, think deeply."

Susan Cain[153]

Illusions

Is a long-term plan a necessary anchor, or a comforting illusion?

It's July 2013, and things are pretty great. Barack Obama has been comfortably reelected and is into his second term, and I'm convinced that America's political trajectory will continue moving inevitably in the direction of progress. I'm healthy, and, for the most part, so are the people I love. My brother Chris and I (and Veto, our perpetually hungry and passive-aggressive cat) have a great apartment in Washington, DC's Mount Vernon neighborhood. I have an awesome group of friends, smart and fun coworkers, and proximity to my grandparents and lots of my extended family, who I now get to see on a regular basis. Erin and I are slowly building a relationship based on coffee dates in the Senate cafeteria and many, many, many text messages (which she will eventually print and compile into two memorable volumes under the meaningful-only-to-us title, "I LIKE CEREAL"). Our relationship is increasingly shaking the foundations of my work-at-all-costs mentality, though not, as it will turn out, fast enough.

On a professional level, things are a bit weird and in flux. Until this point in my 26-year existence, I haven't really had long-term career plans or goals. But this summer, for whatever reason, I've decided to change that. I've chosen a disruptive career plan, determined that it shall be *the plan*, and begun to pursue it at the expense of all other professional possibilities. After four years in politics in DC, I've decided that I will—no, I *must*—move home to Colorado to run for the state House of Representatives in the 2016 election cycle. I haven't yet mapped out the details, but I have a goal I'm excited about and just enough of a plan to make it feel plausible, but without enough of a plan to realize how difficult it will be. I even have a Dropbox folder called "Master Plan." Since I have many good reasons *not* to move back to Colorado right now, I ease my own decision-making process by not really considering any of them. I manage to convince myself that I *have* to move home. I *have* to run in the 2016 election cycle. I *have* to do so in a certain district. I *have* to get back to Colorado as quickly as possible— or else I'll miss "it."

What is "it?" As best I can tell with a few years of hindsight, back then "it" was a combination of things: Staking a public claim to my identity as a Coloradan involved in Democratic politics. Staking a private claim to the same. Measuring my own self-worth in professional political accomplishments (especially the ones that haven't happened yet). Luxuriating in the feelings of motivation, emotional security, and self-assuredness that come from having a fixed plan. Dreaming of political stature until success feels inevitable as long as I work hard and don't let a little doubt get in the way.

Do I stop to think that maybe it's a little odd (and perhaps a little irresponsible) to have never worked in state politics before, but to leave behind a job, friends, family, and a budding relationship to do so? Do I pause to consider that I've only been in Washington for a few years, and that I never planned on moving to DC to work on Capitol Hill before

I moved to DC to work on Capitol Hill, so perhaps I really have no way of knowing whether this new plan is *the plan*? Do I recognize my own history of setting my mind to various life trajectories at the exclusion of all else, and then changing course when I realize they aren't my thing? Do I see how lucky I am that my trial-and-error approach to life has already gotten me to such a good place? Sure, I sense these lingering questions somewhere in the back of my mind. I sense them just enough to cast them aside. I'm all in.

Growing up in Colorado, I loved my state but didn't see it as part of who I was. After all, most of the people I grew up with shared this same trait. There wasn't anything unique or defining about voting in Colorado or having a Colorado driver's license or rooting for the Denver Broncos. No one needed a Colorado "NATIVE" bumper sticker on their car because many of us were born there. Wearing the iconic Colorado "C" from the state flag hadn't yet become cool because the secret of Colorado wasn't out. "When you are part of a place, growing that moment in its soil, there's never a need to say you're from there," Tara Westover reflects in her memoir about growing up in Idaho. "I never uttered the words 'I'm from Idaho' until I'd left it."[154] Similarly, I didn't make "Colorado" a conscious part of my identity until 2005 when I moved to Maine for college. Then, for any number of reasons that probably included loneliness, homesickness, a desire to define myself differently from those around me (i.e., ego), and the general search for identity that any 18-year-old undertakes, I made *my* state supreme and inseparable from the way I saw myself.

That self-identification as a Coloradan continued into my post-college years as I haphazardly drifted into politics in 2009 through, in true millennial style, a series of internships. I held onto this identity as I moved to Washington. Taking great pride in being one of the leaders of the Colorado State Society in DC, I continued refining my self-imposed identity until 2013, when I spontaneously determined that "Democratic politician from Colorado running in the 2016 election cycle" was the only path that would bring me satisfaction. All other possibilities would have to be sacrificed to achieve it.

In truth, I did sacrifice to achieve it. I worked hard to learn the state election process and build the right connections, setting up dozens, perhaps hundreds, of networking coffees in Colorado and DC with this goal in mind. I spent hours mapping out plans, learning about election law, reading about Colorado politics, and thinking about the exciting possibilities of where this would lead. Doing all of this with conviction felt good. It gave me a driving force and a righteous sense of identity. It calmed the terrifying uncertainty of what to do with my life, filling that void with a plan—*the plan!*—that my future would follow.

During this time, although I knew that the security of my self-imposed identity was comforting and inspiring, I failed to see that it was also completely haphazard. I never chose to be born in Colorado. I barely chose to enter politics, having mostly fallen into it through internships and an absence of other (paid) opportunities. I had no idea whether I truly wanted to make a career in politics since I hadn't taken the time to consider any other careers. I'd never really even worked in state politics before deciding to make it my life. Somehow, my great fortune in having these opportunities became my sole purpose and guiding force. Although I didn't use the word "fate," that's more or less how I saw it: All of this randomness and happenstance had set me on this path and, therefore, I must follow it at the expense of all else.

The Plan
The security of the certain plan isn't free

We started this chapter in July 2013. Fast forward four months to November of that year, when I begin to execute *the plan* that has given me such a sense of conviction and identity. I pack up my life in DC, leaving behind a productive career on Capitol Hill and a great group of friends and family, including a relationship with the person I love (and with whom I've recently exchanged the L-word for the first time). In December, shortly after returning to my home state, I start a job in the state Senate. I'm back in Colorado, working at the nexus of state politics, living in a nice apartment in the state House district where I hope to run for office in a couple years' time. I'm just a five-minute drive from my parents, who I now get to see all the time instead of just a few weekends a year. *The plan* is intact and in motion. I'm living the identity I've fixated on so intensely.

But the questions and doubts that I've previously banished to the depths of my mind, along the lines of what Yongey Mingyur Rinpoche describes as a "gnawing low-level disturbance [that] leaves us doubting our own authenticity," aren't as easy to bury now.[155] Why is every networking coffee an exhausting exercise in forcing myself into conversation with feigned conviction? Why am I flying to DC nearly every weekend to see Erin, often cutting work short on Fridays and Mondays to do so, instead of hustling every waking moment to realize my political dreams? Why does every day at work—in the heart of state politics, right where I'd planned to be!—feel like an attempt to mask a growing sense of disingenuousness and unhappiness? Where are the joy and satisfaction that I've assured myself I'll experience once I'm finally living my true identity? Where is the fulfillment I'm supposed to feel now that I'm following *the plan*?

Does Colorado politics not have what I want? Not quite. In reality, I don't know what I want. I may not really know myself at all. I've been trying to maintain an image of myself that I don't actually want to live. I've been wallowing in the comfort and security of having a plan, and relying more on *the plan* to be right the more time, money, and energy I've invested in it. The further I go down that path, the less sure I am about it but the more difficult it is to ignore the doubts and the more terrifying it is to turn back ("sunk cost" 101). I've been so blindly wedded to a single future that I've missed the present right in front of me.

Skip ahead a few more months to February 2014. During an early morning run along the Cherry Creek River in Denver, I make the decision: I will move *back* to DC. Even though I've tried to convince myself that the move to Colorado is "it" and that there's no going back, there will now be a going back. Thus begins *another* journey of networking, job-hunting, and soul searching that will ultimately deposit me back in Washington in November 2014, just short of a year since Erin and I packed up my Volvo and drove me across the country in the opposite direction. This time, I'll have no doubts as to where I want to be (answer: wherever Erin is). But I'll also be physically and emotionally exhausted, financially depleted, and longing for the emotional security of a prescribed plan and a professional identity. "Democratic politician from Colorado" will still sound a lot cooler and a lot more accomplished than "late twentysomething trying to figure out his life," which is what I'll feel I've become.

In reality, of course, that's what I'd been all along. Instead of confronting or accepting the fact that I was one of countless human beings in the middle of some sort of identity crisis, I buried all the uncertainty and stress I felt under a self-imposed mantra of "Democratic politician from Colorado running in the 2016 election cycle." My arbitrary decision to pursue *the plan* gave me plenty of short-term emotional security, but it came at a steep price. That price wasn't just the shock of *the plan* not being a very good plan for me. The price also included the professional and personal costs I incurred along the way.

   With my decision to move back to DC the following year, the bills for all those costs finally came due. From a career perspective, trying to network my way back onto Capitol Hill after moving away with the intention of never returning meant I went, in under a year, from comfortable and self-assured Hill staffer to job-seeker begging for a foot back in the door. It was a jarring hit to the ego that left me feeling pretty sorry for myself. The personal costs were far higher, though. My single-minded determination to pursue my Colorado political dream at the expense of everything else jeopardized my relationship with Erin, which I'd just begun to realize was already giving me a greater sense of fulfillment than anything else in my life. The move had a deep, usually painful, impact on Erin, my brother, my parents, and my extended family and friends. To tally the emotional toll of my brief foray into state politics without including its impact on others would be to overlook perhaps the greatest cost of all.

Ripping away my manufactured identity left me feeling aimless and exposed. Finally admitting that it was a self-insulating façade was painful and scary. And confronting the fragility, shallowness, and uncertainty of it all was unsettling and destabilizing to everything I knew about myself. At the same time, though, it was—and remains—difficult for me to regret it entirely because I learned an enormous amount. (This is the paradox of FOMO, which we'll discuss in the next chapter.) I've come to realize that my true identity, the person I am when I'm living a fulfilled life, isn't an aspiring Democratic politician from Colorado. Yet it took trying and failing to be that person for me to realize this. It took moving away from Erin to understand that I wanted to do whatever it took to be back in the same time zone, and eventually the same city, as her. It took having the secure shell of a self-imposed identity stripped away for me to confront the thrilling, terrifying reality of trying to understand my authentic self in a confusing world.

Identity
Build an identity from the inside out

The fortresses of identity that we build for ourselves are great. They give us a sense of security and a feeling of importance. They make us feel part of something bigger than ourselves. They inspire us with a sense of meaning that helps mask lingering doubts and insecurities. A secure identity can give human beings the strength and conviction to accomplish extraordinary things. But unless these identities are grounded in what makes us who we actually are—in our beliefs, in what fulfills us, in what we love to do, in what we genuinely care about—they're simply fantasies. Yongey Mingyur Rinpoche describes them as "illusory hats that I am wearing on this illusory head, and that live inside this mind that is falsified by confusion and muddled by misperception, hats that have never existed, all of them fake identities, created by a fake-identity mind, sustained by a fabricated constructed self, affirmed by warped perceptions, held in place by habit."[156] They're fleeting and ephemeral images of how we'd like to see ourselves. And they're addictive, because dreaming and talking about all the great things we (or our group) are going to do is far easier than doing them. Yet sometimes even doing them, or striving to do them, masks a greater challenge: building a sense of self that stands on its own, independent of our professional achievements, group memberships, bank accounts, or social status.

I realize all of this now, but back in DC in the winter of 2014, having these life lessons thrust upon me was cold comfort, and a very thin silver lining to an exhausting year. Even though I knew returning to DC was the right move, it still hurt my ego. Even though I was happier back in Washington with Erin, I still felt like a failure for giving up on my Colorado plan (and, confusingly, a little bit guilty for being so much happier once I had). I had made this plan my identity. I'd defined it as my *only* option for professional and personal success. Anything else would be failure. And here I was, a year later, genuinely happier and more fulfilled, but also more unsure than ever about what to do next or how to build a sustainable sense of self. If not "Colorado politician," then who was I? My inability to accomplish an arbitrary goal, such as running for a particular office in a particular election cycle, felt like failure. My experiencing self considered these setbacks to be monumental inefficiencies and costly mistakes that stemmed from personal weaknesses. I had failed. But today my remembering self recognizes these "failures" as humbling and instructive lessons. The true failure, as I came to understand, wasn't returning to DC or altering my life goals. The true failure lay in selecting an arbitrary path, sticking to it blindly, building a self-righteous identity and sense of superiority around it, and ignoring all doubts as I propelled myself forward.

David Brooks writes that "the beauty and meaning of life are in the stumbling—in recognizing the stumbling and trying to become more graceful as the years go by." Ultimately, he observes, "the stumbler is made whole by this struggle."[157] Moving to Colorado and back caused a lot of pain, brought unanticipated insecurities to the surface, and revealed a lot of uncertainties that had been buried under the false comfort of identities and plans. I'm still a stumbler, and I haven't yet been made whole, but I've become a lot more whole than I was. I've found my footing. I've become more aware. I've undertaken the path of deeper self-exploration that has led to this book. And somehow, I've managed to sustain the sense of contentment underlying it all.

That doesn't mean the stumbling and struggling are easy. What's easy, my Colorado foray taught me, is wrapping yourself in an external identity and clinging to it at almost any cost. An identity defined by things out of your control—employer, job title, occupation, professional accomplishment, long-term goal, sports team, religion, political party, race, ethnicity, home—is easy to adopt. It's comforting. And while it's not necessarily bad, it can be addictive. In whatever way you choose to define and characterize your tribe, wrapping yourself in its garments gives you a sense of belonging that can easily morph into relative superiority. The security of an "us" blanket is a feeling that seems to be wired into us, enabling great human progress but also dividing us and pitting us against each other throughout history. A yearning for this sense of security and inherent superiority is at the root of America's, and much of the rest of the world's, poisonous politics today.

My own experience was less apocalyptic and consequential than our current era of resentment and grievance. But in some ways, the core issue was the same: It's hard to build a secure and sustainable sense of identity from the inside out. It's a lot easier to work from the outside in. Moving back to DC was a double cold shower of casting aside my obsessive self-image as a Coloradan and giving up the illusory security of an arbitrary career path. Discarding these crutches was wrenching and terrifying. Ultimately, however, it's proven liberating, and far more fulfilling. Plus, I still get to be a Coloradan. I just recognize there's a lot more to me, too.

Many Paths

There's always another election cycle

In politics, there's always another election. There's always another campaign. There's always another chance to give it a go.* This is just as true in life: There's always another open door somewhere. That's not to say that the next election cycle, campaign, or open door isn't important. It's not to say that you should wait around forever for an opportunity to present itself at some comfortably abstract point in the future. It's not to say that working towards goals doesn't matter (it does) or that career goals are meaningless (they aren't). It's simply to say that perhaps you shouldn't careen down a single path with blinders on, particularly when the pursuit of a self-imposed identity or the fear of missing out might be what's leading you down that path.

To pursue a single plan relentlessly at the expense of all other opportunities is to sacrifice one of life's most powerful forces, which is the fortune of being in the right place at the right time. It's to give up the chance to take advantage of an unexpected opportunity. It's to eliminate the possibility of being wrong about the plan or identity you've created for yourself, potentially leaving you with a lifetime of chasing something you don't really want. It's to assume that at the moment you select that plan, your perspective, worldview, and sense of self-awareness are already honed to perfection. It's to leave no room for error, randomness, or self-discovery. The author Ann Patchett advises, "Never be so focused on what you're looking for that you overlook the thing you actually find."[158] To pursue *the plan* with blind obliviousness is to ensure you'll do just that.

Whether starting an organization, planning a nonexistent political campaign, or even just going from zero to 100 mph on a new habit without thinking it through, I have a lengthy track record of diving impulsively into new ideas. In my eagerness, enthusiasm, and runaway imagination

---

* These statements, even while metaphorical, require a few caveats. Democracy shouldn't be taken for granted. Not every election is free or fair, let alone free and fair. Protecting democratic norms and institutions is critical and urgent. These are important topics, but topics for another book.

for what my mind suddenly decides is possible (or my destiny), I forget that there are an infinite number of ways for a person to find fulfillment in the world. What five minutes ago wasn't a thought in my mind has somehow become inseparable from my identity and a prerequisite for my future happiness. But this mentality of "I won't be happy until I accomplish X" is a recipe for infinite striving and suffering, especially when "X" is nothing more than a vague idea. Instead of obsessively chasing these arbitrary goals, what if I just chose to look more closely at the life already in front of me?

It's an enormous privilege to have the luxury of choice. It's an equally grand privilege to be able to afford, financially, professionally, or otherwise, to take a wrong turn, or several wrong turns, before settling on a path forward. It's fair to say that billions of people around the world do not enjoy these luxuries. But the idea that "there's always another election cycle" is not intended as soothing reassurance for well-off-but-indecisive millennials. It's not an argument for floating aimlessly for years while you try to figure out what your heart is whispering to you. It's not an argument for running from commitment or sacrifice, or for giving up on what's truly important to you. Nor is it an argument for trying a thousand different options in search of the *one true passion* that will bring you peace and purpose.

It's simply an argument for humility in the face of *any* sense of blind conviction. It's an argument for giving yourself the freedom to consider whether the lingering questions at the back of your mind are poisonous self-doubt or genuine issues that merit more attention. It's an argument for allowing yourself to be open-minded about the future, for balancing determination and drive with a willingness to be wrong or change course. It's an argument for pursuing passion projects with intensity and ambition, but without blinders. These arguments transcend where you came from, how old you are, or what resources you have or lack. Don't keep every option open. Don't say "no" to opportunities just in case something else comes along. That's a recipe for inaction and paralyzing indecision. You can be decisive, make plans, and have ambitious goals, *and* you can do so with an open mind. You can welcome the possibility that the path you've selected might be wrong. And you can also welcome the possibility that the path you're already on, which might seem unsatisfying or futile in the moment, could turn out to have everything you need.

"So long as you believe that you are the captain of your own life, you will be drifting farther and farther from the truth," David Brooks suggests.[159] Charting a path that balances action with openness, driving forward while continually scanning the periphery, isn't paralyzing. It's liberating. It marries the drive of goals you believe in with the powerful element of opportunity that characterizes life. It frees you to focus on the things you can control: the skills you can develop, the ways you spend your time, the activities and people you give your attention to, without obsessing over what is out of your control. Is this a naïve and overly simplistic way to see the world? I'd argue it's far more practical and far more realistic than the find-your-one-and-only-true-path approach that many of us are taught and that society urges us to adopt. As the late *New York Times* columnist David Carr once put it, "Just do a good job on what's in front of you. Working on your grand plan is like shoveling snow that hasn't fallen yet. Just do the next right thing."[160] *Just do the next right thing.*

Trajectories
A plan restrains. A trajectory liberates

W hy reframe your path forward as a trajectory rather than a plan? A career plan says you must (and assumes you will) find and land the perfect job that matches the next step of the plan. (The perfect job rarely exists, by the way, but the idea that it's out there is a comforting self-imposed limitation.) A trajectory, on the other hand, tells you to find *a* job that allows you to learn, grow, and develop new skills, and use that job to move broadly in the direction you want to go (which comes with the added benefit of gaining work experience and being able to pay the bills).

Meanwhile, a single life plan (*the plan!*) can be all-consuming, setting you up for potential success but leaving you perilously exposed if you're wrong or if something else goes wrong, often something entirely out of your control. A trajectory keeps you moving in the right direction, but also forces you to build a sustainable foundation of values, principles, and practices that you can control under any circumstances. This foundation helps to anchor you in times of turbulence and in times of exuberance.

Having a plan sets you on a single path for getting where you want to go, often without asking whether it's a healthy and fulfilling path, or even whether the ultimate destination would be a rewarding one. A trajectory, on the other hand, driven by goals and deadlines, keeps you moving forward while helping you spot different paths, or entirely different end goals, along the way. A trajectory allows you to recognize, with humility, that you might be wrong, that you might not know yourself as well as you thought, or that you might change.

In a sneaky way, a detailed plan can actually *prevent* you from acting because it gives you the illusion of action and forward progress. Of course, a certain degree of planning is necessary, and in countless situations it would be irresponsible not to plan ahead. But too much planning can be paralyzing because it masks inaction. You can always come up with more pre-plan plans that feel like action but don't accomplish anything, such as scheduling endless conference calls to talk about the possibility of taking action at some nebulous point in the future. A trajectory recognizes that while planning is a tool for taking action, it's not action itself.

A plan for the future frees you from the burdensome responsibility of having to confront circumstances right in front of you. Why act now when you could just wait for the ideal conditions or perfect opportunity to present itself later? A trajectory, on the other hand, encourages you to dream, but it also demands that you take action and make decisions in the world as it is, not the world as you wish it. A plan trains you to think that happiness will follow only from successful execution of *the plan*. A trajectory, on the other hand, recognizes that the whole thing is a journey, that happiness and fulfillment aren't the result of a linear process of career planning but are actually available to you right now, in this moment. A trajectory allows you to hone a craft over a lifetime without being defined by it or locked into it forever. A trajectory forces you (sometimes rather unpleasantly) to find joy not in life's outcomes but in the process itself, through the real, sustainable purpose that comes from learning, growing, challenging, and forgiving yourself. A trajectory gives you drive and direction, but it also gives you space to fall in love with a career, a side hustle, or a person you never imagined or expected. A trajectory helps you to recognize that you can find fulfillment anywhere, in anything you do, so long as you put it in the right frame.

8

Surrender control (and fight FOMO)

"Our brokenness is also the source of our common humanity, the basis for our shared search for comfort, meaning, and healing. Our shared vulnerability and imperfection nurtures and sustains our capacity for compassion."

Bryan Stevenson[161]

FOMO

We are owned by FOMO

That summer of 2013, when I decided to move home to Colorado, I did so not only because I wanted to make a difference in the state legislature, although that desire was genuine. I also moved, and moved when I did, because I was terrified of missing out if I didn't. One might wonder (as many of my friends did at the time), "Missing out on what, exactly?" Two years before I uprooted my life for this move, I probably couldn't have named more than a few Colorado state representatives or local policy issues. I couldn't have cared less what was happening in the state House. And I had no idea that, two years later, I would feel compelled to try to become a part of it.

Yet here I was, embarking, with absolute conviction, on an audacious and unlikely, not to mention vague and undefined, plan. I had very suddenly decided that I had to move back home and run for a specific state House seat—not in the future, but *now*. And if I didn't...I'd miss out on something. If people didn't soon know me as a rising figure in state politics, I'd miss out. If I didn't have the chance to be an elected official during the Obama era, I'd miss out. If I wasn't quickly recognized as a political force in Colorado, I'd miss out. If I didn't achieve success and renown as a state representative, which would set me on a long and fruitful path toward a high-profile and accomplished political career, I'd miss out. What, *exactly*, would I be missing out on? That was a scarier question—a question much harder to answer and, therefore, much easier to avoid. Instead, I used up all my spare brain space dreaming of how I would give inspiring speeches and change the world through American politics.

When you think so much about an idea or a decision, actions and outcomes can start to feel inevitable. At some point my endless internal strategizing and forecasting tipped me from "eventually moving home to Colorado" to "have to move home now, or *else*." Once crossed, a mental threshold like that can be difficult to uncross. Sometimes it begins to feel as though it's destined to happen, or even that it already has. Like so many mortals unsure about their place in the world, I'd been bested by that powerful illusion that grabs hold of our hopes for the future and the self-image we paint for ourselves, and warps it into a full-blown fantasy that only the most self-confident and self-aware among us are able to resist. I was fully under the illogical spell of FOMO: the fear of missing out.

I don't recall the first time I heard the term "FOMO," but it was revelatory. One simple acronym captured a feeling I'd experienced to some degree my entire conscious life, a feeling that was always lurking in the background of my computer-brain like a piece of malware, guiding my decisions and often keeping me from doing the things that most fulfilled me by dragging me into things that didn't. Like many people, I can point to countless occasions when I made decisions based on FOMO, ranging from the trivial to the seriously consequential. I've taken meetings I wasn't interested in and had no reason to take just so I didn't miss out on making a new contact or having something to fill a half-hour slot on my calendar (or just because I was uncomfortable about saying "no").

I've kept social media accounts open and active just in case someone, sometime, might be looking for me. I've signed up for email newsletters for fear of missing some crucial piece of information or commentary, forgetting that five minutes before signing up I hadn't even known of its existence. I've gone to parties I didn't want to go to, taken trips I didn't want to take, read books and listened to podcasts I didn't want to read or listen to, added items to my to-do list I didn't want or even need to do, attended events I didn't want or need to attend, and said "yes" to all sorts of requests that I didn't want or need to say "yes" to. I've even moved forward with career- and life-altering decisions I didn't really believe in and knew in my heart and mind weren't the right thing for me to do.

Does FOMO have some biological or evolutionary purpose? An urge to blend in with the tribe for survival, maybe? A pre-programmed wariness of being left behind? Perhaps this is just the first time in human history that all the key ingredients for FOMO have come together, as large swathes of the population have the leisure time, technological capability, cultural obsession with striving and accomplishment, and the social expectation of constant connectivity. Whatever the reason, the purpose of FOMO is a mystery to me because, in most instances, it inspires decisions that add little value to our lives and often come at a significant cost. Almost without exception, FOMO demands time and attention that could be put toward doing what *actually* fulfills us or helps us accomplish real goals, rather than checking an arbitrary—and often imaginary—box for the sake of checking the box.

Part of what makes FOMO so insidious and powerful is that we always seem to learn when we missed out on something, yet we almost never hear (or remember) when we didn't miss out. In this very specific regard—lest I be accused of falsely equating FOMO with human tragedy, which I am *not* doing—missing out on something is like a plane crash or a terrorist attack: We only notice it when it happens. We never notice the countless times each day when it *doesn't* happen. We quickly grow accustomed to borderline irrational sacrifices made because of those one-in-a-million happenings. And it's all made more complicated by the fact that some of these "just in case" preparations are actually a good idea.

Let's take this unfortunate analogy even further. Making decisions based on FOMO is like living one's life in fear of a plane crash or a terrorist attack while also continuing to smoke cigarettes or not wear a seatbelt while driving. It's an irrational fear of something highly unlikely that obscures real risk or harm happening right now, right in front of you. And like plane crashes and terrorist attacks, FOMO is made that much worse and that much more illogical by social media. (End of depressing analogy.)* The costs of FOMO are hard to measure. We rarely recognize what we've given up to make FOMO-based decisions, particularly if what we've sacrificed is something as intangible as an hour working on a passion project or recharging with a book. Often, it's only in hindsight that we truly appreciate these costs, if we do at all.

Paradox

When does the FOMO justify the FOMO?

B reaking the grip of FOMO is made even more complicated by the fact that it isn't entirely harmful. It would be far easier to avoid if it were. Yet, like a substance or behavior that can be damaging in excess but, if indulged in responsibly, might also help unlock new opportunities or open your eyes to new perspectives, FOMO isn't all bad. It owes its power, in part, to the fact that we *do* sometimes gain a lot by making decisions because we fear we'll miss out if we don't.

To this day, for example, I can't entirely regret leaving what was an altogether happy life in Washington to return to Colorado because it was a transformative experience. I gained a lot of insight into who I am and what I care about. I made significant strides toward identifying

---

* For the record, one study showed that if you boarded a commercial airplane once a day at random, it would be 26,000 years before you were likely (not even guaranteed) to be involved in a fatal crash. In the meantime, think of all the deep work you could do on those 9.5 million flights!

what I do and don't want to do professionally. I learned, occasionally in a wrenching and hurtful way, that I needed to do whatever it took to be in the same place as Erin, and that my conviction that life should consist solely of career ambitions was profoundly misguided. I got to spend a year living near my parents for the first time in close to a decade.

I moved home to Colorado not because doing so would bring me fulfillment but because I was afraid I would miss out if I didn't. But if I hadn't taken that painful plunge, I might have always wondered what would have happened if I had, and I wouldn't have gained some of the insights that have led directly to this book. I almost surely wouldn't be in the contented place I am now, with a clearer understanding of how I can build a more fulfilling life. It's a classic case of "What if...?"— which, of course, is the quintessential justification for FOMO. Those "What if?" questions aren't entirely misguided, but they can quickly become debilitating if you let them consume every decision you make.

Therein lies the FOMO paradox. Life is too short *not* to try some things just because we don't want to spend the rest of our lives wondering what might have happened. In other words, life's too short not to give FOMO a seat at the decision-making table from time to time. But life is also too short to let FOMO have the deciding vote every time. How do we make any sense of that? How are we supposed to know when the FOMO justifies the FOMO? Even when we recognize that FOMO is us pulling toward a false opportunity—a false projection of greener grass on the other side—we still feel it. Even when we sense the allure of FOMO and know without a doubt that we shouldn't succumb to it because it's neither rational nor helpful, we feel it.

Before trying to make sense of FOMO, it's worth acknowledging how widespread and pervasive it is, and how many different ways it shows up in our lives. There are different versions of FOMO. One, as the writer and professor Scott Galloway described in 2018, is FOBLO, fear of being left out, which Galloway calls "the more hurtful version of FOMO."[162] My brother compiled a list of other derivations, some more succinct than others, which include FOR (fear of regret), FONDWYTYSBD (fear of not doing what you think you should be doing), FOFOMO (fear of FOMO), and FOHMO (fear of having missed out). Of those FOMO-adjacent experiences, FOHMO is perhaps the craftiest because it pressures you to look at what you *didn't* do in the past from the perspective of who you are today.** Measuring your past decisions against your present self doesn't really make sense, but FOHMO makes you do it anyway. I'm sure there are more types of FOMO, all united by a common fear of missing out on *something*. That something is usually intangible and potentially nonexistent, though it's also entirely real in how it manifests in the feeling of fear.

Just how insidious is it? Let's return to my go-to storytelling device of working in politics. As I write these words, it's been more than two years since I left politics and moved to the UK, so I'm far away from the universe in which I spent the first eight years of my professional career. I have a greater sense of fulfillment and stillness than at any point in my life. I've found that many of the things I miss about working on Capitol Hill—the people, the camaraderie, the sense of built-in purpose, the possibility of making a difference—exist elsewhere, too. I've found a great deal of satisfaction writing and publishing my own opinions under my own name. Most importantly, I've found nothing to disprove my conviction that I'll do whatever it takes to be in the same city as Erin.

All of these things are true. I *know* I'm happy and fulfilled here. I *know* I was exhausted and burned out in national politics. I *know* I needed to break free of it for a while. I *know* I wouldn't be happier or more fulfilled there right now. Yet I can still find myself overcome with intense FOMO for political life in Washington. I still wonder what I'm

---

** A decision *not* to do something may have been the "best" or the "right" call at the time you made it. You couldn't have known at the time that Future You would worry that you missed out for not having done it. All you can do is trust that you made the best decision at the time. Yes, you can learn from FOHMO—the "Hmm, today I would probably have said 'yes' to that" instinct isn't a bad one—but you're not really being fair to yourself and your (in)ability to predict the future if you keep beating yourself up for maybe having missed out in the past.

missing for not being there. I still want to be able to say I was there, in the room where it happens. But I don't actually *want* to be there.

Here's a minor, but telling, example. I couldn't care less about watching Donald Trump's State of the Union addresses, a few of which have passed since I began writing this book. I know that my life is calmer and more focused for not watching or experiencing them. If I want to learn what happened, perhaps to write about it later or just to be an informed citizen, I can read about it. There are *zero* reasons I need to see it live. Yet no matter who's in the Oval Office when State of the Union time rolls around each year, a small part of me inevitably feels like I'm missing out—not just by living abroad or not working in politics, but for not being physically present in the U.S. Capitol during the speech. That doesn't make any sense! I know clearly and objectively that I don't want to be there (or anywhere near Donald Trump, for that matter), just as I don't *actually* want to be running for state House in Colorado or even working in politics. But the pull of FOMO is still there, waiting to strike in the weirdest and most unexpected ways. It's real. It's powerful. It's completely illogical. And it's always lurking.

Craving
FOMO isn't a fear. It's a craving

If there's a solution to FOMO, is it, to return to Daniel's Kahneman's concept of the two selves, to ignore the remembering self and try to live only in the moment? Is it to ignore the experiencing self and accept you will spend your life begrudgingly doing things you don't enjoy because it's more important to have done them? Or is the solution to feel the pull of FOMO and think, "Not today, but someday..." so you either do it someday (and perhaps realize it was just FOMO), or you don't do it and spend your life wondering, "What if?" Can the FOMO paradox be resolved?

The only thing even resembling a resolution, I think, is pretty unsatisfying: It's to recognize FOMO and sit with it. It's to be aware of all of FOMO's complexities and contradictions. It's to accept that there isn't a single life mapped out for you if only you open the right door. It's to trust that your life could go in an infinite number of directions, and that while most of what leads to door A instead of door B is beyond your control, you can probably find meaning and fulfillment through either one. It's to recognize that all you can control is a determination to do your best to navigate through life while forgiving yourself and others if and when you fall short. It's to accept that you cannot possibly do everything.

In politics, it took living and working through four elections to realize there's always another election cycle. It took moving abroad to make me realize that no country or culture has a monopoly on fun, hardworking people doing important and inspiring things. It took leaving politics to realize that Capitol Hill, a work environment I loved, where I worked with some of the most impressive people I've ever met, was not the only place I could find professional fulfillment. It took falling in love to make me realize that when you find the right person or activity, you're not missing out on anything because everything you need is right there, *in that moment.*

FOMO is a craving. It's a temptation. It's a reflection of our discomfort with the uncertainty of the future and our desire to be able to "do it all." It's an irrational human instinct exacerbated by social media, fed by constant connectivity, and perpetuated by a general sense, especially in status-conscious environments like politics, that we're getting left behind. To succeed in fighting FOMO is to accept that you *will* inevitably miss out on some things in life, even some things that really matter, and that's ok. And it's to accept that sometimes you *will* have to do things that you don't want to do, for whatever reason.

You can't resolve FOMO. Or fix it. Or make it go away. But you can reframe how you interpret it. You can learn to recognize it, explore it, accept it, and wait for it to pass. You can even begin to appreciate what *The Economist*'s Bartleby columnist calls JOMO, the *joy* of missing out.[163] Fear of missing out is no way to make a decision, let alone live a life. Like any craving, FOMO will always be there. All you can do is try to be aware of it and do your best to choose how you respond to it.

Vulnerability

Let people into your life

W hen I chose to override FOMO in 2014, Ctrl-Z-ing my move to Colorado and returning to DC, I wasn't only altering my professional trajectory, as I'd done many times before (like a good millennial). I was also acknowledging something more fundamental: My priorities had changed. I couldn't eliminate the fear of missing out on whatever it was that had compelled me to strive to become a Colorado politician. I couldn't make that feeling disappear. But in this instance, the more I refused to follow FOMO to its illogical conclusions, the more I found myself capable of resisting it and seeing beyond it. The more I made a conscious decision *not* to succumb to FOMO, the easier it became to recognize it and let it go, and the more I began to see and appreciate the life happening in front of me.

Contrary to what a younger Adam would have assumed, discarding my FOMO-induced compulsions did not leave me with an internal vacuum devoid of inspiration or motivation. Sure, I felt (and still feel) a twinge of emptiness here or a touch of sadness there—the inevitable byproduct of giving up a deeply-held identity—but I increasingly found that FOMO was replaced by something more significant and powerful. Something more meaningful and real. What took the place of FOMO was, quite simply, an openness to the human emotions I was experiencing. To feelings and vulnerability. To life unfolding in front of me.

In hindsight, it's not surprising that this transformation coincided with building and deepening my relationship with Erin. Today, it's obvious to me that her arrival into my life provided the clarity I needed to begin to challenge FOMO, and to be less controlled by the underlying insecurities that precipitate it. It didn't make these fears or insecurities disappear, but it gave me the perspective I needed to see what mattered more. It helped me bring more important stuff to the surface.

Finding a teammate with whom to navigate this weird fleeting thing called life has been, without question, the single most transformative aspect of my adult existence. Welcoming another person into my life has reoriented my worldview, rearranged my priorities, and recalibrated my trajectory. Although she'll roll her eyes when she reads this, I'll say it anyway: Without Erin, I would not have stumbled across the foundational ideas of this book. I would not have reached such a point of steady fulfillment that I'd be compelled to share it with the world. I would not know how to let people into my life. And I might never have learned to embrace one of the most fundamental tenets of the human condition: Feelings are good.

I used to reject the entire premise of emotional vulnerability, sometimes pretty aggressively. I don't know why. Maybe it stems from being a shy kid growing up, or being an introvert in a world designed for extroverts. Maybe it's because I've always been pretty self-conscious (though not always self-aware) and worried about being a burden on those around me. Part of it might be that emotions are hard and complicated, and I found it easier to work on tangible things—skills, creative projects, hobbies, professional responsibilities—that depended only on my own effort and my own time. It didn't hurt that my fellow millennials and I were raised in a world in which success is determined by individual achievements that follow relentless professional striving. More broadly, though, I think I ran from emotions because I wanted to be in control of every aspect of my life. Depending on other people came with rejection, fear, anxiety, and uncertainty—variables I couldn't control—so depending on others was better left to those who had time and energy for that stuff.

Whatever the cause, for years I preached righteously that feelings, vulnerability, and deep personal relationships were the prerogatives of others. I, martyr to the cause of busyness and in full control of my life, was too busy hustling, or telling myself a story of self-sacrifice for work, or running from one FOMO-driven commitment to another. Emotional contentment was a worthwhile sacrifice for realizing professional ambitions. I even found righteously pointless ways to live my stubbornness, such as refusing to use emojis in messages because they expressed emotion. (Now I swear by them—especially Bitmojis).*** In each chapter of my life, I've been fortunate to have strong circles of friends, but if people really wanted to get close to me and get *me* to open up, they had to make the effort and push through my hesitation. And even if they succeeded, I would often retreat by stepping back or making clear that, while I liked spending time with them, I didn't *depend* on them.

The further I progressed through life trying not to acknowledge my feelings and those of others, the scarier (and the more of a "failure") it seemed to consider backtracking and opening a whole new door. I already had enough work in my professional striving and planning and productivity-seeking. Why pile on the additional work of building relationships? The more I tried to control everything about my life and the world around me, the more I saw emotional vulnerability as a risk I couldn't afford.

I suspect I didn't build as convincing a façade of invulnerability as I imagined, but I wanted it to be true nonetheless. I was deeply invested in persuading myself that I could make it through life keeping my heart at arm's length from my head. Superficially, I made these investments in self-deception because I wanted to believe that professional success—an arena I was comfortable in and (wrongly) felt I could control—would bring me personal fulfillment. But it was really because I was scared. Scared of the lack of control and the possibility of rejection that comes with emotional exposure. Scared of the immense task of throwing away the comfort blanket of "Democratic politician from Colorado," or whatever path I'd chosen for myself at a given time. Scared of undertaking the difficult work of building an identity on a more authentic foundation. I was desperate to prove I could extract happiness and fulfillment from

---

*** I can't believe I once scorned emojis. In the digital age, I don't think there's a better way to communicate subtle emotional nuances and prevent misunderstandings (and just make people smile) than using the right emoji. Or, better yet, the right Bitmoji. When it comes to communicating clearly, I'm convinced Bitmoji is the single most important app on my phone.

self-directed professional accomplishments. I was desperate to show I didn't need anyone else. I was desperate to convince myself that I could control every aspect of my existence.

My brother and I have always loved Jon Krakauer's *Into the Wild*, which tells the story of Chris McCandless, a young man who ventures alone into the Alaskan wilderness after college. In the book, Krakauer describes a note McCandless scrawls shortly before his death: "Happiness only real when shared," it reads.[164] *Happiness only real when shared.* That line stuck with me long before my emotional renaissance. Perhaps because, at some level, I knew it was a lesson I needed to take to heart.

When I moved to Colorado in late 2013, I again, entirely unsurprisingly, chose professional ambition and the relentless pursuit of a contrived identity over personal fulfillment. With Erin in DC and my political destiny in Colorado, I very nearly did choose state politics over love. For whatever reason, though, that year fortune both smiled on me and conspired to shake the foundations of my world in the most unsettling manner possible by showing me another way to live. For whatever reason, Erin not only entered my life but decided she liked spending time with me as much as I wanted to spend time with her. For whatever reason, Erin put up with my hesitations and fears of entering into a relationship that would require me to—gasp—sacrifice, compromise, and give up a bit of control. For whatever reason, Erin was patient as I worked up the nerve to make a commitment, and she was infinitely more patient after I announced, out of the blue, that I was moving to Colorado just a few months after we started dating. For whatever reason, Erin didn't give up on our still-nearly-brand-new relationship, even though we spent a year flying back-and-forth from Denver to DC, draining bank accounts and becoming experts in credit card airline rewards. For whatever reason, to this day she remains willing to put up with my habit-oriented neuroses—my determination to read *The Economist* every morning, my insistence on meditating and writing every day, my badgering about "when are we going to work out today?" Thankfully, she continues to nudge me in a healthier and more balanced direction by reminding me it's ok not to do all of these things, perfectly and obsessively, all of the time, because sometimes other things matter more.

Because of Erin, and because of the lessons our relationship has taught me, I began to see the emptiness of what I had been chasing, and what I was sacrificing to chase it. I began to see the hollowness of *why* I was chasing it. And I began, bit by bit, to accept that I would never be able to control every aspect of my existence. I would never be able to guarantee myself permanent happiness. I would never be able to wall myself off from painful or challenging emotions. I would never be able to find fulfillment from a life built only on career-centric striving. I would never be able to fully silence FOMO. So, I changed directions, an emotional reflection of the cross-country U-turn I made driving from DC to Colorado and back again, unsure both times whether I was going the right way. And then suddenly I stumbled into the place of serenity from which this book emerged.

Surrender

"The more you love, the more you can love." [165]

More than six years after Erin and I began our relationship, it's still a little jarring to look back at the amount of *work* that went into getting us here. Years of living in different cities, with all the challenges that come with that. Years, too, in the same city, and all the challenges that come with *that*. Sometimes working just a floor apart in one of the Senate office buildings, and other times juggling that weird balance of career stability for one of us and student life for the other. So far, our relationship has endured a combined eight jobs and three master's degrees in four different cities across three time zones and two continents. There have been plenty of disagreements and plenty of sparring, but also a consistent laughter-to-everything-else-ratio that skews heavily in the direction of LOLs.

For me, the relationship with a partner was the key that unlocked all sorts of love and meaning elsewhere. But, of course, the vulnerability of love isn't limited to romance. We can build profound and rewarding relationships with other human beings in countless ways. Parents.

Grandparents. Siblings. Children. In-laws. Cousins. Aunts. Uncles. Close friends. Distant friends. Colleagues. Mentors. Mentees. Acquaintances. Literal neighbors. Metaphorical neighbors. And so many more. Fulfillment can emerge from open, loving connections of any composition. The moments when I'm laughing with family and friends are the moments when I'm the most present and most fulfilled. My relationship with Erin showed me that the power of human connection was all around me, if only I would choose to open myself up to it.

That all sounds kind of fluffy and mystical. What do I mean by vulnerability to love? At its most fundamental level, being vulnerable means giving up control, and discarding the idea that you'll ever be in control. It means relying on others. Trusting them. Counting on them. Asking them for help. The philosopher Lao Tzu famously observed, "Being deeply loved by someone gives you strength, while loving someone deeply gives you courage."[166] It's scary, it's unpredictable, it's unmanageable, and it can be really, really hard.

It also comes with all sorts of unpleasant side effects. There's the pain of rejection. The fear of hurt or betrayal. The nihilistic queasiness that lingers and infects everything in the middle of a conflict not yet settled. There's the pain of missing someone. The fear of losing them. It's easy, as I did for years, to convince yourself that these downsides outweigh the potential upsides. (As with using social media, excuses for inaction are pretty compelling when couched in the comforting assurance of a positive cost-benefit analysis.)

But what if, instead of rejecting all these scary and uncontrollable feelings outright, you reframe how you see them? The loneliness and longing of missing someone *are* difficult and painful. *And* what a luxury it is to miss someone, and to have them miss you back. Worrying about losing someone *is* wrenching and exhausting. *And* what a blessing it is to have someone to worry about losing, and for them to feel the same way. The grief and pain that follows the death of someone you love *is* devastating and excruciating. *And* what fortune to have had that person in your life, and for them to have had you in theirs. Instead of framing these emotional hurdles as "either-ors," you can try to reframe them as "both-ands."

You can't make these complicated or painful feelings disappear, but reframing them sometimes makes their burden a little more manageable. Sometimes it transforms fear into awareness and appreciation. Awareness that you will have to say goodbye to your family when the holidays end and you have to return to work many time zones away, and with it an appreciation for the reunion you've all been looking forward to for so long. Awareness that someone you love could be taken away at the most unexpected moment, and with it an appreciation of the moments you have—and had—together. Awareness that your insecurities and weaknesses are only human, and with such awareness an appreciation of the insecurities and weaknesses of others. Awareness that we're all riding a roller coaster of emotions and fears, and with it an appreciation of our common humanity and an ability to connect with others in a more authentic and empathetic way. These feelings, unpleasant as they may be, mean you're living life as it's supposed to be lived, with all the highs and lows inherent to the human condition.

So, yeah, I've encountered some downsides to emotional vulnerability. Trying to deny that reality, like trying to bury grief or pain, doesn't serve anyone. Crafting and maintaining any human relationship requires a ton of work. Giving up control is hard. Admitting that you never had much control in the first place is even harder. While some or all of this may strike you as both remarkably obvious and a remarkable understatement, I'm still amazed by how much emotional capital a meaningful, long-term human connection of any kind requires.

But I'm even more amazed by the potential return on investment. I always knew this stuff would be hard. What I didn't know, or perhaps refused to see, was that it would still be worth it. For instance, when I'm with Erin I often encounter a byproduct of an open, vulnerable relationship that's hard to describe. It's a feeling that fills me with warmth, stability, and the "happy jitters."[167] It's a sensation of not feeling compelled to be anywhere else or do anything else. It's a powerful blend of contentment, happiness, fortune, protectiveness, compassion, and fulfillment that comes from finding people with whom to take on the world. Describing his partner Kenyatta, Ta-Nehisi Coates writes that he "had not been prepared for the simple charm of watching someone you love grow."[168] I, too, was unprepared that such a simple charm could be so powerful and fulfilling. And I was completely unprepared for how much I would grow at the same time.

Each chapter in this book, from working deep to building awareness, from making time for what matters to seeking stillness, is a room. These ten rooms (and surely there are more) sit behind doors lined up side-by-side in the same hallway. In any of these rooms, you can find a new way to reframe your day-to-day experience to make it more fulfilling. But there's a door that opens to the hallway itself, a door you can find no matter who or where you are. That door is love. "The more you love," David Brooks writes, "the more you can love."[169] The door of love leads to everything in this book. And when you manage to stumble through it, there's no limit to the fulfillment that awaits you on the other side.

9

Think about death

> *"Among the many lessons that emerge from the geologic record, perhaps the most sobering is that in life, as in mutual funds, past performance is no guarantee of future results."*
>
> Elizabeth Kolbert[170]

Impermanence

Thinking about death reminds us to live

It's 6:15 pm, and I haven't left my apartment all day. It's been a weird day. One of those days when early ambitions of stillness and deep work have been replaced by frantic emails, anxious conference calls full of "Can you believe they did that?" and a lot of frustration with all sorts of people and forces I can't control. Throughout the day, I've been mentally scrapping all of my earlier plans—a scheduled workout class, a quiet 45 minutes of writing, a catch-up call with my Oakland-based brother to plan an upcoming mountain adventure. I've even ditched more substantive work tasks I had planned, not because I don't need to do them but because I've chosen instead to dive headfirst into the world of busyness. As we've discussed, flexibility and forgiveness are important—we can't do everything perfectly every day—but I'm not throwing out my plans because I need some flexibility or self-forgiveness. I'm abandoning my goals for the day because my universe has shrunk to the work crisis in front of me, and I've become wholly fixated on fixing it.

Except I can't fix it, and it's not really a crisis. It's a disagreement, sure, emanating from one of those routine miscommunications that we human beings are prone to, especially in this age of remote working and virtual meetings and constant distractions. I haven't created this sense of crisis out of nothing—there is an underlying issue that needs to be resolved—but I have manufactured the atmosphere of stress, faux-urgency, and franticness that I'm now fully inhabiting. For whatever reason—to prove I'm right, to empty my inbox, to "fix" the situation—or some combination of these reasons, I've willfully handed my day over to pettiness, internal politics, and the technological tools that sustain them.

After a day of this, the sun has begun to set over London, inundating our west-facing apartment with some rapidly disappearing afternoon warmth. I look out the window and think to myself, "It would've been a great day to walk through Regent's Park, if only I had time." I pause for a second. "Well, if only I had *made* the time." And then, in the midst of this self-imposed and obsessive frenzy, I stop. I stop responding to emails. I stop venting to colleagues on WhatsApp. I stop plowing through my to-do list with righteous anger. I stop plotting how I'm going to "win" the situation in which I've found myself.

Instead, I take a step back to consider some questions. Can I do anything about this? Does it really matter right now? Will it matter in a month? What about a year? Will I be thinking about this a decade from now? If I were near death, would it matter to me? Would it matter to anyone at all? If someone needed me right now, or if someone I love were in trouble, would I tell them, "Sorry, I need to resolve this work drama first"? The answer to all of these questions, obviously, is "no." The situation I've gotten so worked up about *doesn't* matter right now. It doesn't really matter at all. So, I stop. I finish what I can for the day and sign off. I call my brother. I go for a run in Regent's Park, catching the very end of the sunset. I press play on an episode of the *Longform* podcast that I've been saving for a while. And I get ready for Erin to come home, and the dinner we'll cook together, and the evening we'll spend catching up and watching something funny and mindless on TV.

Out of nowhere, it seems, came a moment of clarity that turned my day around. Where did that moment come from? In part, it came from practicing the ideas in this book—accepting that I can't do it all, breaking the busyness addiction, trying to nudge each day in a more fulfilling direction, and so on. I've invested countless hours in these practices, so realistically, my day didn't turn around in an instant; I was able to summon some clarity to interrupt the spiral of getting-things-done-ism because of this investment. But in that moment, as the sun descended behind Regent's Park, I still needed a spark of awareness, a spark of perspective, to break free. And that clarity came from a simple realization: Our time is limited. The time of people we love is limited. None of it is guaranteed. Who knows what will happen to any one of us at any time?

In other words, the clarity I needed in that moment came from thinking about death.

In the grand sweep of time, choosing to log off of Outlook and log back into the rest of my life was a microscopically insignificant decision. If I'd spent another hour working instead of going for a run and calling my brother, my life wouldn't have changed much. (As he began his day in California, Chris might even have appreciated having some extra time to go about his morning routine.) But what if this one-off moment of clarity weren't a one-off? What if it were a habit? What if I summoned this sense of perspective more often? It's probably unrealistic—not to mention fairly bleak—to think about death during every living moment. But what if I thought about death a little more frequently than I do now? What if I made remembering my mortality and accepting the finitude of life slightly more significant factors in my internal decision-making algorithms?

In *Being Mortal*, Atul Gawande shares research that suggests that our perception of how much longer we'll live determines how we wish to spend our time. Age is a factor, of course, but the findings go beyond saying that we see the world differently as we get older. The studies

Gawande cites find that any significant life disruption—an illness, a natural disaster, political turmoil, a move to a different country—can alter how we perceive the time we have left. More significantly, this shift in perception can occur even if the disruption hasn't actually occurred, even if we've only been instructed to think about it. "When, as the researchers put it, 'life's fragility is primed,' people's goals and motives in their everyday lives shift completely," Gawande writes. "It's perspective, not age, that matters most."[171] It follows, then, that thinking about death might shift your perception of how much time you have left and, thus, make you think differently about how you spend that time. Why wait for an external event to disrupt your life and put everything in perspective? What better way to prime the fragility of life than to remind yourself of it regularly?

That may sound morbid and depressing, but I've become convinced it's exactly the opposite. Thinking about death reminds you to factor in what matters most to you when you're deciding between working late or ordering takeout with your family. Or weighing whether to read a meaningful book or call into a 9 pm work call that you don't even need to be on. Or considering whether to respond to a comment on an annoying Instagram post with snark or with understanding (or whether to respond at all). Or navigating the inevitable trade-offs of professional ambition and personal fulfillment. When you constantly think about death, you constantly appreciate life. You're reminded that human existence is fleeting and can be taken away, or disrupted immeasurably, at any moment.

While this discussion is about much more than altering how you make tiny decisions on a moment-by-moment basis, thinking about mortality does bring some helpful clarity to life's quotidian challenges—especially when you consider the scale of human history. If you stumble badly during a speech or if someone at work slights you during a meeting, does it matter over the course of a lifetime? Probably not. If you choose not to run for local political office this cycle, would it matter over the course of American history? Almost certainly not. If you fail to achieve your wildest professional dreams—or even if you do—would it matter to human history, let alone planetary history? Unlikely. If that's not a humbling enough exercise, factor in the incomprehensible and ever-expanding size of the universe for an even greater dose of perspective and humility.

By way of example, consider the position of president of the United States, by many measures the most famous and most powerful person in the world. Someone (who happened to be born in America through no choice of his or her own) could spend an entire lifetime striving to be president. Succeeding in this quest requires a great deal of effort and skill, and a far greater amount of luck and fortune. Even if the stars align and this person succeeds, how long will they be remembered for? 100 years? 1,000 years, just maybe? Certainly not much more than that. Did you know that someone named Benjamin Harrison used to be president? ("President of what?" you ask. Of the United States.) Maybe I should have known about Benjamin Harrison, but I didn't. I'm obsessed with U.S. politics, I used to lead tours of the U.S. Capitol, and I read a ton about U.S. history. And I first learned about President Benjamin Harrison just now. On Wikipedia.[172] How about vice presidents, or defeated opponents, or all of the other aspiring candidates who fell short? As John Adams, one of the rare successful presidential aspirants, once noted about the human obsession with legacy, "For what folly it is! What is it to us what shall be said of us after we are dead? Or in Asia, Africa, or Europe while we are alive? There is no greater possible or imaginable delusion."[173]

These wise reminders occur throughout history. Marcus Aurelius was once a leader of great power and prominence, known and (presumably) feared by millions. We know his ideas only because a few written notes managed to survive for two millennia.[174] As he once wrote, "Is it your reputation that's bothering you? But look at how soon we're all forgotten. The abyss of endless time that swallows it all."[175] A couple-thousand years later, Nina Riggs describes the concept of "memento mori" that emerged during the era of Marcus and his fellow Stoics.[176] Memento mori, Riggs writes, "was a phrase that originated with the ancient Roman practice of a successful general returning from battle being assigned a slave to follow him around, whispering in his ear: '*Respice post te. Hominem te memento.*' 'Look to the afterlife,' the slave was instructed to say in an effort to help the general avoid haughtiness from all the praise he received in the wake of his victory, 'and remember you're only a man.'" Riggs puts it more simply: "Remember, says the world—you must die."[177]

There are many such examples. Arthur Brooks observes that throughout history some cultures have practiced contemplating death to train themselves to fear it less. Consider the darkly-named concept of "corpse meditation." "Many Theravada Buddhist monasteries in Thailand and Sri Lanka display photos of corpses in various states of decomposition for the monks to contemplate," Brooks writes. "Psychologists call this desensitization, in which repeated exposure to something repellent or frightening makes it seem ordinary, prosaic, not scary. And for death, it works."[178] Pointing to psychological research which suggests that thinking about death is scarier for people who are *not* dying (at least in the immediate sense), Brooks concludes, "For most people, actively contemplating our demise so that it is present and real (rather than avoiding the thought of it via the mindless pursuit of worldly success) can make death less frightening; embracing death reminds us that everything is temporary, and can make each day of life more meaningful."[179]

Inevitability
Death's inevitability is invigorating

Like the writers I've just cited, I've been thinking about death a lot. I'm not sure exactly why. I imagine it's a combination of experiencing the emotional renaissance I discussed in the last chapter, gaining perspective from moving abroad, exploring the ideas in this book more deeply, doing some aging of my own, attending a number of unexpected memorial services, and beginning to grapple with the mortality of people I love. I don't claim to have any secrets to making sense of death. The fact that a person can be here one moment and not here the next—but also continue to be here in so many meaningful ways—still floors me. I suspect it always will. Yet rather than try to solve it or run from it, I've sought to reframe how I approach the act of living and the certainty of dying.

Death is humanity's great equalizer. It's the great limiter, but also the great liberator. As Yuval Noah Harari writes bluntly, "As far as we can tell, from a purely scientific viewpoint, human life has absolutely no meaning. Humans are the outcome of blind evolutionary processes that operate without goal or purpose."[180] Is that a depressing idea because it means nothing matters? Or, is it liberating because it empowers us to focus on the things that really *do* matter? Are the inevitability of death and the smallness of the individual depressing because they mean our potential is inherently limited? Or, are they liberating because they free us from futile and compulsive striving and suffering?

Life is defined by uncertainty, but at least one thing is certain: At some point, it will end. Some might see this perspective as a recipe for selfish nihilism, pure libertarianism, or just giving up and hoarding immediate pleasures. Others might see thinking about death as fatalistic or morbid. But there's another way to frame it. As Paul Kalanithi observes beautifully and simply, "even if I'm dying, until I actually die, I am still living."[181] *Until I actually die, I am still living.* Thinking about death reminds us that we're alive.

The arc of the moral (and actual) universe, whether it bends toward justice or not, is really long, and life is really short. It existed before us and will continue after us. Knowing that death is inevitable puts this in perspective, unlocking a clarifying sense of awareness. "The problems that beset modern people at the peak of their family and work lives," Yongey Mingyur Rinpoche writes, "closely parallel issues that arise for people everywhere at the end of life: an inability to accept impermanence, grasping at what is not available, and not being able to let go."[182] By focusing on the present and finding fulfillment in today, we can begin to free ourselves from needless striving and self-imposed suffering.

♦

The awareness of mortality can also spark and sustain a sense of urgency. Death's inevitability makes it invigorating. It helps us prioritize and focus on what matters. It's a line of reasoning similar to why Ta-Nehisi Coates says his blunt assessments of America's lack of progress fighting racial injustice aren't a reflection of hopelessness, but rather a reflection of clarity. "I don't ever want to lose sight of how short my time is here. And I don't ever want to forget that resistance must be its own reward, since resistance, at least within the life span of the resistors, almost always fails," Coates writes. "I don't ever want to forget…that the larger story of America and the world probably does not end well. Our story is a tragedy. I know it sounds odd, but that belief does not depress me. It focuses me."[183] Openness to a brutal, painful reality empowers Coates to better confront it. That's reason for focus, not fatalism. Action, not apathy. The awareness that death is coming for everyone can depress us, or it can focus us. It can paralyze us, or it can invigorate us. "Nothing endures but change," writes Yongey Mingyur Rinpoche. "Accepting this has the potential to transform the dread of dying into joyful living."[184] Recognizing the inevitability of death reminds us that whatever trajectory we're on—whatever our goals, whatever our dreams, whatever we're striving toward—it could all be interrupted at any moment, probably without warning.

I've become convinced that no matter when the end comes, we will succeed if we manage to find meaning and moments of joy on the way to achieving our goals, in the little moments of progress and presence along the way. We will succeed if the process, and not the product, is our purpose. But if the only frame through which we see "success" is an end point or finish line, with our happiness and fulfillment dependent on achieving some far-off future goal, then our success is far from guaranteed. If we refuse to accept that this could all end later today, well, we better hope we're lucky enough to hang on as long as our striving requires. We better prepare to discover that the grass on the other side of our achievements and accomplishments might not be as green as we'd hoped. And we better get used to missing all the life happening in front of us right now.

Impossibility

What does it mean to live?

I don't understand how someone can be here one moment and not here the next. This is, as I mentioned earlier, one aspect of death I can't figure out. (I can't figure out most of them, but let's hone in on this one for now.) The transition from here to not here simply does not compute for me. Scientifically, I get it. I understand the basics of how the body dies, or at least I accept that the science exists and is not in doubt. I understand physical impermanence. But I can't seem to wrap my mind around the impermanence of all the other aspects of life. I can't seem to make sense of it because when a person passes away, *so much* of that person can continue to live.

They can remain alive in big, profound, meaningful ways, in cherished memories, personal and professional legacies, networks of colleagues and friends, new generations of children and grandchildren, the stories they told and the stories told about them. They can continue to live in small, but equally profound and meaningful, ways, too. Their clothes. Their keepsakes that meant little to anyone but them. Their routine possessions, like cell phones and keys and wallets and well-worn shoes. The things they wrote—text messages, emails, grocery lists, memos, books, holiday cards—and the things they created. The plans they had. That's the one that really gets me, I think. This person had plans. Not just big goals and ideas and ambitions, but the mindless, forgettable stuff they were going to do tomorrow, or next week, or in a few months after the holidays. They had routine, everyday, boring life stuff to do—and then they didn't have it to do anymore. Yet none of that has entirely disappeared because it clearly still exists, even if the person at the center of it has passed.

Here's an analogy that hopefully doesn't trivialize my befuddlement. My first apartment in Washington, DC, was at 13th Street and Massachusetts Avenue NW. I haven't lived there since the summer of 2012, which, as I'm writing this, is more than seven years ago. It's safe to assume that apartment has seen at least a few tenants since I moved out. Yet if I walked into apartment 716 in that building and found all of my stuff still there, arranged how I'd left it, as if I'd just been out of town for the last seven years, I wouldn't be all that surprised. Sure, it would be weird, and I would probably be shocked and confused, but I wouldn't be *that* surprised. In some corner of my mind, that space, which meant a lot to me because of how much I grew as a person while I lived there, still exists, even though its physical manifestation is long gone.

That's sort of how I feel about death. No matter how long it's been, if I walked into a coffee shop and saw someone sitting there who I know has died, I would be shocked and confused, but would I really be *that* surprised? Or would I just be overjoyed and excited to have the opportunity to catch up? Who knows, since this scenario hasn't actually happened to me. But I strongly suspect we'd just pick up where we left off. "Being alive" is more than a biological, physical state. Being alive is about how you spend your time and who you spend it with. It's about how you *spent* your time and who you *spent* it with. It's about memories, dreams, stories, conversations, lessons, plans, things that have happened. Death might make future memories impossible, but it can never take away the memories we already have—the good times had, the laughs shared, the ideas exchanged, the routine conversations and everyday business of life conducted. That outlasts any one of us. And that's where I get hung up. Religious beliefs aside, we're taught that death is permanent. That someone dies, and then they're gone. But in so many ways, they're not. They're here, then they're not. But they still sort of are.

Or, maybe I'm just in denial about the inevitability of death and the inevitable passage of time. Maybe I feel like I could walk back into my first DC apartment because some part of me is pretending it's still there so I don't have to confront the fact that it's not. Maybe I don't feel like people I loved who have passed away are truly gone because I refuse to accept that they are. Maybe I'm not terrified of my own death because—despite everything I've just written—I haven't honestly admitted to myself that it's inevitable and will almost certainly come at a time when I'm not ready for it. Fear of one's own mortality, and fear of the mortality of the people we love, are distinct types of fear. But would my outlook change if I suddenly got an unexpected diagnosis or had a close call of my own?

Nostalgia

To live is to embrace life's most complicated emotions

Clearly, I don't know what to make of the possibility—no, the certainty—of my own death or the deaths of people who I love. What I do know is that I need to keep exploring it and keep being aware of it. I also know that, like mentally noting a difficult emotion to lessen its grip, embracing the inevitability of death can supplement anxiety with appreciation and awareness—appreciation for what we have, and awareness of the richness of being alive.

For me, no sensation illuminates these bittersweet contradictions and complexities more vividly than nostalgia. Nostalgia is that moment when suddenly, as we go about our lives, caught up in the day-to-day obligations and distractions that come with human existence in the twenty-first century, the past floods into the present. We've all had these moments: Driving by an old apartment and remembering when it was home. Seeing someone who reminds you of your first boss or a childhood classmate you'd forgotten about. Stumbling across a TV show you watched as a kid. Hearing a song you loved in high school. Catching a whiff of something, often food, that transports you back in time. Searching for an email and encountering a forgotten conversation from a decade ago. "Sitting in the space between dendrites," David Carr writes, "memories wait to be brushed by a smell or a taste, and then they roar back to life."[185]

These moments unleash powerful questions. They force us to reflect on all the life we've lived and all the time that's somehow vanished quietly into our subconscious. How can once-meaningful chapters fade away so quickly? How much have you forgotten about who you once were? How well do you really know yourself? It's unsettling that something—a sport you played passionately while growing up, for instance—can be so central to your world one day, and then nonexistent the next. It just happens. Skiing was a huge part of my life growing up. I didn't decide, one day in my mid-twenties, "Starting tomorrow, I will not think about skiing." I never filed paperwork with my brain that announced, "By order of management, beginning next week, tenant will no longer devote time or attention to skiing." If forgetting were this intentional, losses and breakups and painful experiences would be way easier to endure, and I probably wouldn't be writing this chapter about death.

You don't decide to think your last thought about something. You just don't think about it anymore. Possibly forever, unless something jogs your memory. Then, surprisingly and usually without warning, this trigger unearths waves of memories and archived experiences from the depths of the memory bank. Nostalgia is what you feel when those waves, especially the positive and formative ones, crash into the present. It's beautiful, rich, sad, and confusing.

By traditional legal standards, I'm the same person today I was in the past. That's true for most of us. Yet moments of nostalgia can make you feel thoroughly disloyal to your former self. You think you've always been who you are today, right now, until an unanticipated glimpse of the past, perhaps triggered by a flood of memories from a forgotten chapter, tells you that's not true. These moments remind you that past, current, and future you are inseparable, but not identical. They show you that you're continually redefining who you are, that what matters to you today may not matter tomorrow, and what mattered before may be irrelevant or even antithetical to what matters to you today. And even if an activity or person or place doesn't really concern you anymore, the fact that it once mattered means something.

Our future-obsessed culture expects us to constantly strive for and focus on the next potential achievement, making these nostalgic realizations even more bewildering. We rarely carve out time to reflect on our personal evolution, so it's startling to have thrust into our consciousness such vivid reminders of the methodical passage of time. Nostalgia is driven by the past. Fear of death is driven by the future. Yet both feelings force you into the present with heavy doses of raw self-awareness. They take you out, however briefly, of your minute-by-minute march forward of plans and tasks and to-do lists. They make you reflect on how much living you've done, and how quickly and subtly it can slip away. Nostalgia and death remind you, at once, of the impossibly long and impossibly short nature of life.

There are different types of nostalgia, of course. The sentiment I'm describing here is distinct from the yearning for a mythical past that plagues much of Western politics today. As an American former congressional staffer now living in the UK, large parts of the two political worlds I inhabit have been taken hostage by this desire to turn back the societal clock. These movements are born of frustration and buoyed by grievance and resentment. The nostalgia I'm describing, on the other hand, is more personal and generally more unpredictable. It's not a way of imagining how the *world* might once have been but rather a reminder of who *I* used to be. It's more likely to make me smile wistfully than tweet angrily. It's both happy and sad, bitter and sweet.

The writer Daniel H. Pink has observed that "meaningful endings," in books, movies, or really any experience, are rooted in "one of the most complex emotions humans experience: poignancy, a mix of happiness and sadness."[186] All of us have painful memories, some more difficult or traumatic than others. There may be chapters we don't want or aren't ready to confront. But we're all constantly evolving as human beings so, like it or not, from time to time we will all encounter poignant reminders that take us back to earlier versions of ourselves.

Over the past few years, my grandfather, Seymour, has been exploring these moments through a series of essays. One tells the story of January 20, 1965, when he and a friend managed to get tickets to an inaugural ball commemorating Lyndon Johnson's swearing-in. Somehow, Grandpa Sy found himself seated at a dinner table next to Omar Bradley, the five-star Army general and World War II hero. In the piece, Sy reflects on how he'd completely forgotten about that night until suddenly bumping into an old friend brought the night back to the surface of his memory. "It may be true what I have read," he writes. "The mind works like a computer. Long-forgotten memories come forth if you punch the right key."[187]

Awareness practices like meditation have helped me appreciate the power of recognizing and sitting with complicated sentiments, rather than trying to bury or fix them. Just as Grandpa Seymour did when he rediscovered that memorable evening in Washington, DC, I've been trying to dive more deeply into nostalgia whenever it hits. Once, for instance, I was driving through Summit County, Colorado, and heard aspen leaves rustling on the trees. I was immediately taken back to summer days hiking with my family and doing jumps on bikes with Chris. For a few extra moments, I made a conscious effort to hold on to those complex feelings, as well as the steering wheel of the car.

Another time, nostalgia nearly overwhelmed me on a work trip to LEGO headquarters in Denmark. Like a lot of kids, I was once obsessed with LEGOs. Seeing these toys again reopened chapters in my life I hadn't thought about in twenty years. Being surrounded by the memories they sparked was like meeting a long-lost friend whose presence reminds us of how much *we've* changed. Like skiing, LEGOs were once central to my life, but I didn't consciously decide not to think about them anymore. I just stopped. Grew up. Moved on. Moved out. I'm sure I didn't know it at the time, but there was a day when I played with my last LEGO before I put the toys away. There was a time when I thought my last thought about them before they were filed away in my mental archives. And then, two decades later, on a visit to Billund, Denmark, of all places, these memories came flooding back into the present.

How do you reconcile your former, current, and future selves? How do you build a life in which you appreciate the present? How do you confront the inevitable passage of time in an honest way? How do you recognize the majesty of living without being overwhelmed by the fear of it being taken away? How do you cultivate awareness of who, or what, you love, while also preparing for the possibility of loss and finality? These questions don't have easy answers, or even any answers. But we explore them anyway because the quest itself makes life richer and more meaningful.

It might be nostalgia, mortality, or loss. Or it might be any one of the myriad other painful reminders of the impermanence of life. When these feelings force tough questions into your consciousness, momentarily pushing aside the countless other short-term things you're working on and worried about, you're given an opportunity. Whether it's a fond memory or a painful one, whether it generates feelings of joy or feelings of regret, when you're gifted a moment of clarity and presence, you can embrace the complicated unknowns that come with it. You can step back from the nonstop rush of your busy life. You can tweak your priorities. You can reframe how you're experiencing life right now. You can sit with nostalgia. You can sit with death. You can sit with mortality. You can sit with these heavy, complicated feelings and, even if just for a moment, you can see where they take you.[188]

10

Embrace the craft of life

> *"Joy, as I have heard countless Black preachers say, is different
> from happiness, because happiness is predicated on 'happenings,'
> on what's occurring, on whether your life is going right, and
> whether all is well. Joy arises from an internal clarity about
> our purpose."*

Brittney Cooper[189]

Joyful Struggle
Find joy in the struggle

When it comes to building more fulfilling days, any progress I've made over the past decade can probably be summarized as living, learning, and making adjustments as I go, and trying to do so with as much awareness as possible. In practice, that's meant limiting activities and commitments that don't bring me fulfillment to focus more on those that do. It's meant replacing the compulsion for professional striving with presence and the recognition that other activities matter to me more. It's meant slowly and haltingly rejecting the tempting idea of "doing it all." It's meant reframing my life as a craft in which each day is a chance to do a little work, make a little progress, and find a few moments of stillness.

I'm convinced that this process of self-discovery has made me a better person for those around me. And I'm convinced that anyone can tilt their life in a more fulfilling direction by making similar tweaks at the margins. But what about the world beyond the individual?

On Wednesday, November 9, 2016 (the day after Erin's birthday, sadly), I took the 5:00 am Amtrak train from New York to Washington. Erin was studying at Columbia that fall, and I was due back at my desk in the Senate by 9:00 am. I wasn't worried about the early hour; I'd taken that train almost weekly for months, and until the night before I had expected that Wednesday to be pretty easy in the office—send out a few celebratory press statements, follow the president-elect through her day on cable news, and spend a lot of time scrolling victoriously through Twitter. On election night, Erin and I had gone for a birthday dinner at the Red Rooster in Harlem before walking a dozen blocks back to her apartment to watch the results come in. Like many people, I expected an early night. And like many people, I woke up on Wednesday morning having gotten very little sleep and having no idea what to think, do, or feel.

Remembering that morning still leaves me almost overwhelmed with sadness and bleakness. I'll never forget glancing at the front page of the *New York Times* that morning as I staggered, bleary-eyed and shell-shocked, anxious and angry, through Penn Station. I spent nearly the entire three-hour train ride on Twitter, trying to find even a hint of explanation or understanding. I found neither, but at some point, I came across a series of tweets by Twitter user 5'7" Black Male (@absurdistwords) that stuck with me and have stayed with me since:

> I'm talking to you now surprised white people. I wanna bring you in for an empathy moment. This feeling you have right now. Amazement that the country could be so short-sighted, that it could embrace hate so tightly? Welcome. This despair and dread you feel. The indignation, the bewilderment, the hurt, powerlessness, the fear for family and livelihood? Welcome. That knot in your stomach, that feeling of heartache? That uncertainty about your safety? The deep sense of fundamental injustice? Welcome. For many marginalized people, this spike in distress you feel this morning is what we feel EVERY morning.[190]

In some ways, my journey of recent years has been learning to take different elements of this Twitter wisdom to heart. On a societal level, the 2016 election prompted a similar awakening in many parts of the United States, particularly among white men like me whose extraordinary privilege and lack of awareness was thrust back into focus with inescapable clarity. In my case, the awakening wasn't just one of gaining knowledge, history, and an understanding of injustice in America, although it was certainly all of those things. It was also one of learning what to do with that knowledge, history, and understanding. Of learning to sit with its uncomfortable, hard, and painful truths. Of learning to appreciate that overcoming injustice is a generations-long struggle, not a task that can be accomplished or undone by a single presidential election. Of learning to see that building a better society is a craft to be honed.

At the risk of sounding presumptuous, in my individual evolution of consciousness—the journey I've tried to capture in this book—I see reflections of our national journey. Instead of feeling uncomfortable emotions, for instance—instead of sitting with them, trying to understand them, and seeing where they come from—I buried them, just as many Americans bury the chapters in our history that make us uncomfortable or don't fit our desired narratives. Even having the option to bury them is a privilege in itself; as the previous tweets reflect, not everyone gets to choose whether they run from or live with these sentiments.

For years, I sold myself the self-image and identity of an unfeeling workaholic, using busyness to mask vulnerabilities and hustling single-mindedly to execute *the plan*. Similarly, the United States sells itself the image and identity of being on the single, righteous path that we call the American Dream. Anyone or anything that deviates from this meritocratic, equal-opportunity narrative is un-American and unpatriotic. That we, as a country, are walking along the path toward liberty and prosperity for every individual is inevitable. It is to be accepted and celebrated righteously, not challenged or questioned.

Yet what has made my life so fulfilling, and what I'm most proud of, is the vulnerability and the struggle. The journey. The process.

The *work*. The craft of living that progresses slowly and imperceptibly, day by day. What makes America great, meanwhile, isn't a flawless track record of achievement and progress. What makes it great is an aspirational vision of a free and democratic society that leaves no one behind. What makes it great isn't just the progress we have made but our willingness to reckon with the progress we have not—our willingness to bear the painful responsibilities of the past and do the work of the present. What makes it great is the collective awareness and acceptance that the American Dream has never been a reality for all people—not even close—and that we don't yet live the values to which we aspire.

In other words, the Dream is a trajectory, not a plan. We can't just check things off the list and move on, absolved of further responsibility. Racism? *Fixed it—check.* Opportunity? *Created it—check.* Freedom? *Got it—check.* We should have these values on our minds every day so that we prioritize them at least as much as the little stuff, but they aren't items that we do once, and then forget. Bringing the American Dream to life is the struggle—the craft—of generations. No matter what any politician might promise, we can't change, heal, or achieve it overnight. The best we can hope for is to make a little progress at the margins, day after day after day, to nudge ourselves further in the right direction.

What is the role of any one person in this collective journey? Sometime in late 2016, I wrote the following post-election exploratory sentences: "My role: lift others up who may be caught in despair, anxiety, anger— that's what I can offer. Grateful for relentless optimism flame that keeps burning—sometimes takes time to heat up, but always comes back." There's something there, I think. Sometimes, we don't need to fix anything. (As Erin has to remind me on a regular basis, not every difficulty is a problem I need to solve right then and there.) We just need to be there. Simply being present and engaged can be enough. Offering what David Brooks calls "a ministry of presence" can be enough.[191]

Whether it's a painful national reckoning following a presidential election, the ups and downs of a generations-long struggle for justice, or just a call from a friend who's hurting, we can't solve everything at once. As Lincoln advised his Union general, let's look for honor and meaning simply in doing our part. Can you find ways to be more present, for more people, more often? Can you contribute to the struggle by supporting those in the struggle? Can you find ways to lead, not necessarily by being the first or the loudest or the most prominent, but perhaps by helping those around you step back from the chaos and see their lives through a different frame? Can you sustain a long-term perspective in a world increasingly dominated by short-term, reactionary thinking? Can you serve as a counselor or mentor, offering alternatives to the cynical worldview of the media and popular culture? Can you live as a calm, steady reminder that it's ok to focus on what truly matters?

Day-by-Day
Reframe life as a craft, one day at a time

In 1726, a young Benjamin Franklin departed London for his home in Philadelphia. As Walter Isaacson captures in his biography of Franklin, during many months at sea Franklin crafted what he called a "Plan for Future Conduct." Its aim, Isaacson writes, was "to perfect the art of becoming...a reliable person."[192] If anyone is an authority on self-help, it's Ben Franklin. (Isaacson considers him the "patron saint of self-improvement guides."[193]) Throughout his long life, Franklin constantly sought to improve his future conduct, both through little tips and tricks— what today we might call life-hacks—and broader philosophies on life. "Let me, therefore, make some resolutions, and some form of action, that, henceforth, I may live in all aspects like a rational creature," Franklin wrote.[194] He set meaningful goals that felt modest on a day-to-day scale but, as we now know, proved impactful over the course of his lifetime and beyond.

Franklin, as much as anyone, seemed to see the world as infinitely interesting, with ideas to be explored, insights to be gleaned, and knowledge to be learned. He certainly had his flaws and shortcomings, but the curiosity for life that appears to have driven him is worth exploring. Maybe I'm projecting here, but Franklin seems to have seen life as a craft—something at which he could always improve, but would never perfect. Something he would be tinkering with until the very end. Like any craft, there would never be a point when Franklin truly "finished" life—except for the final moment, and no one knew what would happen beyond that. Given such uncertainty, Franklin's life seems to suggest, we might as well embrace the journey while we're on it, and enjoy it for as long as we have the privilege to do so.

At its most fundamental, that's what this book is about: reframing life as a craft. A craft is tweaked, honed, and embraced over time—over many days and nights of struggle and setback and imperceptible progress—not overnight. A craft is something that we continue to learn and improve, finding meaning and satisfaction in the little moments of success and the obstacles overcome along the way. A craft is something for which the ultimate aim isn't immortality or fame, riches or achievement, but rather something much more fundamental: fulfillment. The kind of fulfillment that emerges from confidence, clarity, and stillness. The kind of fulfillment that can only come from within, but because of that, can come from within any one of us at any time.

A careful (or confused) reader may have noticed that I haven't yet defined fulfillment. That's partly intentional, and partly a reflection of the fact that I don't know exactly what it is. Life, as these chapters reflect, is a constant search for this definition. It's a search we undertake knowing that while we may never find exactly what we're looking for, we can, over time, get a little bit closer. Fulfillment can be many things. It's presence in *this* moment, without feeling pulled anywhere else. It's focus, the intense concentration of working deep and mastering a craft, no matter how trivial a particular task may appear. It's a sense of contented exhaustion at the end of the day. It's the perspective and clarity that comes from knowing what matters most to us. It's humility, accepting that we can't predict the future or control most of what's going on around us. It's confidence built on an identity that has nothing to do with job title, salary, or status. It's the peace that comes from having people at our side with whom we're ready to take on the world. It's the validation that emerges from loving and mutually vulnerable relationships with other human beings. It's the awareness that life as we know it can change dramatically at any moment, and with it the joy that comes from appreciating that moment.

"You know," Harry S. Truman once wrote, "when people can get excited over the ordinary things in life, they live."[195] Fulfillment is about embracing the fact that life—regular, everyday, ordinary life—is a craft. We're all learning as we go. And there's no single right way to go about it.

Goals

Set modest but meaningful goals

"I may say my life has not been entirely vain," wrote Thaddeus Stevens, the abolitionist congressman from Pennsylvania, shortly before his death. Considering one aspect of his legacy of public service, Stevens concluded, "I think my life may have been worth the living."[196] Few of us may have as significant an impact on society as Stevens, but what he articulates is a worthy goal for all of us: to make our lives worth living by doing the best we can, as often as we can. To do the right thing, on balance, more often than not. To have big and ambitious goals, but not at the cost of discarding the life right in front of us. To forgive ourselves and others when we all inevitably stumble from time to time. To wake up the next day—not every day, but most days—determined to keep nudging our journey in a more fulfilling direction.

Instead of judging the success or failure of a life on impossible aims beyond your control—instead of hanging your self-worth on professional achievements, for instance—you can set modest but meaningful daily goals. You can strengthen your character slowly but surely, honing your craft as you go. You can develop an inner sense of self-awareness that reminds you how little you control of the world around you. You can give other people the benefit of the doubt, even those whose actions or words are hurtful, and you can wish them well. You can recognize pain and insecurity in their anger, and you can recognize your own pain and insecurity in your rush to judgment. You can show up for people you care about. You can approach every day with curiosity.

As human beings, we can hear each other. We can notice each other. We can smile at each other. None of us can do all of these things all of the time, but we can strive to do a little bit better each day. And, from these little bits, a fulfilled life can emerge.

It's an incredible luxury to choose to spend part of one's life conducting a self-driven search for meaning. Many people have neither the time nor the resources to indulge in such an exploration. I've certainly benefited from having the resources to study and flail and fail and change plans—the trial-and-error approach to life with which we began this book. And I've benefited from the structural forces in society that give financially secure straight white men like me the chance to make a *lot* of mistakes with little risk of consequence. Not everyone can get away with so many stumbles or so much self-exploration. Nor does everyone have a choice in the matter. As Holocaust survivor and author Viktor E. Frankl captures vividly in *Man's Search for Meaning*, this search and discovery has too often been thrust upon our fellow human beings in the most horrific ways.[197] History offers no shortage of reminders of that.

But history also reminds us that the search for meaning and fulfillment is a universal undertaking, regardless of income, vocation, background, or circumstances. In my case, moving overseas during a challenging time for the United States gave me space to reflect on my own expectations, commitments, and hopes. What this process has shown me, more than anything, is that we control very little of our existence. We have no choice but to fall into that chaos and embrace it. We have no choice but to forgive ourselves for not being able to plot a path to professional superstardom and perpetual happiness. Surrendering to the unpredictability and absurdity of life frees us to find what we love, and who we love, wherever we are.

Whether it's a day full of pointless meetings or a presidential election that shakes your foundations or the loss of a loved one that leaves your emotional compass spinning wildly, the stresses and burdens of life will always pull at your time and attention. But there's joy in this struggle. There's strength in the solidarity of going through it together. We are all just human beings doing the best we can in the short time we have.

I'm saying this to myself as much as to anyone else: No matter the tumult surrounding us today, let's focus on the moments with the people who matter most to us. Let's sit with whatever emotions come our way. Let's give each other the benefit of the doubt. Let's forgive ourselves for being human. Let's reframe today to make a little more space for love. If we manage to do that, you know what? We'll be just fine.

Afterthoughts

"Write some thoughts down for yourself. Grab what you can,
pin it to the page. Look at that! How long you been hanging
on to those?"

Lin-Manuel Miranda[198]

Processing

I t took me more than two years to write this book, so as you can imagine,
there are now hundreds of drafts of different sections sitting in dozens
of folders on my computer and in the cloud. I could just leave them there.
After all, as we discussed toward the end of chapter four, by getting these
words out of my head and onto the digital page, writing has already, for
me, served its core purpose of helping me make sense of the world. Why
publish the creative output of all this processing?

I think about this question a lot these days, particularly in the
context of writing this book and in my side hustle of writing about U.S.
politics. Today, most of my involvement in politics consists of arm's-
length online commentary. The evolution from a full-time job in the
trenches of Capitol Hill to an on-the-side-and-as-time-allows passion
project has left me wondering: What's the value of writing to the causes
I believe in? Writing about politics on the internet—let alone writing a
book about personal fulfillment—doesn't knock on doors or pass bills
or raise money for candidates whose votes could alter public policy. It
feels a little presumptuous to try to convince myself I'm helping others

by committing my thoughts to the page, when I could be spending my time canvassing potential voters, making phone calls for a congressional candidate, or trying to get legislation through on the Hill.

The writer Tim Ferriss reflects on what would happen if he were to choose a different line of work, perhaps one with fewer solitary hours at the keyboard. "If I stop writing," he wonders, "perhaps I'm squandering the biggest opportunity I have, created through much luck, to have a lasting impact on the greatest number of people."[199] Ferriss has built a particularly large and influential platform, but many writers share a similar desire to touch people through their writing. Is this hope realistic, or is it a self-serving justification to give ourselves permission to spend a huge amount of time doing something we enjoy? Is this about service, or is it really just ego?

The way I see it is that the act of publishing, of sharing one's thoughts with the world, is a conscious choice *not* to assume that, just because I've stumbled across an idea, the rest of the world already knows it. It's to hope that others might find inspiration, clarity, or solidarity—or at least a useful tool for self-reflection—in my experiences and perspectives. It's to aim to give readers a sense of community and, if I'm lucky, to help them make sense of the world, by providing something they're missing or hadn't yet considered. But it's also to accept that, even though I might not achieve any of these goals, I should press ahead anyway. To publish one's own writing is to welcome the possibility that the writing has already served its sole purpose—to help the author process the world—and to recognize that purpose as worthy enough in itself.

Starting

Like all great works throughout history, this manuscript began… with an iPhone note full of nonsensical brain dumps and half-finished thoughts. In early 2018, after Erin and I had settled into life in the UK, I found myself newly liberated from the always-on mentality of working in American politics and, thus, with a lot more time to reflect and process. As we'd prepared for the move overseas, I hadn't known what to expect. Would I be lonely? Aimless? Bored? Feeling FOMO? Missing the action of Capitol Hill? The answer to all those questions turned out to be "yes," at least to some extent, but mostly I found myself surprised by how quickly an exhausting career and life transition evolved into feelings of sustained fulfillment as Erin and I moved further into this new chapter. I even began to experience occasional moments of serene contentment—brief points in the day when I felt completely at peace.

I didn't know why. Was it because I'd escaped Trump-era politics? Because I'd honed my meditation practice? Because I was working less and reading and exercising more? Was it because I was taking on a new adventure with my partner? Because I was learning to separate my identity from my job? Because I was getting older?* Or was it simply because I was finally creating some space to reflect on how I could make my days a little more fulfilling?

I wasn't sure. I just knew I was experiencing a sustained sense of contentment and stillness in my life, and I wanted to know why. Sometime in February 2018, as I thought about this puzzling-yet-pleasant evolution while riding a train from Oxford to London, I tapped out the following note on my iPhone:

A manifesto for simple living:

- reclaim attention (read, single task)
- reclaim self-confidence (no social media)
- cultivate awareness (meditate)
- spend time with family (and friends)
- create something (don't just react)
- simplify (things, content, schedule, goals)

---

*   As Atul Gawande writes, "Studies find that as people grow older they interact with fewer people and concentrate more on spending time with family and established friends. They focus on being rather than doing and on the present more than the future." So, maybe this whole book should just be called *I'm Getting Older.*[201]

This note was a spur-of-the-moment brain dump. But over the following weeks, months, and (at this point) years, I kept writing, editing, and writing some more. Before I knew it, the iPhone note had grown to 70,000 words. I had more to process and more to say than I'd realized. And as I was saying it, I was beginning to appreciate just how much satisfaction I derived from the process of writing and rewriting.

The author and meditation teacher Sharon Salzberg recounts feeling particularly discouraged about a book she was working on. One day, feeling as if she might have to settle for some unspecified mediocrity, her friends took her to see Lin-Manuel Miranda's musical, *Hamilton*. Leaving the theater, she says, "I walked out knowing I had to give writing this book all that was in me."[201] I sometimes think about the remarkable volume of creative energy Miranda poured into that musical—and the hours and hours of *work* it required (not to mention all of the work that went into Ron Chernow's biography that inspired it). Thinking about the intensity of that craft is inspiring. It's a reminder that human beings are capable of creating great things. It shows that when we choose to invest our time and attention in such pursuits with steady, sustained effort, we might manage to produce art of majesty and complexity. (This is the good kind of productivity!) It makes us wonder whether *we* might be capable of more than we think, and whether *we* might be able to create something new. Creativity, it seems, begets creativity. And the creative struggle is enormously fulfilling.

At some point in 2016, when moving to the UK was still a far-off possibility among a range of potential future trajectories, something prompted me to jot down the following thought: "What is dream goal?—contentedness? fulfillment?—Quiet noise in mind to hear the answer." Although I asked those questions only a few years ago, the journey to that thought, and later to this book, had begun long before. Almost as soon as I graduated from Colby College in May 2009, I began a process of self-exploration and self-education, of which this project is just the latest incarnation. As this book reflects, I've called this journey any number of things—the hustle, self-help, personal improvement, learning, hacking my life/body/work/career, reflection, mindfulness, an attempt to make sense of it all. The driving force has always been the same: There's a lot of knowledge out there, and pursuing it and filtering it through one's own life is invigorating and inspiring, fun and fulfilling.

Over the past decade, this pursuit, and the subsequent ideas sparked and lessons learned, has manifested in many forms. Sometimes, it's something fundamental, like a new habit that has stuck. Other times, what I've learned has been distilled as to-dos or New Year's resolutions. But more often than not, what I've encountered along this journey has led to nothing more than a fleeting thought or passing remark in a conversation. Occasionally it's been jotted down somewhere as a Kindle highlight or an iPhone note, but usually it's just buried deep in my subconscious. Regardless of the specific shape these ideas have taken, though, or whether they've taken any shape at all, each has represented an attempt to make some sense out of the thoughts bouncing around in my brain. They've been processed over many years, in part thanks to many conversations over many coffees and many beers with many good friends.

Throughout this book, I've done my best to cite every source and where I found it. But many of these ideas came from the countless mental notes I made in passing, so I hope I'll be forgiven if, say, an idea I heard on a podcast a few years ago took root in my brain and has ended up in these pages unattributed. As Salzberg says of *Hamilton*, I'm continually inspired by and grateful for all of the creative energy that human beings past and present have poured into the content I've consumed. In some ways, I see this book as an opportunity to pay tribute to it and to pay it forward.

Home

Before moving back to Colorado in 2013, I'd entertained (and quickly buried) second thoughts about whether my decision to leave was the right one. The skeptical thoughts intensified once I was back in Denver, trying to make *the plan* a reality. I'd had a growing suspicion that something might not be quite right, that perhaps I should've looked around a bit before haphazardly following blind ambition across the country. Still, I was the guy who for years had made Colorado my identity, telling people I was a Coloradan who would inevitably return home. It would all eventually click into place, right?

Less than a month after I moved, my friend Anthony asked me, "How good does it feel to be home?" It was a logical question, given how frequently and fervently I'd said how good it would feel to be home. But in that instance, I found myself responding with only hesitation and uncertainty (and a few tears). "Home," I was beginning to realize, is defined by people, not places. Home is where the people I care about are. Home is wherever Erin and I are when we're together. And there's nothing in this book that leaves me more fulfilled than the conviction that I've truly found *home*, and the knowledge that it doesn't depend on any time zone or area code.

For everything in this book, and for the life I've been so fortunate to live, I'm grateful to the people with whom I'm most at home. That's Erin, of course; my brother, Chris ("Young Christopher"); my parents, Elaine ("Bird") and Steve ("Esteban"); my in-laws, Cathy Carlson and Tom Galloway; my grandparents, Seymour Efros and Robert and Betty Lowenstein, with whom I'll never tire of discussing what we're currently reading and what we want to read next; and our extended families and friends. It's when I'm with them that I truly understand that lesson from *Into the Wild*: "Happiness only real when shared."[202]

While we're at it, there's a little more gratitude in order. Many people read drafts of this manuscript and provided detailed comments and feedback. Others talked through ideas with me or helped to keep me motivated during the writing process. For all of that, I'd particularly like to thank (in alphabetical order!) Beth Lowenstein, Camilla Vogt, Cathy Carlson, Chris Lowenstein, Elaine Sabyan, Erin Galloway, Kerry Donovan, Maddy Broas, Micael Johnstone, Nicole Chan, Shad

Murib, Stephanie Bennett Vogt, and Steve Lowenstein. Many others not named above have contributed ideas and insights to this book. Please know that I'm grateful to all of you.

It's pretty surreal to see an idea you've thought about for so long finally come to life. This project's transformation from idea to ISBN couldn't have happened without the guidance of the team at SilverWood Books, including Helen Hart, Martina Tyrrell, Catherine Blom-Smith, Eleanor Hardiman, and Kirsty Ridge. Their feedback, edits, efforts, insights, design, and support made this book immeasurably more personal and immeasurably better. Any remaining errors are, of course, mine alone. (Is this where I remind everyone that RTs do not equal endorsements?)

Nothing brings ideas to life more vividly than art. I'm grateful to Jesse Brown for crafting the amazing cover image and chapter-by-chapter illustrations. His work conveys in a quick glance what has taken me thousands of words to write. Check out more of his work on his website, www.jessebrown.co.uk.

While I spent far too many hours writing and rewriting and re-rewriting this book, the real source of this project isn't me, or something I read, or my trial-and-error stumble toward fulfillment. It's the person named in some parts of the book and referenced obliquely in others, but whose influence runs throughout the entire thing. Erin has been the catalyst for my personal transformation from striving to fulfillment, from future to present. She has helped me see what I was missing, and she has caught me, time and again, when I've fallen back into my old work- and productivity-obsessed habits. While this book is a giant acknowledgment of her impact on my life, I want to use this section to thank her again. (This is an acknowledgments section, after all.)**

**   After Erin read a draft of this section, she turned to me and said, "It's going to be really awkward when we break up. This is like a rapper making a music video for his girlfriend. This is our J. Lo and P. Diddy moment!" That made me happy. Well, at least the P. Diddy part did. I think?

It's because of Erin that I was shaken out of my striving-working-planning obsession and dropped into the vulnerable, scary, joyful present. It's because I've found fulfillment living each day with her that I've been able to work backwards from there and see what else in my life contributes to the same feelings of being content, being whole, being home—just *being*. She has given more to me—and to us—than she could possibly know. In so many ways, the lessons in this book are the lessons love has taught me.

Endnotes

Cover

1   Brooks, David. (2015). *The Road to Character*. Random House.

Chapter 1: Create stillness

2   Miranda, Lin-Manuel. (2018). *Gmorning, Gnight!: Little Pep Talks for Me & You*. Random House.

3   Petersen, Anne Helen. (2019, Jan. 5). "How Millennials Became The Burnout Generation." *BuzzFeed News*: https://www.buzzfeednews.com/article/annehelenpetersen/millennials-burnout-generation-debt-work.

4   Hobbes, Michael. (n.d.; accessed 2019, Nov. 19). "Millennials Are Screwed: Why millennials are facing the scariest financial future of any generation since the Great Depression." *Huffington Post*: https://highline.huffingtonpost.com/articles/en/poor-millennials/.

5   Petersen, Anne Helen. (2019, Jan. 5). "How Millennials Became The Burnout Generation." *BuzzFeed News*: https://www.buzzfeednews.com/article/annehelenpetersen/millennials-burnout-generation-debt-work.

6   Petersen, Anne Helen. (2019, Jan. 5). "How Millennials Became The Burnout Generation." *BuzzFeed News*: https://www.buzzfeednews.com/article/annehelenpetersen/millennials-burnout-generation-debt-work.

7   Agrawal, Sangeeta and Wigert, Ben. (2018, Jul. 12). "Employee Burnout, Part 1: The 5 Main Causes." *Gallup*: https://www.gallup.com/workplace/237059/employee-burnout-part-main-causes.aspx.

8   Pendell, Ryan. (2018, Jul. 19). "Millennials Are Burning Out." *Gallup*: https://www.gallup.com/workplace/237377/millennials-burning.aspx.

9   Strauss, Karsten. (2016, Aug. 8). "Survey: Too Much Work, Too Much Stress?" *Forbes*: https://www.forbes.com/sites/karstenstrauss/2016/08/08/survey-too-much-work-too-much-stress/.

10   Fitzmaurice, Rosie. (2019, Feb. 4). "Sleep, sunlight and fresh air: 40 things Brits don't get enough of in life." *Evening Standard*: https://www.standard.co.uk/lifestyle/health/40-things-brits-dont-get-enough-of-a4056716.html.

11 *See books such as*: Pinker, Steven. (2018). *Enlightenment Now: The Case for Reason, Science, Humanism, and Progress*. Penguin Books.; Rosling, Hans. (2018). *Factfulness: Ten Reasons We're Wrong About the World—And Why Things Are Better Than You Think*. Sceptre.

12 Weller, Chris. (2017, Sept. 20). "Barack Obama has a one-question test that proves how good the world is today." *Business Insider*: https://www.businessinsider.com/president-barack-obama-speech-goalkeepers-2017-9.

13 Wootton, David. (n.d.; accessed 2019, Nov. 19). "The Impossible Dream: How have we come to build a whole culture around a futile, self-defeating enterprise: the pursuit of happiness?" *Lapham's Quarterly*: https://www.laphamsquarterly.org/happiness/impossible-dream.

14 Harari, Yuval Noah. (2015). *Sapiens: A Brief History of Humankind*. HarperCollins Publishers.

15 Seidman, Dov. (2007). *How: Why How We Do Anything Means Everything*. Wiley.

16 Mingyur Rinpoche, Yongey. (2019). *In Love with the World: A Monk's Journey Through the Bardos of Living and Dying*. Spiegel & Grau.

17 Sapolsky, Robert M. (2004). *Why Zebras Don't Get Ulcers: The Acclaimed Guide to Stress, Stress-Related Diseases, and Coping (Third Edition)*. Henry Holt & Company.

18 Lewis, Michael. (2018). *The Fifth Risk*. W. W. Norton & Company.

19 Wright, Robert. (2017). *Why Buddhism Is True: The Science and Philosophy of Meditation and Enlightenment*. Simon & Schuster.

20 O'Donohue, John. *Excerpted from a conversation between the late John O'Donohue, Irish poet, author, and philosopher, and Krista Tippett*. (2008, Feb. 28). "John O'Donohue: The Inner Landscape of Beauty." *On Being with Krista Tippett*: https://onbeing.org/programs/john-odonohue-the-inner-landscape-of-beauty-aug2017/.

21 Newport, Cal. (2016). *Deep Work: Rules for Focused Success in a Distracted World*. Hachette Book Group.

22 Grant, Ulysses S. *Cited in*: Chernow, Ron. (2017). *Grant*. Penguin Books.

23   Brach, Tara. (2003). *Radical Acceptance: Embracing Your Life with the Heart of a Buddha*. Bantam Books.

24   Coates, Ta-Nehisi. (2017, Jan./Feb.). "My President Was Black." *The Atlantic*: https://www.theatlantic.com/magazine/archive/2017/01/my-president-was-black/508793/.

25   Coates, Ta-Nehisi. (2017). *We Were Eight Years in Power: An American Tragedy*. One World.

26   Leonhardt, David. (2017, Apr. 18). "You're Too Busy. You Need a 'Shultz Hour.'" *The New York Times*: https://www.nytimes.com/2017/04/18/opinion/youre-too-busy-you-need-a-shultz-hour.html.

27   Lowenstein, Steven R. (2009, Jan. 27). "Tuesdays to Write … A Guide to Time Management in Academic Emergency Medicine." *The Society for Academic Emergency Medicine*: https://onlinelibrary.wiley.com/doi/abs/10.1111/j.1553-2712.2008.00337.x.

28   Lowenstein, Steven R. (2009, Jan. 27). "Tuesdays to Write … A Guide to Time Management in Academic Emergency Medicine." *The Society for Academic Emergency Medicine*: https://onlinelibrary.wiley.com/doi/abs/10.1111/j.1553-2712.2008.00337.x.

29   Newport, Cal. (2016). *Deep Work: Rules for Focused Success in a Distracted World*. Hachette Book Group.

30   Newport, Cal. (2016). *Deep Work: Rules for Focused Success in a Distracted World*. Hachette Book Group.

31   Holiday, Ryan. (2014). *The Obstacle Is the Way: The Timeless Art of Turning Trials into Triumph*. Portfolio/Penguin.

32   Aurelius, Marcus. (2002). *Meditations: A New Translation, with an Introduction*, by Gregory Hays. The Modern Library.

33   Brach, Tara. (2003). *Radical Acceptance: Embracing Your Life with the Heart of a Buddha*. Bantam Books.

Chapter 2: Build awareness

34   Salzberg, Sharon. (2017). *Real Love: The Art of Mindful Connection*. Flatiron Books.

35   Wright, Robert. (2017). *Why Buddhism Is True: The Science and Philosophy of Meditation and Enlightenment.* Simon & Schuster.

36   Salzberg, Sharon. (2017). *Real Love: The Art of Mindful Connection.* Flatiron Books.

37   Harris, Dan. (2014). *10% Happier: How I Tamed the Voice in My Head, Reduced Stress Without Losing My Edge, and Found Self-Help That Actually Works—A True Story.* HarperCollins.

38   Harris, Dan. (2014). *10% Happier: How I Tamed the Voice in My Head, Reduced Stress Without Losing My Edge, and Found Self-Help That Actually Works—A True Story.* HarperCollins.

39   Harris, Dan. (2014). *10% Happier: How I Tamed the Voice in My Head, Reduced Stress Without Losing My Edge, and Found Self-Help That Actually Works—A True Story.* HarperCollins.

40   Holmes, Lindsay. (2015, Oct. 4). "This Simple Meditation Video Will Convince Even The Non-Believers To Start Practicing." *Huffington Post:* https://www.huffingtonpost.co.uk/2015/04/10/meditation-video_n_7001156.html.

41   Harris, Dan. (2014). *10% Happier: How I Tamed the Voice in My Head, Reduced Stress Without Losing My Edge, and Found Self-Help That Actually Works—A True Story.* HarperCollins.

42   Salzberg, Sharon. (2017). *Real Love: The Art of Mindful Connection.* Flatiron Books.

43   Brach, Tara. (2003). *Radical Acceptance: Embracing Your Life with the Heart of a Buddha.* Bantam Books.

44   Cain, Susan. (2012). *Quiet: The Power of Introverts in a World That Can't Stop Talking.* Broadway Books.

45   Wright, Robert. (2017). *Why Buddhism Is True: The Science and Philosophy of Meditation and Enlightenment.* Simon & Schuster.

46   Salzberg, Sharon. (2017). *Real Love: The Art of Mindful Connection.* Flatiron Books.

47   Aurelius, Marcus. (2002). *Meditations: A New Translation, with an Introduction,* by Gregory Hays. The Modern Library.

48   Wright, Robert. (2017). *Why Buddhism Is True: The Science and Philosophy of Meditation and Enlightenment*. Simon & Schuster.

49   Bredlau, Amy-Lee. (2016, Mar. 8). "Where Do You Put the Pain?" *Journal of the American Medical Association*: https://www.researchgate.net/publication/297750371_Where_Do_You_Put_the_Pain.

50   Bredlau, Amy-Lee. (2016, Mar. 8). "Where Do You Put the Pain?" *Journal of the American Medical Association*: https://www.researchgate.net/publication/297750371_Where_Do_You_Put_the_Pain.

51   Mingyur Rinpoche, Yongey. (2019). *In Love with the World: A Monk's Journey Through the Bardos of Living and Dying*. Spiegel & Grau.

52   Klein, Ezra. *Excerpted from a conversation between Yuval Noah Harari and Ezra Klein*. (2017, Feb. 28). "Yuval Harari, author of Sapiens, on how meditation made him a better historian." *The Ezra Klein Show:* https://www.vox.com/2017/2/28/14745596/yuval-harari-sapiens-interview-meditation-ezra-klein.

53   Harari, Yuval Noah. (2015). *Sapiens: A Brief History of Humankind*. HarperCollins Publishers.

54   Harris, Dan. (2014). *10% Happier: How I Tamed the Voice in My Head, Reduced Stress Without Losing My Edge, and Found Self-Help That Actually Works—A True Story*. HarperCollins.

55   Brach, Tara. (2003). *Radical Acceptance: Embracing Your Life with the Heart of a Buddha*. Bantam Books.

56   Mingyur Rinpoche, Yongey. (2019). *In Love with the World: A Monk's Journey Through the Bardos of Living and Dying*. Spiegel & Grau.

57   Brach, Tara. (2003). *Radical Acceptance: Embracing Your Life with the Heart of a Buddha*. Bantam Books.

Chapter 3: Make work a craft

58   Newport, Cal. (2016). *Deep Work: Rules for Focused Success in a Distracted World*. Hachette Book Group.

59   Newport, Cal. (2016). *Deep Work: Rules for Focused Success in a Distracted World*. Hachette Book Group.

60 Newport, Cal. (2016). *Deep Work: Rules for Focused Success in a Distracted World*. Hachette Book Group.

61 Newport, Cal. (2016). *Deep Work: Rules for Focused Success in a Distracted World*. Hachette Book Group.

62 Newport, Cal. (2016). *Deep Work: Rules for Focused Success in a Distracted World*. Hachette Book Group.

63 Newport, Cal. (2016). *Deep Work: Rules for Focused Success in a Distracted World*. Hachette Book Group.

64 Gallagher, Winifred. (2009). *Rapt: Attention and the Focused Life*. Penguin Books. *Originally cited in*: Newport, Cal. (2016). *Deep Work: Rules for Focused Success in a Distracted World*. Hachette Book Group.

65 Newport, Cal. (2016). *Deep Work: Rules for Focused Success in a Distracted World*. Hachette Book Group.

66 Lifehacker. (2010, Jan. 28). "Productivity in 11 Words." *Lifehacker*: https://lifehacker.com/productivity-in-11-words-30931567.

67 Resnick, Brian. (2018, Jun. 13). "The Stanford Prison Experiment was massively influential. We just learned it was a fraud." *Vox*: https://www.vox.com/2018/6/13/17449118/stanford-prison-experiment-fraud-psychology-replication.

68 Resnick, Brian. (2018, Jun. 13). "The Stanford Prison Experiment was massively influential. We just learned it was a fraud." *Vox*: https://www.vox.com/2018/6/13/17449118/stanford-prison-experiment-fraud-psychology-replication.

69 Lewis, Michael. (2012, Sept. 11). "Obama's Way." *Vanity Fair*: https://www.vanityfair.com/news/2012/10/michael-lewis-profile-barack-obama.

70 Lifehacker. (2010, Jan. 28). "Productivity in 11 Words." *Lifehacker*: https://lifehacker.com/productivity-in-11-words-30931567.

71 Pink, Daniel H. (2018). *When: The Scientific Secrets of Perfect Timing*. Riverhead.

72 Pink, Daniel H. (2018). *When: The Scientific Secrets of Perfect Timing*. Riverhead.

73   Pink, Daniel H. (2018). When: The Scientific Secrets of Perfect Timing. Riverhead.

74   Graham, Paul. (2009, Jul.) "Maker's Schedule, Manager's Schedule." *Paul Graham*: http://www.paulgraham.com/makersschedule.html. *Graham is co-founder of the venture capital fund Y Combinator. I first encountered his maker-manager concept on the Farnam Street website*: "Maker vs. Manager: How Your Schedule Can Make or Break You." (2017, Dec.) *Farnam Street*: https://fs.blog/2017/12/maker-vs-manager/.

75   Graham, Paul. (2009, Jul.) "Maker's Schedule, Manager's Schedule." *Paul Graham*: http://www.paulgraham.com/makersschedule.html. *Graham is co-founder of the venture capital fund Y Combinator. I first encountered his maker-manager concept on the Farnam Street website*: "Maker vs. Manager: How Your Schedule Can Make or Break You." (2017, Dec.) *Farnam Street*: https://fs.blog/2017/12/maker-vs-manager/.

76   Dalio, Ray. (2017). *Principles: Life and Work (Unabridged Audiobook).* Simon & Schuster Audio.

77   Graham, Paul. (2009, Jul.) "Maker's Schedule, Manager's Schedule." *Paul Graham*: http://www.paulgraham.com/makersschedule.html. *Graham is co-founder of the venture capital fund Y Combinator. I first encountered his maker-manager concept on the Farnam Street website*: "Maker vs. Manager: How Your Schedule Can Make or Break You." (2017, Dec.) *Farnam Street*: https://fs.blog/2017/12/maker-vs-manager/.

78   Cain, Susan. (2012). *Quiet: The Power of Introverts in a World That Can't Stop Talking.* Broadway Books.

79   Cain, Susan. (2012). *Quiet: The Power of Introverts in a World That Can't Stop Talking.* Broadway Books.

80   Newport, Cal. (2016). *Deep Work: Rules for Focused Success in a Distracted World.* Hachette Book Group.

81   Pressfield, Steven. (2002). *The War of Art: Break Through the Blocks and Win Your Inner Creative Battles.* Black Irish Entertainment.

82   Pressfield, Steven. (2002). *The War of Art: Break Through the Blocks and Win Your Inner Creative Battles.* Black Irish Entertainment.

83   Pressfield, Steven. (2002). *The War of Art: Break Through the Blocks and

Win Your Inner Creative Battles. Black Irish Entertainment.

84 Pressfield, Steven. (2002). *The War of Art: Break Through the Blocks and Win Your Inner Creative Battles*. Black Irish Entertainment.

85 Pressfield, Steven. (2011). *Do the Work: Overcome Resistance and Get Out of Your Own Way*. Do You Zoom, Inc.

86 Pressfield, Steven. (2002). *The War of Art: Break Through the Blocks and Win Your Inner Creative Battles*. Black Irish Entertainment.

87 Robertson, David C. with Breen, Bill. (2013). *Brick by Brick: How LEGO Rewrote the Rules of Innovation and Conquered the Global Toy Industry*. Crown Business.

88 Robertson, David C. with Breen, Bill. (2013). *Brick by Brick: How LEGO Rewrote the Rules of Innovation and Conquered the Global Toy Industry*. Crown Business.

89 Shenk, Joshua Wolf. (2005). *Lincoln's Melancholy: How Depression Challenged a President and Fueled His Greatness (Unabridged Audiobook)*. HighBridge.

90 Lincoln, Abraham. *Cited in*: Shenk, Joshua Wolf. (2005). *Lincoln's Melancholy: How Depression Challenged a President and Fueled His Greatness (Unabridged Audiobook)*. HighBridge.

91 Dalio, Ray. (2017). *Principles: Life and Work (Unabridged Audiobook)*. Simon & Schuster Audio.

92 Shenk, Joshua Wolf. (2005). *Lincoln's Melancholy: How Depression Challenged a President and Fueled His Greatness (Unabridged Audiobook)*. HighBridge.

93 Pressfield, Steven. (2002). *The War of Art: Break Through the Blocks and Win Your Inner Creative Battles*. Black Irish Entertainment.

94 Truman, Harry S. *Cited in:* McCullough, David. (1992). *Truman*. Simon & Schuster.

Chapter 4: Consume content intentionally

95 The Economist. (2009, Mar. 20). "Herbert Simon: Guru." *The Economist*: https://www.economist.com/news/2009/03/20/herbert-simon.

96   Mod, Craig. (2019, May 29). "The Glorious, Almost-Disconnected Boredom of My Walk in Japan." *WIRED*: https://www.wired.com/story/six-weeks-100s-miles-hours-glorious-boredom-japan/.

97   Newport, Cal. (2016). *Deep Work: Rules for Focused Success in a Distracted World*. Hachette Book Group.

98   West, Kanye (@kanyewest). (2018, May 21). *Twitter*: https://twitter.com/kanyewest/status/998641417072271360. *This excerpt includes minor edits for clarity.*

99   The Hoarse Whisperer (@HoarseWisperer). (2018, May 21). *Twitter*: https://twitter.com/HoarseWisperer/status/998647591557615617.

100   Lewis, Paul. (2017, Oct. 6). "'Our minds can be hijacked': the tech insiders who fear a smartphone dystopia." *The Guardian*: https://www.theguardian.com/technology/2017/oct/05/smartphone-addiction-silicon-valley-dystopia.

101   Thompson, Nicholas. (2017, Jul. 26). "Our Minds Have Been Hijacked by Our Phones. Tristan Harris Wants to Rescue Them." *WIRED*: https://www.wired.com/story/our-minds-have-been-hijacked-by-our-phones-tristan-harris-wants-to-rescue-them/.

102   Center for Humane Technology. (n.d.; accessed 2019, Nov. 19) "Take Control." *Center for Humane Technology*: http://humanetech.com/take-control/.

103   *See also*: Bowles, Nellie. (2018, Jan. 12). "Is the Answer to Phone Addiction a Worse Phone?" *The New York Times*: https://www.nytimes.com/2018/01/12/technology/grayscale-phone.html.

104   Tolentino, Jia. (2019, Apr. 22). "What It Takes to Put Your Phone Away." *The New Yorker*: https://www.newyorker.com/magazine/2019/04/29/what-it-takes-to-put-your-phone-away.

105   Jackson, Tom. *Cited in:* Charman-Anderson, Suw. (2008, Aug. 28). "Breaking the email compulsion." *The Guardian*: https://www.theguardian.com/technology/2008/aug/28/email.addiction.

106   *As told to*: Ferriss, Timothy. (2017). *Tribe of Mentors: Short Life Advice from the best in the World*. Houghton Mifflin Harcourt.

107   Rhodes, Ben. (2018). *The World as It Is: A Memoir of the Obama White House*. Random House.

108   Harari, Yuval Noah. (2015). *Sapiens: A Brief History of Humankind*. HarperCollins Publishers.

109   Harari, Yuval Noah. (2015). *Sapiens: A Brief History of Humankind*. HarperCollins Publishers.

110   Ellis, Joseph J. (2018). *American Dialogue: The Founders and Us*. Alfred A. Knopf.

111   Obama, Barack H. and Robinson, Marilynne. (2015, Nov. 19). "President Obama & Marilynne Robinson: A Conversation—II." *The New York Review of Books*: https://www.nybooks.com/articles/2015/11/19/president-obama-marilynne-robinson-conversation-2/.

112   Brooks, David. (2015). *The Road to Character*. Random House.

113   The Economist (2019, Nov. 14). "Who will win the media wars? Netflix, Disney and the battle to control eyeballs." *The Economist*: https://www.economist.com/leaders/2019/11/14/who-will-win-the-media-wars.

114   Shenk, Joshua Wolf. (2005). *Lincoln's Melancholy: How Depression Challenged a President and Fueled His Greatness (Unabridged Audiobook)*. HighBridge.

115   Coates, Ta-Nehisi. (2017). *We Were Eight Years in Power: An American Tragedy*. One World.

116   Pink, Daniel H. (2018). *When: The Scientific Secrets of Perfect Timing*. Riverhead.

117   Riggs, Nina. (2017). *The Bright Hour: A Memoir of Living and Dying*. Simon & Schuster.

118   Kalanithi, Paul. (2016). *When Breath Becomes Air*. Random House.

119   Grant, Ulysses S. *Cited in*: Chernow, Ron. (2017). *Grant*. Penguin Books.

120   Chernow, Ron. (2017). *Grant*. Penguin Books.

121   *I previously published a version of this section on Medium*: Lowenstein, Adam M. (2019, May 30). "The clarifying power of writing and storytelling." *The Writing Cooperative*: https://writingcooperative.com/the-clarifying-power-of-writing-and-storytelling-48efef2c6256.

Chapter 5: Resist the productivity obsession

122   Semler, Ricardo. (2004). *The Seven-Day Weekend: Changing the Way Work Works*. Portfolio. *I originally encountered a version of Semler's advice here*: Cowan, Katy. (2019, Jun. 24). "Frank Chimero on causing 'good trouble' and re-imagining the status quo to combat achievement culture." *Creative Boom*: https://www.creativeboom.com/features/frank-chimero/.

123   Murphy, Kate. (2014, Jul. 25). "No Time to Think." *The New York Times*: https://www.nytimes.com/2014/07/27/sunday-review/no-time-to-think.html.

124   Brach, Tara. (2003). *Radical Acceptance: Embracing Your Life with the Heart of a Buddha*. Bantam Books.

125   Kreider, Tim. (2012). *We Learn Nothing: Essays*. Simon & Schuster. *Originally cited in*: Ferriss, Tim. (2016). *Tools of Titans: The Tactics, Routines, and Habits of Billionaires, Icons, and World-Class Performers*. Houghton Mifflin Harcourt.

126   Young, Scott. (2018, Feb. 23). "Lesson Three: Why You'll Always Be Too Busy." *Cited in an email newsletter distributed by Cal Newport*.

127   Ferriss, Tim. (2016). *Tools of Titans: The Tactics, Routines, and Habits of Billionaires, Icons, and World-Class Performers*. Houghton Mifflin Harcourt.

128   Markovits, Daniel. *Excerpted from a conversation between Daniel Markovits and Ezra Klein*. (2019, Sept. 23). "When meritocracy wins, everybody loses." *The Ezra Klein Show*: https://www.stitcher.com/podcast/the-ezra-klein-show/e/64086855. *This excerpt was edited slightly for clarity*.

129   The Walden Woods Project (n.d.; accessed 2019, Nov. 20). "Mis-Quotations: This page contains quotations either misquoted or erroneously attributed to Henry D. Thoreau." *The Walden Woods Project*: https://www.walden.org/thoreau/mis-quotations/. *In popular (mis)attribution, "industrious" is often replaced with "busy." According to the Walden Woods Project, "The correct quotation appears in Thoreau's letter to his friend, H.G.O. Blake, on 16 November 1857."*

130   Griffith, Erin. (2019, Jan. 26). "Why Are Young People Pretending to Love Work?" *The New York Times*: https://www.nytimes.com/2019/01/26/business/against-hustle-culture-rise-and-grind-tgim.html.

131   Griffith, Erin. (2019, Jan. 26). "Why Are Young People Pretending to Love Work?" *The New York Times*: https://www.nytimes.com/2019/01/26/business/against-hustle-culture-rise-and-grind-tgim.html.

132   Griffith, Erin. (2019, Jan. 26). "Why Are Young People Pretending to Love Work?" *The New York Times*: https://www.nytimes.com/2019/01/26/business/against-hustle-culture-rise-and-grind-tgim.html.

133   Gawande, Atul. (2014). *Being Mortal: Medicine and What Matters in the End*. Henry Holt.

Chapter 6: Make time for what matters

134   Kahneman, Daniel. (2011). *Thinking, Fast and Slow*. Farrar, Straus and Giroux.

135   Holiday, Ryan and Hanselman, Stephen. (2016). *The Daily Stoic: 366 Meditations on Wisdom, Perseverance, and the Art of Living*. Portfolio.

136   McCullough, David. (1992). *Truman*. Simon & Schuster.

137   Pink, Daniel H. (2018). *When: The Scientific Secrets of Perfect Timing*. Riverhead.

138   *As told to*: Ferriss, Timothy. (2017). *Tribe of Mentors: Short Life Advice from the best in the World*. Houghton Mifflin Harcourt.

139   Newport, Cal. (2016). *Deep Work: Rules for Focused Success in a Distracted World*. Hachette Book Group.

140   Pasricha, Neil. (2016). *The Happiness Equation: Want Nothing + Do Anything = Have Everything*. Putnam.

141   The Economist. (1955, Nov. 19). "Parkinson's Law." *The Economist*: https://www.economist.com/news/1955/11/19/parkinsons-law.

142   The Economist. (2018, Jun. 30). "Tortured by meetings: You take minutes and waste hours." *The Economist*: https://www.economist.com/business/2018/06/30/tortured-by-meetings.

143   The Economist. (1955, Nov. 19). "Parkinson's Law." *The Economist*: https://www.economist.com/news/1955/11/19/parkinsons-law.

144   Fried, Jason and Heinemeier Hansson, David. (2018). *It Doesn't Have to Be Crazy at Work*. HarperCollins.

145   Kahneman, Daniel. (2011). *Thinking, Fast and Slow*. Farrar, Straus and Giroux.

146   Kahneman, Daniel. (2011). *Thinking, Fast and Slow*. Farrar, Straus and Giroux.

147   Kahneman, Daniel. (2011). *Thinking, Fast and Slow*. Farrar, Straus and Giroux.

148   Gawande, Atul. (2014). *Being Mortal: Medicine and What Matters in the End*. Henry Holt.

149   Kahneman, Daniel. (2011). *Thinking, Fast and Slow*. Farrar, Straus and Giroux.

150   Fried, Jason and Heinemeier Hansson, David. (2018). *It Doesn't Have to Be Crazy at Work*. HarperCollins.

151   *Walt Disney Studios*. (2018). *Christopher Robin*. See also: Wright, Robin. (2018, Aug. 23). "The Moral Clarity of 'Christopher Robin.'" *The New Yorker*: https://www.newyorker.com/culture/culture-desk/the-moral-clarity-of-christopher-robin.

152   *I previously published a version of this chapter on Medium*: Lowenstein, Adam M. (2019, Jun. 1). "Working In Politics Taught Me to Make Time for What Matters." *The Ascent*: https://medium.com/the-ascent/working-in-politics-taught-me-to-make-time-for-what-matters-35a3bb0de142.

Chapter 7: Have a trajectory (not a plan)

153   Cain, Susan. (2012). *Quiet: The Power of Introverts in a World That Can't Stop Talking*. Broadway Books.

154   Westover, Tara. (2018). *Educated: A Memoir*. Random House.

155   Mingyur Rinpoche, Yongey. (2019). *In Love with the World: A Monk's Journey Through the Bardos of Living and Dying*. Spiegel & Grau.

156   Mingyur Rinpoche, Yongey. (2019). *In Love with the World: A Monk's Journey Through the Bardos of Living and Dying*. Spiegel & Grau.

157   Brooks, David. (2015). *The Road to Character*. Random House.

158   Patchett, Ann. (2017, Nov. 9). "Word for the Day." *Cited in: A Network for*

Grateful Living: https://us10.campaign-archive.com/?e=f56835f930&u
=ebb9f9f588051c1f7a7fc8f09&id=7460c9dd21.

159 Brooks, David. (2015). *The Road to Character*. Random House.

160 Carr, David. (2014). "University of California Berkeley School of Journalism Commencement Address." *The Desk*: https://thedesk.matthew keys.net/2015/02/david-carr-berkeley-commencement-speech/.

Chapter 8: Surrender control (and fight FOMO)

161 Stevenson, Bryan. (2014). *Just Mercy: A Story of Justice and Redemption*. Spiegel & Grau.

162 Galloway, Scott. (2018, Nov. 2). "Coarseness and Coddling." *No Mercy/ No Malice*: https://www.profgalloway.com/coarseness-and-coddling.

163 The Economist. (2019, Jan. 31). "The two tribes of working life." *The Economist*: https://www.economist.com/business/2019/01/31/the-two-tribes-of-working-life.

164 Krakauer, Jon. (1996). *Into the Wild*. Random House.

165 Brooks, David. (2015). *The Road to Character*. Random House.

166 Lao Tzu. *Cited in*: Salzberg, Sharon. (2017). *Real Love: The Art of Mindful Connection*. Flatiron Books.

167 Bender, Jeremy. (2013, Oct. 8). "19 Reasons Why Long-Distance Relationships Are Better Than You Think." *BuzzFeed*: https://www.buzzfeed.com/jeremybender/reasons-why-long-distance-relationships-are-better-than-y.

168 Coates, Ta-Nehisi. (2017). *We Were Eight Years in Power: An American Tragedy*. One World.

169 Brooks, David. (2015). *The Road to Character*. Random House.

Chapter 9: Think about death

170 Kolbert, Elizabeth. (2014). *The Sixth Extinction: An Unnatural History*. Henry Holt.

171 Gawande, Atul. (2014). *Being Mortal: Medicine and What Matters in the End*. Henry Holt.

172   *Harrison was a Republican from Indiana who was preceded and succeeded by Grover Cleveland. Who knew?*

173   Adams, John. *Cited in*: Ellis, Joseph J. (2018). *American Dialogue: The Founders and Us*. Alfred A. Knopf.

174   Sellars, John. (n.d.; accessed 2019, Nov. 21). "Marcus Aurelius (121—180 C.E.)." *Internet Encyclopedia of Philosophy*: https://www.iep.utm.edu/ marcus/. *As Sellars notes, "The modern text [of Meditations] derives primarily from two sources: a manuscript now in the Vatican and a lost manuscript… upon which the first printed edition (1558) was based."*

175   Aurelius, Marcus. (2002). *Meditations: A New Translation, with an Introduction*, by Gregory Hays. The Modern Library.

176   Riggs, Nina. (2017). *The Bright Hour: A Memoir of Living and Dying*. Simon & Schuster. *See also*: Holiday, Ryan. (2017, Jun. 27). "Why You Should Pretend Today Is the End." *The Observer*: https://observer. com/2017/06/why-you-should-pretend-today-is-the-end-memento-mori-stoicism-philosophy/.

177   Riggs, Nina. (2017). *The Bright Hour: A Memoir of Living and Dying*. Simon & Schuster.

178   Brooks, Arthur C. (2019, Jul.). "Your Professional Decline Is Coming (Much) Sooner Than You Think." *The Atlantic*: https://www.theatlantic. com/magazine/archive/2019/07/work-peak-professional-decline/590650/.

179   Brooks, Arthur C. (2019, Jul.). "Your Professional Decline Is Coming (Much) Sooner Than You Think." *The Atlantic*: https://www.theatlantic. com/magazine/archive/2019/07/work-peak-professional-decline/590650/.

180   Harari, Yuval Noah. (2015). *Sapiens: A Brief History of Humankind*. HarperCollins Publishers.

181   Kalanithi, Paul. (2016). *When Breath Becomes Air*. Random House.

182   Mingyur Rinpoche, Yongey. (2019). *In Love with the World: A Monk's Journey Through the Bardos of Living and Dying*. Spiegel & Grau.

183   Coates, Ta-Nehisi. (2017). *We Were Eight Years in Power: An American Tragedy*. One World.

184   Mingyur Rinpoche, Yongey. (2019). *In Love with the World: A Monk's*

Journey Through the Bardos of Living and Dying. Spiegel & Grau.

185 Carr, David. (2008). *The Night of the Gun: A Reporter Investigates the Darkest Story of His Life. His Own.* Simon & Schuster.

186 Pink, Daniel H. (2018). *When: The Scientific Secrets of Perfect Timing.* Riverhead.

187 Efros, Seymour. (2016, Apr. 19). "Memory 21." *Distributed via email.*

188 *I previously published a version of this section on Medium*: Lowenstein, Adam M. (2019, Jun. 14). "The unexpected moment when the past floods into the present." *The Startup*: https://medium.com/swlh/ the-unexpected-moment-when-the-past-floods-into-the-present-4aad6e43de4d.

Chapter 10: Embrace the craft of life

189 Cooper, Brittney. (2018). *Eloquent Rage: A Black Feminist Discovers Her Superpower (Unabridged Audiobook).* Macmillan Audio.

190 5'7" Black Male (@absurdistwords). (2016, Nov. 9). *Twitter*: https:// twitter.com/absurdistwords/status/796333455248359426. *This excerpt includes minor edits for clarity.*

191 Brooks, David. (2015). *The Road to Character.* Random House.

192 Isaacson, Walter. (2003). *Benjamin Franklin: An American Life.* Simon & Schuster.

193 Isaacson, Walter. (2003). *Benjamin Franklin: An American Life.* Simon & Schuster.

194 Franklin, Benjamin. *Cited in*: Isaacson, Walter. (2003). *Benjamin Franklin: An American Life.* Simon & Schuster.

195 Truman, Harry S. *Cited in*: McCullough, David. (1992). *Truman.* Simon & Schuster.

196 Stevens, Thaddeus. *Cited in*: Trefousse, Hans L. (1997). *Thaddeus Stevens: Nineteenth-Century Egalitarian.* The University of North Carolina Press.

197 Frankl, Viktor E. (1959). *Man's Search for Meaning.* Beacon Press.

Afterthoughts

198   Miranda, Lin-Manuel. (2018). *Gmorning, Gnight!: Little Pep Talks for Me & You*. Random House.

199   Ferriss, Tim. (2016). *Tools of Titans: The Tactics, Routines, and Habits of Billionaires, Icons, and World-Class Performers*. Houghton Mifflin Harcourt.

200   Gawande, Atul. (2014). *Being Mortal: Medicine and What Matters in the End*. Henry Holt.

201   Salzberg, Sharon. (2017). *Real Love: The Art of Mindful Connection*. Flatiron Books.

202   Krakauer, Jon. (1996). *Into the Wild*. Random House.